Social Science and Public Policy in the United States

Irving Louis Horowitz
James Everett Katz

The Praeger Special Studies program—utilizing the most modern and efficient book production techniques and a selective worldwide distribution network—makes available to the academic, government, and business communities significant, timely research in U.S. and international economic, social, and political development.

Social Science and Public Policy in the United States

PRAEGER SPECIAL STUDIES IN U.S. ECONOMIC, SOCIAL, AND POLITICAL ISSUES

Praeger Publishers   New York   Washington   London

H
61
H6845
1975
Cop. 2

Library of Congress Cataloging in Publication Data

Horowitz, Irving Louis.
    Social science and public policy in the United States.

    (Praeger special studies in U.S. economic, social,
and political issues)
    Includes bibliographical references and index.
    1. Social sciences.   2. Policy sciences.   3. Social
scientists—United States.   I. Katz, James Everett,
joint author.   II. Title.
H61.H6845   1975   309.2'12   74-33034
ISBN 0-275-05310-5
ISBN 0-275-89160-7 pbk.

PRAEGER PUBLISHERS
111 Fourth Avenue, New York, N.Y. 10003, U.S.A.

Published in the United States of America in 1975
by Praeger Publishers, Inc.

Printed in the United States of America

This one is for Wright

This volume was initially prepared on behalf of the Organization for Economic Cooperation and Development (OECD) under the general supervision of Irving Louis Horowitz as principal investigator and James Everett Katz as assistant investigator. In its draft form the findings were submitted and delivered before the International Intergovernmental Group on Social Science Policy of OECD on June 10 and 11, 1974, in Paris, France. We wish to express our appreciation and gratitude for the intellectual support rendered by the director of the science policy section of OECD, Jean-Jacques Salomon, and his able associate director, Georges Ferné.

PREFACE

The title of this study is comprised of six big words, and three awesome realities: social science, public policy, and the United States. The unvarnished truth is that the subject of social science and public policy has as much to do with political-economic systems as with national systems. What makes the United States an especially intriguing case is not the size of this nation or even its peculiar history but rather the conditions of doing policy-oriented social science under a neocapitalist system of either a late industrial or postindustrial variety. Rather than leave to the imagination what this means, let us state quite simply that the United States is a social system largely directed by a bureaucratic sector responsive, but not always responsible, to older social classes. Beyond that, in the contemporary United States we are dealing with a mass society without a mass base, a society in which numbers count for much at the level of consumer power and purchasing power but for less at the level of political power, at least beyond the voting process.

In such a context, social science links up with policy efforts, first to satisfy the bureaucratic needs of managing a postindustrial economy (and that means managing the competing needs of entrenched social classes), and beyond that to satisfy perhaps equally powerful intermediate sectors of a nondescript and nonpolarized variety, ranging from secretaries to schoolteachers. Social science also relates to the second part of our paradigm concerning postindustrial capitalism: it satisfies the needs of people who themselves are largely without voice even though they sometimes have the vote. In that peculiar sense, the role of social science involves advocacy as well as analysis—that is, giving voice or representation to that difficult-to-grasp phenomenon called "the people," and also giving expression to an even more ubiquitous concept called the "general interest" as over and against special interests.

Thus, rather than emphasize the national aspects of problems dealt with in this study, we will emphasize the universality of problems faced by social science in its relationship to public policy. By such an emphasis we shall hopefully provide meaning to those outside—as well as to those inside—the United States, moving towards the wider implementation of research techniques and design in the policy sector.

Briefly, our study emphasizes problems of openness, publicity, legitimization, reward, the work ambiance, funding, information dissemination, and implementation—all of which are faced in common by the social sciences. Likewise, a heavy emphasis is placed upon problems of the policy sector: issues connected with secrecy, partisanship, implementation, planning, costs, and benefits of research arising from any piece of social research. In so doing we hope that this series of propositions about the interpenetration of social science and public policy are generalizable and worthwhile across national space, if not necessarily beyond this particular historical period.

Irving Louis Horowitz
Rutgers University

CONTENTS

LIST OF TABLES

LIST OF ABBREVIATIONS

AAP	Association for the Advancement of Psychology
ACDA	Arms Control and Disarmament Agency
ADAMHA	Alcohol, Drug Abuse and Mental Health Administration
AID	Agency for International Development
APA	American Psychological Association
CEA	Council of Economic Advisors
DOD	Department of Defense
DOS	Department of State
FAP	Family Assistance Plan
GWIE	Graduated Work Incentive Experiment
HEW	Department of Health, Education and Welfare
IDA	Institute of Defense Analysis
INR	Bureau of Intelligence and Research
IRP	Institute for Research on Poverty
ISA	International Security Affairs
ISA/SOMS	International Studies Association, Section on Military Studies
MARC	Metropolitan Applied Research Center
M-Reit	Mutual Real Estate Investment Trust
NAM	National Association of Manufacturers
NAS	National Academy of Science
NASA	National Aeronautics and Space Administration
NCM	new civilian militarist
NIH	National Institute of Health
NIMH	National Institute of Mental Health
NLF	National Liberation Front
NORC	National Opinion Research Center
NSB	National Science Board
NSF	National Science Foundation
OEO	Office of Economic Opportunity
OEP	Office of Emergency Preparedness
OMB	Office of Management and the Budget
ONR	Office of Naval Research
ORO	Operation Research Office
OST	Office of Science and Technology
OAS	Organization of American States
PIRG	Public Interest Research Group
SDC	Systems Development Corporation
SORO	Special Operations Research Organization
SSRC	Social Science Research Council
USIA	United States Information Agency

Social Science and Public Policy in the United States

CHAPTER

1

SOCIAL SCIENCE AND PUBLIC POLICY IN THE UNITED STATES: AN INTRODUCTION

Any examination of how the social sciences impart policy guidelines in the United States and the ways in which the policy-making apparatus supports and underwrites social science activity is a thoroughly ubiquitous exercise. The magnitude of the undertaking invites skepticism at least and scorn at most. Cries and whispers will be evoked concerning the autonomy of the social sciences, followed by declarations that policy has no more dependency on social science research than apples have on oranges. Beyond that is the lurking suspicion that American social science may employ a different rhetoric but scarcely exhibits a noticeable or notable superiority to social sciences elsewhere in the world. Given these and other herculean objections to this sort of study, it is perhaps necessary to set forth plainly and frankly the scope and limits of this ambitious, yet exploratory, effort.

Alternating between case-study materials and empirically grounded theory, this extended monograph attempts to set forth the intriguing relationships between the community of social scientists and the still larger cluster of policy makers in the United States. This is a large-scale task. And it cannot be emphasized too strongly that this contribution is only intended to set forth those main points in this interrelationship that may have a particular bearing on future developments within the policy complex outside the United States.

The work emphasizes throughout the institutional setting of policy research rather than the headier realm of ideology. This emphasis is necessary by virtue of the simple fact that in the great majority of cases policy research is sponsored research. What is involved is an exchange system of buyers and sellers of information that is presumably scarce or difficult to generate. Beginning elsewhere—with a general system of ideas, for example—would exaggerate the role of an intelligentsia and therefore only becloud and falsify the actual context in which policy-oriented research takes place in the United States.

The study examines measures taken by various parts of the U.S. government to bring about a closer cohesion between those who govern and those who would exploit social science toward that end. At this level specific case studies are employed to achieve a clearer perspective of the relationship between government policy needs and social science delivery capabilities. *Social Science and Public Policy in the United States* seeks to deal systematically with the strains and tensions inherent in any relationship between those charged with political success through policy achievements and those whose self-appointed task is to search for truth and meaning. If there is an interaction between social science and public policy, there must also be a training ground for this nexus of interconnections. We address the educational framework that now exists and permits such a fusion of applied effort.

So much emphasis has been placed on the role of the federal government as patron and donor in social-policy research that there has been a short-sighted tendency to ignore the ways that social scientists participate in community, local, city and state policy making. Indeed, a considerable amount of successful if unheralded work goes on at those subnational levels. One finds there a high degree of isomorphism between social science and policy implementation. As a result, our work considers in detail how each social science discipline, through its own inner history, responds to the policy-making demands of the present. The level of sophistication and stage of professionalization heavily influence the exact impact a particular social science has upon policy making. Our analysis is selective (that is, based on case-study material), attempting to show how each social science discipline provides unique mechanisms to deal with particular policy issues.

Large-scale policies, involving explicit social science participation, are examined in case studies of social science involvement in foreign affairs and domestic affairs. This separation is made imperative by the widely held (and largely accurate) assumption that the failure rate in overseas research, like the success rate in domestic research, hinges on a prior existence with the body politic of either a consensus or a dissensus. Social science involvement in the policy process must therefore focus sharply on public opinion, on the minds and hearts of the citizenry.

A final theme that characterizes our work throughout is the examination of interactional frameworks and paradigms governing the relationship between social scientists and the administrators and perpetrators of public policy. We focus on the sorts of problems that social science researchers throughout the world can expect to encounter when they involve themselves with the policy process. Beyond that, we present a number of modest recommendations that should enable researchers to avoid the pitfalls encountered in the United States. We do not, however, suggest that social scientists should discard the effort to use scientific knowledge to solve practical human problems.

Lest the reader of this report think our attempt all-encompassing, we should point out what is exluded from its purview. First, we have not considered work in social science of a purely historical or theoretical character that may have informed the decisions of certain policy makers—for example, the influence of Metternich on the thought of Kissinger. Second, we have omitted work of a primarily critical character—for example, studies concerned with demonstrating how things do not work or how events cannot be controlled. Third, we have overlooked work that is oracular, which, despite its future orientation, necessarily fails to stipulate the costs as well as the benefits of reaching stated goals. The difference between policy planning and futurology is sometimes difficult to establish, but a sense of a present time and space framework is clearly important to such a distinction. Stated affirmatively, policy-oriented social science research assumes a meliorative capability in respect to the costs and benefits involved in any decision-making process and a definitely temporal and spatial framework within which to operate. It might well be that these assumptions are mere presumptions, that, in point of fact, social science dedicated to policy processes is foredoomed by larger cosmic, metaphysical, or historical tendencies that are simply not subject to the constraint and will of human intervention. Yet this very restriction sets the outer limits of social science involvement in the process of policy formation.

One might imagine that by rigorously limiting the parameters and purposes of policy-related social science research most theoretical problems could be put aside, if not entirely resolved. This, however, is not the case, for within the interconnection of social science and public policy there exists a set of larger ethical and valuational issues that cannot be resolved. Simply put, it is debatable whether the involvement of social science in the policy process implies a set of moral imperatives quite beyond the research itself, or whether social science is simply a precise tool for setting forth the most efficacious policy recommendations for the least possible fiscal and political costs.

The degree to which "policy making" as a separate function has permeated current social research on major public issues is suggested in the following statement from an introduction to a study of the effects of day care on labor-force participation:

> The paper concludes that the provision of free and adequate day care services to low-income mothers will lead to an increase in labor force participation; in fact, a ten percentage point increase (from 32 to 42 percent) in participation is estimated. The paper also notes the possibility that the provision of subsidized day care may result in an increase in the number of hours worked by employed mothers but that it may not be cost-effective and may lead to an increase in unemployment rates. These findings are not used to make policy decisions. It is left to the policy maker to determine if the impact is sufficient to justify the costs associated with the support of subsidized day care [Ditmore and Prosser 1973].

One can detect in the preceding formulation the resurfacing in modern guise of the old fact-value dualism, with the assumption that, somehow, information provided and decisions made are discrete entities. We do not think that it is an exaggeration to say that a considerable amount of current thinking in the United States is predicated on that central assumption. Lasswell's idea of a "science of policy-making" (Lasswell 1951:3-15) has largely given way to a de facto operational view that because of the fragmentation of power the social scientist is primarily concerned with facts, while the policy makers are concerned primarily with the strategies necessary to implement desired legislation rather than social goals as a whole (Coleman 1973:1).

While a considerable amount of analysis is based on the assumption that the research performed is utterly distinct from the applications devised, a growing body of social science opinion operates on an entirely different set of premises: what might be referred to as the monist—in contrast to the dualist—framework. For example, discussing policy implications in a recently concluded piece of research on mobility among blue-collar workers, the author states:

> One of the purposes of this study is to help provide direction for Federal upgrading programs in general and for the Training Incentive Payments Program (TIPP) in particular. . . . [T]he National Manpower Advisory Committee listed five principal justifications for Federal intervention in the area of upgrading. Two of these justifications are of direct concern to this study: (1) To broaden access to minority groups to better jobs. In the absence of Federal assistance they might not have an equal chance to be promoted. (2) Federal support would make possible experimental and developmental efforts aimed at helping redesign their upgrading structures with an aim of increasing the opportunities for upgrading [Steinberg 1973:116-17].

This analysis of upward mobility among blue-collar workers focuses on racial and sexual variables precisely because of the author's predisposition to make the research policy relevant. The question remains whether such intentions as exist in the monistic framework actually lead to different policy implications than those enunciated by the dualists (who simply assume a disjunction and scarcely worry about it). But whatever the answer to that question might be, it is of no small interest that the interrelationship of social science and policy making involves and invokes fundamental considerations of the connection of theory and practice that are at least as old as Aristotle and Marx and are by no means confined to the special aspect of life in the United States.

It is important to state flatly that although we have carefully circumscribed the nature of policy analysis, we have left the matter of causal priority wide open. Whether the circuit starts with a sociopolitical "need to know," leading to a social-scientific attempt to satisfy such practical requisites intellectually or whether the circuit really commences with a social-scientific problematic situation that stimulates a practical policy response is not going to be resolved by this study. This does not mean that the causal priority of social science or public policy is little more than a question of which came first, the chicken or the egg. The senior author of this study has done considerable writing on the theme of causal priority (Horowitz 1972:414-30). However, in terms of the limits of this study, any effort at settling such large, metaphysical issues would represent a digression from out main aims. Hence, the question of whether we live in a "policy science" climate or a "Mandarin" climate will be set aside in favor of the less ambitious but presumably more realizable goal of setting forth the contents and contours of the connection of social science to policy making in the United States.

REFERENCES

Coleman, James
   1973   "Ten Principles Governing Policy Research," *Footnotes* Vol. 1 (March):1.
Ditmore, Jack and W. R. Prosser
   1973   *A Study of Day Care's Effect on the Labor Force Participation of Low-Income Mothers.* Washington, D.C.: Evaluation Division, Office of Planning, Research and Evaluation, Office of Economic Opportunity.
Horowitz, Irving Louis
   1972   *Foundations of Political Sociology.* New York and London: Harper & Row.
Lasswell, Harold D.
   1951   "The Policy Orientation," in *The Policy Sciences,* ed, Danial Lerner and Harold D. Lasswell. Stanford: Stanford University Press.
Steinberg, Edward
   1973   *Upward Mobility of Low-Income Workers: A Research Report to the United States Department of Labor.* New York: Institute of Public Administration.

CHAPTER

2

PERSONNEL AND FUNDING
FOR SOCIAL SCIENCE INPUTS
INTO POLICY MAKING

The relationship between social science and public policy in the United States largely involves an exchange of monies for information. Therefore, it is entirely appropriate, if not especially exciting, to begin with the best available raw data on the numbers of social scientists involved in the policy process, the amounts of money involved, and the breakdown of personnel, first by social science discipline and then by government and subgovernment agencies. In this way, the actual magnitude of social science involvement in the policy process can be properly framed. And if we cannot possibly achieve a comprehensive review of social science policy akin to what has already been achieved in the physical sciences (OECD 1968), by starting with the foregoing data, we can better appreciate the limits as well as the scope of this effort.

The rate of growth in federal support for human resources has approximately doubled every three years for the last 12 years. This rate of growth is even more striking in recent years, if one takes into account a general tapering off in expenditures by the federal government for most other research and development (R and D). Some idea of the dramatic increase in both the priorities and rate of growth of human-resource expenditures is provided by Table 2.1. Human resource expenditures are government-wide programs in six functional areas: education, manpower, health, income security, civil rights, and crime reduction. One should note, in particular, that outlays for human resources have increased without much relationship to the political party in power or even to the relative calm or volatility of economic performance as a whole.

Table 2.2 breaks up the growth of human resource spending into categories by programs for the 1970s. This expansion ranges from approximately 33 percent in education and manpower to slightly less than 25 percent in veterans benefits and services programs. These growth rates for human services have a special meaning for social science. Above all, the shift in federal priorities from defense and space activities to human resources means simply that more R and D funds are available to social scientists than at any time in the past. As a result, more

6

TABLE 2.1

Percent of Budget Representing Outlays for Human Resources

Year	Outlay for Human Resources (percent)
1955	21
1958	26
1961	30
1964	29
1967	32
1970	37
1973	45

Source: Biderman and Sharp (1972).

TABLE 2.2

Outlays for Human Resources, by Type of Program (millions of dollars)

Year	Education and Manpower	Health	Income Security	Veterans Benefits and Services	Total
1971	8,654	14,463	55,712	9,776	88,606
1972	10,140	17,024	65,225	11,127	103,516
1973	11,281	18,117	69,658	11,745	110,801

Source: Biderman and Sharp (1972).

social science positions are available in applied programs, signifying a shift from an academic to a policy-oriented work life for social scientists. All of this adds up to growth in the size and power of the social science professions, leading to a still greater impact by the social scientific community on policy construction, implementation, and evaluation.

While research and development funds for military weapons and the space program are shrinking, R and D funds for social agencies have increased 33 percent since 1967 and have doubled since 1965. R and D funds for agencies that employ both the social and physical sciences, such as the departments of

Transportation, Agriculture, Commerce and the Interior, have also increased. Their overall growth rate has been approximately 20 percent between 1965 and 1971 (see Table 2.3).

Table 2.4 consists of two parts. The first line shows the rapid increase in the number of social scientists receiving federal support. The most striking increase is in sociology, which has seen its support base more than double in the four years between 1966 and 1970. Growth has been slower in economics, which has been an area of high past utilization; but growth has been considerably more rapid in psychology, another area of high past utilization. The number of social scientists receiving federal support has increased by one-third over the four years for which data exist. This increase is even more dramatic when the "pipeline" effect of manpower production is considered (Berelson 1960). It takes an average of six years of post-graduate work to produce a social scientist. Each year, only a limited cohort of social science trainees can be injected into the training system, and it will be six years before the cohort emerges at the other end of the training cycle. But quite beyond this time factor is the absorption of social science personnel as a professional work category apart from college and university teaching.

In the second part the data show the high percentage of social scientists supported by the federal government in education and especially in nonprofit institutions. This material also reveals that significant percentages of social scientists are also supported in sectors such as industry, business, and local subnational units of government. As the bottom line demonstrates, an average of one-third of all social scientists receives some sort of fiscal support from the federal government. And this would have to be reckoned a modest estimate, since the data are concerned only with direct fiscal aid.

The number of social scientists employed by independent nonprofit institutions is also sharply higher than in the past (Biderman and Sharp 1971, p. 28). These institutions are important vehicles for the introduction of new policy initiatives within American society. Nonprofit organizations can experiment in areas in which the federal government cannot trespass. These areas of experimentation allow inquiries into processes that may then lead to entirely new policy initiatives. The experiments by the Ford Foundation with "gray areas" opened the path for the government's "war on poverty"; at the very least, they occurred simultaneously. Since 1967 the number of scientists and engineers has declined in all fields except the social science, where it has increased markedly, in contrast to the general trend of employment in nonprofit institutions. Americans are confronted with a faith in social science solutions at a time when conventional forms of diplomacy and policy seem less efficacious.

The data in tables 2.5 to 2.11 examine federal human and social-resources programs in order to determine the gross shape of the government's commitment to policy construction, administration, and evaluation. Since there are no specific categories for policy-oriented work utilized on a government-wide basis, each major program must examine policy work within each social program. Thus, comparability can be established only by comparison of isomorphic rather than genotypic areas.

The yearly growth of civil rights outlays by the federal government is shown in Table 2.5. The most robust area of growth has been for equal opportunity

TABLE 2.3

Federal Obligations for Research and Development, Various Fiscal Years, 1965-71[a] (millions of dollars)

Department or Agency	1965	1967	1969	1971
Grand total[b]	15,709	16,723	16,164	15,810
Total (excluding NASA)[b]	10,208	11,711	12,119	12,456
Major agencies				
DOD	6,728	7,809	7,869	7,762
NASA	5,093	5,012	4,045	3,354
NIH/NIMH	587	842	896	930
AEC (weapons)	527	499	552	481
NSF	195	314	301	384
Subtotal	13,130	14,476	13,663	12,911
Other, primarily social, agencies				
HEW (excluding NIH/NIMH)	374	423	418	529
HUD	—	11	18	60
OEO	4	47	35	90
VA	43	48	53	65
Dept. of the Int. (water-pollution control)	33	83	112	134
Dept. of Justice	—	3	6	29
Subtotal[c]	454	615	642	907
Other, primarily industrial, agencies				
AEC (excluding weapons)	994	980	1,155	1,078
Dept. of Transp.	99	106	129	226
Dept. of Agric.	218	269	278	306
Dept. of Commerce	74	79	74	99
Dept. of the Int. (excluding water-pollution control)	82	126	129	137
Subtotal	1,467	1,560	1,765	1,846
Addendum: basic research[d]	1,547	1,875	2,134	2,024

Tabulations by John M. Deutch, MIT, on the basis of data from *Special Analyses: Budget of the United States, Fiscal Year 1971* and from publications of the NSF.
[a]Includes obligations for R and D facilities.
[b]Includes relatively minor R and D obligations of smaller agencies not listed in table.
[c]Since data on the R and D obligations of the departments of the interior and justice are not available in all years, some small part of each annual change shown by these subtotals reflects changes in statistical coverage rather than changes in obligations.
[d]Included in agency totals.

Source: Biderman and Sharp (1972).

TABLE 2.4

Number and Percent of Social Scientists, Receiving Federal Support in Various Types of Employment by Field, 1966, 1968, and 1970

	Economics			Sociology[a]			Anthropology			Political Science[b]		Psychology			Total[c]		
	1966	1968	1970	1966	1968	1970	1966	1968	1970	1968	1970	1966	1968	1970	1966	1968	1970
I. Number	**13,150**	**11,510**	**13,386**	**3,640**	**6,638**	**7,658**	**919**	**1,217**	**1,325**	**5,176**	**6,493**	**19,027**	**23,077**	**26,271**	**36,736**	**42,442**	**48,640**
II. Percent, by type of employment																	
Education	30	31	27	35	33	28	38	37	31	21	16	43	43	36	38	38	32
Federal and military	100	100	100	100	100	100	100	100	100	100	100	100	100	100	100	100	100
Nonprofit	42	47	43	47	57	46	42	40	46	42	45	45	46	48	45	47	47
Industry and business	10	17	16	22[d]	32	31	50[d]	64[d]	73	40	41	31	33	29	16	25	23
All other	15	22	23	28	19	20	30[d]	34[d]	19	20	19	24	27	23	22	25	23
All types	30	38	35	37	35	30	40	39	31	29	23	43	43	38	37	40	36

[a] Increase from 1966 to 1968 partially due to change in NSF *Scientific Register* listing criteria for this field.

[b] No 1966 data available from *Scientific Register*.

[c] Excludes political science.

[d] Based on fewer than 25 cases.

Data from National Science Foundation, *American Science Manpower 1968: A Report of the National Register of Scientific and Technical Personnel* (Washington. D.C.: U.S. Government Printing Office, 1969), pp. 178-80 (NSF 69-38); *American Science Manpower 1966: A Report of the National Register of Scientific and Technical Personnel* (Washington, D.C.: U.S. Government Printing Office, 1967), pp. 156-58 (NSF 68-7), and *American Science Manpower, 1970: A Report of the National Register of Scientific and Technical Personnel* (Washington, D.C.: U.S. Government Printing Office 1971), pp. 162-67 (NSF 71-45).

Source: Biderman and Sharp (1972).

TABLE 2.5

Federal Rights Outlays for Enforcement
(millions of dollars)

	1971	1972	1973
Federal service equal employment opportunities	27.80	30.80	32.30
Military service equal opportunities	5.95	20.30	28.25
Private sector equal employment opportunities	34.43	49.89	66.29
Equal educational opportunities	70.30	122.90	400.00
Fair housing	7.55	9.07	10.88
Enforcement and investigation	34.15	46.48	50.07
Program direction, research, and information dissemination*	4.96	5.88	7.01
Indian programs	0.40	0.70	0.80
Civil rights conciliation and prevention of disputes	4.20	5.60	6.50
Total	189.74	291.62	602.10

*Area of social policy input funding.

Source: Office of Management and Budget (1973: 210).

education. Like most areas of civil rights enforcement this constitutes programmatic support rather than specific research and administrative support. The program direction, research, and information dissemination category (which represents the policy portion) is quite small in relation to the larger "transfer of funds" programs. When program direction is compared to other means of problem avoidance, such as conciliation and prevention of disputes, the funding provided is approximately equal. The distinction may be viewed as that between juridical and social science emphases of conflict resolution within the larger program of civil rights. Program direction is equal to 40 percent of the funds committed to enforcement and investigation of civil rights complaints. Although funds provided for the policy sector are small when compared to overall federal civil rights spending, policy-oriented programs represent a significant percentage of the actual administrative conduct of civil rights enforcement.

Table 2.6 documents the significance of research and direction spending in comparison to the larger federal manpower program. Research and direction constituted 4 percent of the entire manpower program in 1973 and is growing at a faster rate than the overall program. Half of the research and direction budget is devoted to program direction. Program direction implies administrative guidance and social-science-related information gathering. Two major

TABLE 2.6

Federal Outlays for Research and Direction in Manpower Programs* (millions of dollars)

Program	FY 1971	FY 1972	FY 1973
Research and Development	24	30	29
Evaluation	3	3	3
Program direction	84	98	106
Labor market information	30	34	38
Planning and technical assistance	14	23	26
Total	155	188	202
All manpower outlays	3,145	4,310	5,141

*Agencies include the Department of Labor, Veterans Administration, ACTION, and Equal Opportunity Commission.

Source: OMB, Special Analysis of the 1973 Budget, 1973: 145, 152.

constituents of the program direction category are the Committee on Civil Rights, which is an independent fact-finding agency, and the Women's Bureau of the Department of Labor, which deals with issues relating to the utilization of womanpower and the economic, social, legal and civil status of women.

Table 2.7 reveals that nearly 6 percent of the federal outlays for crime are devoted to planning and research with policy implications. Once again, the

TABLE 2.7

Federal Outlays for Crime Reduction (millions of dollars)

Program	FY 1971	FY 1972	FY 1973
Crime-related statistics	7.5	13	25
Research on criminal behavior and sociology of crime	23.0	33	45
Planning and coordination of crime-reduction programs	29.0	37	63
Total	59.5	83	133
All crime-reduction outlays	1,353	1,974	2,321

Source: Special Analysis of the 1973 Budget, Office of Management and Budget, 1973: 227.

planning and research segment of the program is growing faster than the general program.

The largest segment of the federal human resources programs is related to elementary and secondary education. Twelve percent of the program is devoted to research and innovation with policy implications. Again, the specific segment incorporating policy studies is growing faster than the program of which it is a part as shown in Table 2.8.

The extraordinary growth in the policy sectors of the health-care delivery system of the United States is documented in Table 2.9. For example, research, planning, and coordination of drug-abuse programs has expanded 350 percent within two years. The size of the improvement program of health care (through

TABLE 2.8

Federal Outlays for Research and Innovation in Elementary and Secondary Schools (millions of dollars)

Program	FY 1971	FY 1972	FY 1973
Research and Development (HEW)			
National Institute of Education	—	2	50
Office of Education R and D	85	92	54
Subtotal	85	94	104
Innovation and Demonstration (HEW)			
Office of Education			
Educational renewal	109	125	135
Follow through	48	69	60
Teacher Corps	34	41	41
Career education model development and training	5	6	10
National priority programs	3	20	37
Statistics and evaluation	5	15	21
Supplementary services	112	132	142
Education for the handicapped	54	60	65
Other	29	43	52
NSF and other	41	40	45
Subtotal	440	551	608
Total, research and innovation	**525**	**643**	**712**
Total, federal outlays for elementary and secondary education	**5,059**	**5,762**	**6,345**

Source: Special Analysis of the Budget, Office of Management and Budget 1973: 121, 126.

TABLE 2.9

Federal Outlays for Improving Organization and
Delivery of Health-Care Services
(millions of dollars)

Program	FY 1971	FY 1972	FY 1973
Planning	72	82	98
Technology	39	42	49
Manpower utilization	36	41	46
Health-care systems improvement	183	221	242
Total	331	386	435
Drug abuse			
Treatment and rehabilitation	78.8	189.6	230.2
Education and training	36.8	64.4	64.4
Research, planning, and coordination	16.6	56.1	70.6
Total	132.2	310.1	365.2
Grand Total (billions of dollars)	20.2	23.8	25.5

Source: Office of Management and Budget, 1973: 163,173.

research, training, and planning) is miniscule in proportion to the federal health outlay, making up less than 1 percent of the total program, but in terms of actual dollars available to social scientists it is highly significant. This segment of the health-care program devotes over $800 million to planning, sociotechnics, education, and coordination.

Table 2.10 documents that the Department of Defense spends approximately a half-billion dollars for social scientific research and studies annually. Of this sum, 14 percent is aimed at policy-planning. These policy-planning studies examine the options available to the U.S. military forces, and thus determine the international security situation (cf. Tax 1967).

Table 2.11 breaks down the policy-planning studies funds available to the office of the director of Defense Research and Engineering. Defense Research and Engineering is the "lead-in" office that explores future developments and capabilities for the office of the secretary of Defense. The role of the RAND Corporation, which absorbs fully one-third of the funds available for policy-planning, is paramount.

Social science expenditures for a particular discipline tend to be concentrated in specific departments. For example, economics is in the Bureau of Labor Statistics; political science, in the Department of Defense; history, in the Department of Agriculture; sociology and anthropology, in the Department of Health, Education and Welfare. In addition to the clustering effect the reader

TABLE 2.10

DOD Behavioral and Social Science Outlays
for Research and Studies, 1970
(millions of dollars)

Programs	Cost
Policy-planning studies*	6.4
Human performance	6.3
Manpower selection and training	25.3
Human factor engineering	3.7
Foreign military security environments	6.9
Total	48.6

*Includes strategic planning in response to changing patterns of political power and analysis; contingency planning; force structure; R and D requirements.

Source: U.S. Dept. of State Foreign Area Research Coordination Group, September 1969: 2.

TABLE 2.11

Funds for Policy-Planning Studies,
Office of Defense Research and Engineering
(thousands of dollars)

Area	1972	FY 1973	Request 1974
International security affairs	900	900	900
RAND Corporation	200	500	500
Total	1100	1400	1400

Source: Senate Armed Services Committee, Budget request, DOD; Fiscal 1974.

should notice that although the social sciences are smallest of all the sciences in terms of federal funds, they are the fastest growing, now representing a significant proportion of federal outlays for research (see Appendix A). Considering how recent this swing is to the utilization of the social sciences, even the fiscal aggregates represent an impressive amount. Beyond that, since a considerable amount of federal spending for social science is "buried" within other auditing categories, such as "environmental sciences" and "psychology" considered as a separate category, the actual expenditures in this area are quite large scale (see Appendix B).

A significant amount of funds for the social sciences are provided to individual social science departments by the larger universities of which they are a part. These funds, which were expanded by approximately 25 percent between 1968 and 1970, provide a source of policy research that retains an academic footing. The chief sources of these university funds among public institutions are state governments, followed by student tuition and fees. Among private institutions the chief source of nonfederal funds are, in order, student tuition and fees, endowment earnings, foundations, and individual gifts. Endowment earnings, foundations and individual gifts are also part of the incoming funds of public institutions applied to social science departments. Voluntary health agencies, industry and endowment principal are among other sources of income available to universities and colleges.

Table 2.12 demonstrates the significant financial commitment to the social sciences by nongovernment agencies. This commitment is especially marked in contrast to the federal funds devoted to social science academic departments. This private participation, furthermore, is growing. Sociology, for instance, registered a 6-percent increase in funds from universities and colleges from fiscal years 1969 to 1970, and economics and psychology grew 16 percent and 12 percent respectively over the same time span. The rate of growth for economics and psychology is greater than for any other science, including life sciences, physical science, and engineering.

The rapid expansion of the non-profit sector, specifically foundations, in the postwar era has multiplied the sources of public policy supports. As Table 2.13 indicates, nearly one-half of all foundations were established in 1950-59 and nearly one-fourth between 1960-69. The area of research that is directed toward something other than the promotion of particular industries or toward supplementing the U.S. defense posture has been greatly enlarged. Large sums

TABLE 2.12

Average Expenditure for Research and Education in Selected Social Science Fields (thousands of dollars)

Department	Avg. Nonfederal Source	Avg. Federal Source
Sociology	377	150
Economics	476	95
Psychology	483	306

Note: Figures rounded to nearest thousand.

Source: National Science Foundation (1973).

are being directed toward international studies, community services, program studies, and civic uses, all with considerable social science policy implications. Even so, the federal government alone spends 150 times more than all private foundations, and the larger differences of impact between an independent private foundation and an elected government is beyond quantification. This strengthens the possibility that the federal government may, in the future, circumvent political obstacles to engage in similar research activities. The increased range of policy research over time legitimates its value and enhances the possibilities for wider public acceptance. Indirectly, foundations serve to liberalize public policy. This effect is complex, however, and needs explanation, especially since such liberalization is one of the main reasons that foundations are criticized by political groups.

The liberalizing effect of foundations upon public policy is the outcome of two factors: first, the concern by the major foundations not to witness the American system eroded through internal strife; second, government reliance, especially on the part of executive agencies, upon the foundations to provide an

TABLE 2.13

**Period of Establishment of 5,436 Foundations, by Decades
after 1900—Latest Asset Classes**

Period	Total Founda- tions	Per- cent	$10 Million or More		$1 Million- Under $10 Million		Less Than $1 Million	
			Number	Per- cent	Number	Per- cent	Number	Per- cent
Before 1900	18	a	1	—	14	1	3	a
1900-09	16	a	6	2	9	a	1	a
1910-19	75	1	22	7	36	2	17	1
1920-29	157	3	32	10	88	5	37	1
1930-39	259	5	64	19	118	6	77	2
1940-49	1,134	21	97	29	463	25	574	18
1950-59	2,546	47	79	24	799	44	1,668	51
1960-69[b]	1,231	23	30	9	303	17	898	27
Total	5,436	100	331	100	1,830	100	3,275	100

[a]Less than 0.5 percent.
[b]Record incomplete for recent years.

Note: Information on year of organization was unavailable for 18 directory foundations.

Source: Lewis (1971).

umbrella for innovative programs, both domestically and overseas, that are clearly beyond the purview of the government as such.

Of the 25,000 foundations currently in existence the 12 largest, or a small fraction, control some $7.5 billion in assets, or roughly 30 percent of the resources of all the foundations put together (see Table 2.14). How these top 12 foundations were created, how they spend their money, what criteria they use in spending it, and their performance record, especially for the social sciences, which share disproportionately in the top 12, are all issues of great importance (Nielsen 1972). For our restricted purpose we simply want to indicate the magnitude of support given to the social and behavioral sciences, shown in Table 2.14. The top 12 foundations have displayed greatest concern with problems of race, crime, and international affairs—in short, areas that most invite social science participation. So in the foundation-supported researches social science has been riding a crest of policy interest in sensitive areas and deriving the benefits of such large-scale support.

The combined 1970 and 1971 major-field expenditures by dollars and percentages of the foundation sector reveal that education and welfare account for more than one-half of all expenditures, with a total funding of nearly $1

TABLE 2.14

Assets of the 12 Largest Foundations, 1969,
Compared with Their Assets in 1965
(dollar figures in millions)

	1969		1965	
Foundation	Rank	Assets	Rank	Assets
Ford Foundation	1	$2,902	1	$3,050
Lilly Endowment	2	778	7	320
Rockefeller Foundation	3	757	2	854
Duke Endowment	4	510	3	692
Kresge Foundation	5	433	*	173
Kellogg (W.K.) Foundation	6	393	4	492
Mott (Charles Stewart) Foundation	7	371	5	424
Pew Memorial Trust	8	367	10	273
Sloan (Alfred P.) Foundation	9	303	8	309
Carnegie Corp. of New York	10	283	9	289
Hartford (John A.) Foundation	11	277	6	342
Mellon (Andrew W.) Foundation	12	234	*	245
Totals	12	$7,608	12	$7,463

*Not in the first 12 in 3d edition.

Source: Lewis (1971).

billion for both years. A breakdown of these totals on an annual basis shows that education and welfare both received significant dollar boosts in outlays, whereas the total percentage of outlays dropped in favor of areas such as humanities and international activities.

Social science research is included under different categories. As Table 2.15 shows, $77 million, or 38 percent of the field of science and technology, goes for social science research. Social science is frequently a major component in the establishment, conduct, and evaluation of science and technology programs in general (Orlans 1972). Not only are the social science portions often disguised (not as a result of any sort of conspiracy but simply as a function of the novelty of using social science personnel), they are also closely tied to military and defense activities. Appendix C, for example, indicates the significant military overtones that are contained in the federal research support to private or nonuniversity research instruments. Because the data are broken down in a way that makes getting at the social science portion difficult, it is hard to determine with any exactitude just what is or is not the social science component in national policy research.

The federal government can promote liberal policies with minimum obstacles by virtue of either an earlier acceptance they may have gained under foundation sponsorship or as a result of joint funding. As one foundation spokesman put it to some skeptics who questioned the value of government-foundation cooperation: "foundations can be valuable to society by probing and supporting risky or highly experimental projects in fields in which a government impact sooner or later will be necessary" (Magat 1969:6). McGeorge Bundy, president of the Ford Foundation, notes that foundation efforts in many fields preceded those of the government: "The reasons for the time lag between foundation and government action are not identical in all cases, but there are some similarities: a tendency on the part of government to be wary of fields that may initially be 'controversial' (population and public broadcasting); delay in the development of an interested and lively public constituency (public broadcasting and the arts); the intense competition for federal funds, and the difficulty, even when need is recognized and public interest has grown, in defining just what the specific role of government should be" (Bundy 1974:v-xii).

"In most of the fields cited," Bundy writes, "needs are so great that they cannot be met without action by others (most importantly, the federal government) that is larger than private foundations can take. In most of these fields the federal government is a larger factor than the largest foundation in the field," he continues, "and in all of them it is now clear that in quantitative terms the role of public authorities generally continues to grow at a faster rate than that of foundation authorities. Despite shared action in various fields, the private foundation and the government are essentially autonomous. We never suppose that we must take whatever role the government proposes, and the various parts of government can and do exercise their own judgment on causes or programs that interest us. When we match public money . . . it is because we believe the particular cause is good. Certainly there are cases where we help to supply a missing element that in a different world the government would itself provide. . . . But the preponderant nature of the relation between a foundation's effort and the

TABLE 2.15

**Foundation Support for Physical, Biological,
and Social Sciences, 1970-71**

Category	Amount (thousands of dollars)	Percent
General science	3,920	2
Physical sciences		
General	891	
Astronomy and space	1,059	
Chemistry	7,697	
Earth sciences and oceanography	3,123	
Mathematics	540	
Physics	931	
Total	14,241	7
Life sciences		
General	88	
Environmental studies	14,898	
Agriculture	7,013	
Biology	12,735	
Medical research	66,094	
Total	100,828	50
Social sciences		
General	1,642	
Anthropology and archaeology	1,114	
Business and labor	19,337	
Economics	3,329	
Political science	15,935	
Law	17,045	
Psychology	3,598	
Sociology	15,929	
Total	77,929	38
Technology	6,694	3
Grand total	203,612	100

Source: Lewis (1971).

government's effort, when they are both large-scale grant-makers in the same field, is one of mutual reinforcement and a fitting division of labor" (Bundy 1974).

In addition to promoting government policy aims, foundations conduct research on problems that remain outside the scope of direct action by a private foundation, such as arms control. In such circumstances, research and analysis themselves become legitimized methods of action. "Government, like any other very large institution, is only imperfectly attentive to the need for self-examination, and it would be dangerous if an unavoidable monopoly of authority were combined with an avoidable monopoly of research and analysis. The government and the public stand to gain from the existence of independent studies by independent analysts" (Bundy 1974).

A more active form of research consists of experimental programs related to possible reform in public policy. Foundations support both analysis and experimental action in its approach to housing, community development, drug abuse, and the improvement of police effectiveness.

This assortment of data adds up to a steadily increasing set of federal expenditures for human resources, public welfare, environmental improvement, education, and other economic and social purposes. This increase takes place against a backdrop of declining federal expenditures for other areas: national security and directly military outlays are being reduced to absorb the new social services (cf. Weidenbaum 1971:88-89). In order to service this changeover properly, manpower-resource allocations have shifted from the physical and engineering sciences to the social and behavioral sciences. Thus, we are no longer dealing with the sort of marginal expenditures for social sciences customary in the past, but a new priority that raises profound qualitative considerations by the very fact of the magnitude of expenditures and outlays for the "soft" sciences by federal agencies, private foundations, and a host of other American economic and social institutions.

REFERENCES

Berelson, Bernard
  1960   *Graduate Education in the United States.* New York: McGraw-Hill.
Biderman, Albert and Laurie M. Sharp
  1972   *The Competitive Evaluation of Research Industry.* Washington, D.C.: Bureau of Social Science Research, Inc.
Bundy, McGeorge
  1974   "The President's Review" *Ford Foundation Annual Report.* October 1, 1972 to September 30, 1973. New York, March 24, 1974.
Lewis, Marianna O. (ed.)
  1971   *The Foundation Directory* (4th edition). Prepared by the Foundation Center. New York: Columbia University Press.
Magat, Richard
  1969   *Foundation Reporting.* Address to the Ninth Biennial Conference on Charitable Foundations, May 19, 1969.

Neilsen, Waldemar A.
    1972   *The Big Foundations.* New York: Columbia University Press (A Twentieth Century Fund Study).
Office of Management and Budget
    1973   *Special Analysis of the 1973 Budget.* Washington, D.C. U.S. Government Printing Office.
Organization for Economic Cooperation and Development
    1968   *Reviews of National Science Policy.* United States, Paris: OECD.
Orlans, Harold
    1972   *The Nonprofit Research Institute.* New York: McGraw-Hill.
Tax, Sol (editor)
    1967   *The Draft: A Handbook of Facts and Alternatives.* Chicago and London: The University of Chicago Press.
U.S. Department of State, Foreign Area Research Coordination Group
    1969   *Horizons* 2 (September, 1969) Washington, D.C.: U.S. Government Printing Office.
U.S. Congress, Senate Armed Services Committee
    1974   *Budget Request, FY 1974. Department of Defense.* Washington, D.C.: U.S. Government Printing Office.
U.S. National Science Foundation
    1973   *Federal Funds for Academic Science.* Washington, D.C.: U.S. Government Printing Office.
    1974   *Federal Funds for Research, Development, and Other Scientific Activities.* Washington, D.C.: U.S. Government Printing Office.
U.S. Congress, Senate Committee on Appropriations
    1973   *Legislative Branch Appropriations, 1973 and 1974.* Washington, D.C.: U.S. Government Printing Office.
Weidenbaum, Murray
    1971   "Changing Priorities in Government Investment in Technology," *The Use and Abuse of Social Science,* edited by Irving Louis Horowitz. New York: Transaction/E. P. Dutton.

CHAPTER

3

TRENDS IN THE
POLICY IMPLEMENTATION
OF SOCIAL SCIENCE
RESEARCH

Without the steadily increasing support from the federal agencies documented in Chapter 2, the relationship between social science and public policy in the United States would have been stillborn. Thus, we must turn our attention to the qualitative side of this picture: to specific legislative, executive, and judicial efforts to incorporate social science research in governmental practices and procedures. Beyond that, we must show how, even in such activities as lobbying by private enterprise, the role of the social sciences in setting forth public policy has been enhanced, if not entirely secured, in recent years.

The infusion of social science in public policy owes far less to any specific discoveries of the behavior sciences than to the general success of science as such in American life (Biderman 1970). Nearly 90 percent of the scientists and engineers the world has even known are still alive, and half of them live in the United States. Many of the presumably good things in American material life have been attributed to science; the word itself has acquired a mystique that has rubbed off on all those who wear the scientist's mantle. Thus, the degree of "softness" of any particular social science counts for less than the absorption into the American ideology of the idea that one can study sociological, political, and economic activities in a scientific manner. And thus, the spin-off of a portion of the American gross national product for social science, as well as for physical science, activities is largely the result of a faith in science as a whole. Determining whether such a spin-off is warranted on empirical grounds—i.e., in terms of the actual discoveries of the social sciences—is not the purpose of this study. But to ignore the milieu of a science-oriented culture would be to leave unexplained the unique role of the United States in the transformation of the social sciences from a small, ancillary activity performed behind university walls to a large-scale, central service performed in the full view of the body politic.

CONGRESS AND THE FULL OPPORTUNITY
AND SOCIAL ACCOUNTING ACT

In hearings before the Government Operations Committee (Senate Government Operations Committee 1968:322-33) Senator Walter Mondale described the four objectives of the Full Opportunity and Social Accounting Act (Senate 5: Title I):

1. Declaration of "full social opportunity for all Americans as a national goal";
2. formation of the Council of Social Advisors, which "advisory council to the President would draw from disciplines of social science in analyzing and evaluating progress in social reform";
3. issuance of an annual social report that "would enable the President to dig deeply into aspects of American life that are presently only touched upon" (by the executive branch); and
4. creation of the Joint Congressional Committee on the Social Report, "like the present Joint Committee on the Economic Report." (Senate Government Operations Committee 1968:322-33).

Following a series of major hearings, legislation for this bill was introduced in 1967. The Government Operations Committee held an informal seminar in June 1967 on the objectives of the legislation and the concept of social accounting, followed by four days of formal hearings in July 1967. A revised Full Opportunity Act was reintroduced to the 91st Congress by Mondale. In December 1969 Senator Jacob Javits, along with Senator Mondale, introduced an amendment to establish an office of goals and priorities analysis as an arm of the Congress. This office would submit an annual report to Congress, setting forth goals and priorities in the general context of needs, costs, available resources and program effectiveness. With some amendments the subcommittee established the office as Title II of the Full Opportunity and Social Accounting Act in April 1970. The bill was passed by the Senate in September 1970; however, the House took no action on this measure. In January 1971 Mondale and Javits introduced the identical bill in the 92d Congress. Testimony was heard from five witnesses on July 13, 1971, by the Subcommittee on Evaluation and Planning of Social Programs, which reported favorably on the bill, without amendment, in December 1971.

The informal seminar of the 90th Congress focused primarily on the idea of a national social accounting system, emphasizing the valuable contribution such a concept could make to governmental decision making. Although there are many difficulties inherent in trying to work with "soft" social data, seminar participants agreed that new mechanisms to deal with social needs and social programs were sorely needed.

At the hearings that followed the seminar, virtually all the witnesses testified on the paucity of information available to public policy makers in fields such as education, welfare, job training, health care, and antipoverty programs. Bertram

Gross pointed out: "Executive officials and Members of Congress alike are misled today by inadequate interpretation of bad information, based on obsolete concepts and inadequate research and collected by underfed and overlobbied statistical agencies" (Gross 1965; Gross 1966).

Many witnesses reiterated the complexity of putting social health into some system of indicators while pushing for immediate implementation of the program; for example, Howard Freeman, a member of the HEW panel on social indicators, also recommended that concurrent research be undertaken to constantly improve the system of social accounts. Concerning the roles of the various levels of government, private concerns, and institutions in the process of social accounting, the consensus of both the hearings and the seminar seemed to be that a strong federal effort and a national focus were essential with cooperation and coordination among all the bodies concerned. Philip Hauser also pointed out that the creation of a council of social advisors and a presidential social report would be an effective way to attract public attention and concern to needs and goals in the social areas.

An important question raised in further hearings of the Senate committee was whether the social sciences were ready to provide the kind of social indicators and cost-benefit analyses that are implied by this legislation. In response to this question, Otis Dudley Duncan said that the concept and feasibility of a social report had been demonstrated as long ago as 1933 with the pioneering study "Recent Social Trends." That study has been reinforced in recent years by the publication of such volumes as *Social Indicators* (Bauer 1966a), *Social Indicators and Sample Surveys* (1966b); *The Corporate Social Audit* (Bauer and Fenn 1972); and the HEW sponsored report, *Toward a Social Report* (Bell 1969).

While some witnesses questioned the advisability of another White House advisory unit, the general opinion was that a council of social advisors would greatly strengthen the president in identifying needs, establishing priorities, and evaluating programs. A council advising the White House would also help rectify the general lack of total, comprehensive, long-range social policy. Furthermore, it was felt, only a White House office could lend the necessary visibility and prestige to the effort to take social account of the nation's condition and progress.

Senator Charles Percy testified that the office of goals and priorities analysis would fill the large gap felt by Congress in the areas of independent counsel and perspective on national program and policy design. He also noted that the executive branch already surpassed Congress in that it had the services of a computer-based program-management and evaluation and information system. It was agreed that the tools provided for in the Full Opportunity Act would not only restore some balance between the executive and legislative branches but would also improve the quality of work in the executive branch.

In the hearings held in the 92d Congress Raymond Bauer (OMB 1972) in discussing the arrangements for the new office, stressed that we would have to allow a new Council of Social Advisors ten or 15 years to reach maturity. Sol M. Linowitz, chariman of the National Urban Coalition, pointed out that the office created by the Full Opportunity Act would provide congressmen with the means to analyze the budget as a whole for the first time, thus filling an "information vacuum."

Concerning the responsibilities of a council of social advisors, Nicholas J. Demerath III, who was then executive officer of the American Sociological Association, told the subcommittee that the social sciences were "now well along with the methodological revolution which is producing far greater rigor in handling more complex phenomena. . . . In the case of sociology, this has involved the development of methodological techniques largely borrowed from econometrics, as a matter of fact, which have ushered in a shift from static to dynamic and from descriptive to causal analysis" (Government Operations Committee 1968).

The committee estimated the costs that would be incurred in carrying out this bill for fiscal years 1973, 1974, and 1975 would be $1.5 million for each of the three years for Title I and $3 million for each of the three years for Title II. Both the congressional leaders and the social scientists took it for granted that such new forms of research would generate not only fresh data but also new answers to old problems. Few questioned such efficacy, and fewer still introduced any discordant notions that such capabilities could possibly be misapplied and might continue to service special interests instead of the general interest, precisely as a consequence of the new form of information retrieval. The professional societies of the social sciences, for the most part, located in Washington, D.C. had done their job very well.

NATIONAL FOUNDATION FOR THE SOCIAL SCIENCES

The proposal to establish a national foundation for the social sciences was developed and examined in a series of hearings held in 1966 and 1967 by the Subcommittee on Government Research of the Senate Committee on Government Operations (1967). Senator Fred Harris, chairman of the subcommittee, became the sponsor of the bill to establish the foundation. He stated that a separate foundation for social science would "give the recognition, status, visibility and prestige the social sciences need." In addition, Harris also pointed out that the National Science Foundation would, of necessity, continue to be dominated by physical scientists, and that there were too many risks in depending on mission-oriented agencies for new support for innovative programming.

The stated purpose of the Harris bill was the establishment of a national foundation for the social sciences, separate from the operating agencies and departments of the federal government (such as the National Science Foundation and the Department of Defense), to encourage and support research in the social and behavioral sciences. In addition, the foundation would serve as a contracting agency for the other departments and agencies to secure unclassified, scholarly research in the social and behavior sciences (Government Operations Committee 1967).

A number of government witnesses testified, in response to the proposed bill, but no general consensual position from the administration emerged. The director of the National Science Foundation opposed the creation of a separate foundation and outlined the basis for an expanded social science program for the NSF: representatives from the Department of Defense (DOD) and the Office of Economic Opportunity (OEO) stated they thought it would be unwise to set up a separate foundation. The secretary of Labor could not give a definite opinion on the proposal but did emphasize the need to strengthen social science research in the sciences' own departments; others, such as the representative of the Department of State and the Peace Corps, agreed that a new foundation would give the social sciences a substantial boost in the federal government (Lyons 1969:291-92).

The testimony of social scientists also varied greatly. Kingsley Davis, an eminent demographer from the University of California at Berkeley (and the first social scientist to be elected to the National Academy of Sciences), strongly supported the Harris bill. Warren Miller, director of the Inter-University Consortium for Political Research at the University of Michigan, also strongly supported the bill, arguing that only a federal foundation run by social scientists could be expected to fight for the support needed to use the newest developments in the social sciences.

The most direct opposition to a national foundation for the social sciences came from Herbert Simon, a political scientist and psychologist from Carnegie-Mellon University (and also a member of the NAS). Simon asserted his belief that there was a scientific and practical necessity for maintaining a single scientific organization, the NSF. He felt that social scientists should seek more recognition from the principal science policy-making agencies, the President's Science Advisory Committee (PSAC) and the Office of Science and Technology (OST), rather than multiply organizational layers. Simon's view has largely prevailed in social science circles.

Harris proceeded to report his bill out of the subcommittee with a favorable recommendation in the middle of 1968. However, no companion bill had come up for hearings in the House of Representatives. Instead, the House Committee on Science and Astronautics proposed a bill to amend the NSF that would give the NSF official authority to support the social sciences. With the restrictions on spending imposed by the priorities of the Vietnam War there seemed little prospect of immediate political success or immediately available funds, even if the bill were to be passed. Senator Harris reintroduced the bill in 1969, with 32 Senators co-sponsoring the legislation (there were 19 original co-sponsors), but again the bill was not enacted (Lyons 1969 289, 295).

Despite the legislative failure of the national foundation for the social sciences, the Harris bill had far-reaching effects on the development of a focused policy on the federal level for social science. The idea of a foundation devoted exclusively to the social sciences became an important element in the general reassessment in the federal government of the role of the social sciences, which was undertaken by three different social science policy study groups in late 1968. These groups were the Advisory Committee on Government Programs in the Behavioral Sciences, set up by the National Academy of Sciences-National Research Council; a joint project sponsored by the NAS and the Social Science Research Council to survey the state of the art and the future needs of the social sciences; and the NSF-sponsored Special Commission on the Social Sciences, set up to explore ways to strengthen the social sciences and make them more responsive to the needs of society.

Congress employs the services of social scientists in another aspect of policy making: technology assessment. The Office of Technology Assessment, established in 1972, although emphasizing physical science, recognizes the potential of social science contributions to its concerns. For example, social scientists will be employed on the following proposed analyses: economists and public policy analysts will examine using tax structures as instruments for upgrading the quality of the environment; public policy analysts, sociologists, and public opinion specialists will investigate social and attitudinal obstacles to food irradiation and the causes of these obstacles; consumer analysts will study waste-paper recycling; urban planners will look at possible employment of geothermal energy; experimental psychologists, energy economists, and political scientists will analyze the breeder reactor; experimental and social psychologists will study automotive air bags; specialists in the areas of public safety, national security, economics, and international affairs will be involved in the study of nuclear-materials safeguards; sociologists, economists, health care administrators, population statisticians, and demographers will examine genetic engineering (Office of Technology Assessment 1973:69-100).

Such legislative pressures did move the older NSF toward a more empathetic view of the social sciences, reflected not simply in increased expenditures but also in a special section led by a series of prominent social scientists, whose task was to broaden the mission of the NSF. The absence of legislative follow-through on the specific measures is due to many factors: grass-roots indifference as reflected in the generally negative attitude of members of the House of Representatives; opportunistic rather than principled reasons for supporting social-science and social-indicators legislation (for example, the potential for higher support to poorer states without regard to the actual present strengths and concentrations of social science personnel); and, finally, an indecisive response from professional social scientists themselves (cf. Westin and Baker 1972:341-405). While most testimony reflected strong support, there was a noticeable absence of like-minded enthusiasm in home universities, foundations, and private research establishments. Nonetheless, legislative relief or not, budgetary allocations for social scientists went soaring and thus relieved any great pressure for new congressional measures. What could not be accomplished through the act of Congress could clearly be achieved through the Bureau of the Budget.

SOCIAL INDICATORS AND NATIONAL GOALS

In September 1929 Herbert Hoover announced the formation of the Research Committee on Social Trends. The mission of the committee was "to examine and to report upon recent social trends in the United States with a view to providing such a review as might supply a basis for the formulation of large national policies looking to the next phase in the nation's development" (President's Research Committee on Social Trends, 1933:xi). "The various inquiries which have been conducted by the Committee are subordinated to the main purpose of getting a central view of the American problem as revealed by social trends." (President's Research Committee on Social Trends 1933:xiii). The report released by the committee advocated the application of knowledge to social action. The introduction of the report explained: "The Committee's procedure, then, has been to look at recent social trends in the United States as interrelated, to scrutinize the functioning of the social organization as a joint activity. It is the express purpose of this review of findings to unite such problems as those of economics, government, religion, education, in a comprehensive study of social movements and tendencies, to direct attention to the importance of balance among the factors of change" (President's Research Committee on Social Trends 1933:xiii).

The committee was financed by the Rockefeller Foundation and administered through the Social Science Research Council (SSRC). Wesley Mitchell, famed economist and a friend of Hoover's, and Charles Merriam, political scientist and a founder of the SSRC, played a profound role in the establishment and functioning of the committee (cf. Karl 1963:37-81). The report and committee were private, rather than governmental, operations. Of the 30 authors of the report, only one was a member of the federal government. Fully 20 had university affiliations, while the remaining nine were from various foundations.

Following the precedent established by Hoover, another Republican, Dwight Eisenhower, established the Commission on National Goals, which made its report in 1960. Rather than attempting a broad survey of American life, such as urged by the Hoover report, Eisenhower's commission focused on prescriptive goals. Its policy aims included, among others, "an ending [of] discrimination in higher education by 1970" while "states make progress in good faith toward desegregation of publicly supported schools" (Commission on National Goals; 1960:4). Whereas the Hoover committee gave only slight attention to international affairs, the world situation was a central focus of the Eisenhower commission. Interestingly, the cold war fueled much of this support: "Communist aggression and subversion . . . threaten all that we seek to do at home and abroad. . . . Communist China's blatant hostility to the United States makes it especially urgent to strengthen our Pacific defenses and our ties with our Pacific allies" (1960:18).

Frank Pace, Jr., vice-chairman of the National Commission on Goals and at the time chairman of the board of General Dynamics, commented: "My conception of what this Commission has tried to do is to set out the things for which we should strive over the long term and to identify areas in which inaction might cost us dearly. It should be recognized that the Commission task was to point out what the nation should do. It could not enter into the more difficult and detailed problems of priorities and the exact costing and paying for goals achievement" (1960:30).

One of the first calls for social indicators was contained in Gunnar Myrdal's classic study of American racial attitudes, *An American Dilemma* (Myrdal 1944). The study was funded by the Carnegie Foundation. He proposed the establishment of a yearly or decennial index on the progress of black achievement of equality. However, this proved to be an isolated cry in the policy wilderness. The next major broadening step beyond "economic philistinism" occured almost 20 years later, in the early years of the Kennedy administration, when Wilbur J. Cohen (later undersecretary of Health, Education and Welfare) initiated the annual HEW *Trends* and the monthly HEW *Indicators* (cf. Report of the Special Commission on the Social Sciences of the National Science Board 1969:56-58). These publications have grown increasingly sophisticated and comprehensive (Bauer 1966a:xiii-xiv).

In 1962 the PSAC issued a report, *On Strengthening the Behavioral Sciences* (1962). Among its recommendations the PSAC report called for more "systematic collection of basic behavioral data for the United States" (1962). Bauer (1966b:341) credits this report with stimulating several small research programs on social indicators at the University of Michigan's Survey Research Center in Chicago. At this same time, Wilbert Moore and Eleanor Sheldon of the Russell Sage Foundation were working on new methods of "monitoring social change" (Bauer 1966b:341). This foundation has continued its interest in social indicators (cf. Henriot 1972; Bauer and Fenn 1972).

In 1962 the National Aeronautics and Space Administration (NASA) began working with the American Academy of Arts and Sciences on a project to determine the "second order consequences" of a vast space program on American society. In order to discover or predict such changes, the need for societal monitoring devices, such as social indicators, was appreciated. Raymond Bauer became the director of research on the academy's program on social indicators, which released an issue of its journal, *Annals*, devoted entirely to the question of social indicators (1967). This issue, in conjunction with Bauer's *Social Indicators* (1966a), helped to fuel the social indicators' movement.

NASA's project gave a great deal of impetus to the social indicator research movement. The project has been described by Earl Stevenson, chairman of the Committee on Space, American Academy of Arts and Sciences, as "a pioneer among government agencies in its sensitivity to the wide ranging nature of its effects on society and in its awareness of the need to develop methods of anticipating these effects—and if possible—bringing them under some degree of conscious control" (Bauer 1966a:vii). At the same time, in 1966, the National Commission on Technology, Automation and the Economy pointed out in its report that the social measures lagged seriously behind the ability to measure strictly economic changes. The report called for a system of social accounts (not social indicators per se) to broaden the concept of cost and benefit beyond economic terms and emphasized four areas of development: measurement of social costs and net returns from innovations; improved measuring of "social ills"; "performance budget" in areas of social need, such as housing and education; and development of indicators on economic opportunity and social mobility.

The emergence of social indicators within the federal government occurred when Bertram Gross was able to stimulate Douglas Cater, special assistant to the White House for social questions, and John Gardner, secretary of HEW, to take positive action. Cater and Gardner liked the idea so well that they convinced President Johnson to establish the HEW Panel on Social Indicators (Bell 1969).

The panel consisted of 41 social scientists and an equal number of statisticians and administration experts. The joint chairmen were Daniel Bell and William Gorham (who was replaced by Alice Revlin in 1968). It might be added that this executive route of the social indicators movement, like its legislative counterpart, represented a fusion and meeting of minds between liberal politicians and academicians.

In March 1966 the office of Lyndon Johnson directed the secretary of HEW to "search for ways to improve the Nation's ability to chart its social progress." In particular, the president's office requested that HEW "develop the necessary social statistics and indicators to supplement those prepared by the Bureau of Labor Statistics and the Council of Economic Advisors. With these yardsticks we can better measure the distance we have come and plan for the way ahead" (Johnson 1967; Johnson 1971).

The Health, Education and Welfare Panel of Social Indicators responded to Johnson's directive with *Toward a Social Report*, delivered on January 11, 1969 (Bell 1969). It urged, in HEW Secretary Cohen's words, "the continued allocation of staff resources in the Executive Branch to prepare a comprehensive social report to the Nation with emphasis on the development of social indicators which will measure social change and be useful in establishing social goals" (U.S. Department of Health, Education and Welfare 1970:111). However, panel member Raymond Bauer noted at the time that the HEW panel "doesn't have either muscle or autonomy of an independent agency to generate the necessary initiative to keep a social indicator movement alive" (Government Operations Committee 1968:p. 90).

On July 13, 1969, President Richard Nixon established a National Goals Research Staff (NGRS) within the White House. In establishing the staff, Nixon stated, "It is not to be a 'data bank'. It might more accurately be referred to as a key element in a management information system. For the first time it creates within the White House a unit specifically charged with the long perspective; it promises to provide the research tools with which we at last can deal with the future in an informed and informative way" (National Goals Research Staff 1970:222).

> This will be a small, highly technical staff, made up of experts in the collection, correlation, and processing of data relating to social needs, and in the projection of social trends. It will operate under the direction of Leonard Garment, Special Consultant to the President, and will maintain a continuous liaison with Daniel P. Moynihan in his capacity as Executive Secretary of the Council for Urban Affairs, and with Arthur Burns, Counsellor to the President, in his capacity as head of the Office of Program Development (ibid.).

The functions of the NGRS were to include forecasting future developments and assessing the longer-range consequences of present social trends; measuring the probable future impact of alternative courses of action, including measuring the degree to which change in one areas would be likely to affect another; estimating the actual range of social choice; developing and monitoring social indicators that can reflect the present and future quality of American life and the direction and rate of its change; summarizing, integrating, and correlating the results of related research activities being carried on within the various federal agencies, and by state and local governments and private organizations (National Goals Research Staff 1970:221-22).

The National Goals Research Staff can be contrasted to earlier efforts of the Hoover commission, the HEW report, and especially the Commission on National Goals established by Eisenhower. Those groups had been oriented toward identifying specific goals and measuring the nation's progress in achieving them. There were no such targets for the NGRS: "The Staff did not have a goal-*setting* function; neither did it have a planning function. Rather its purpose has been to pull together analyses into a comprehensive, long-range view of policy alternatives that can serve as an aid in the process of decision" (Ibid:22). Originally mandated to produce "annual reports," the NGRS was disbanded shortly after producing its first report. Since 1970 the Office of Statistical Policy of the Office of Management and the Budget (OMB) has taken limited "responsibility for setting up a consistent system of social indicators and publishing the results" (Cazes 1972:10).

The Office of Management and Budget produced this report in the early part of 1974. The study is a survey of eight indicators (health, public safety, education, employment, income, housing, population, and leisure and recreation). Although most of the data composing the broad indicators are well-established federal statistics, some information originates from private sources (1974). The goal of the report is to provide composite indexes (in graphic form) of important variables. The study is designed to appeal to the public and provide a central and usable source of information on salient features of American life for professionals. Many federal agencies have cooperated in the construction of this report. OECD and the United Nations have both provided encouragement and advice to this project (OMB 1974).

The social indicators movement is a step toward bringing social science information to bear upon public policy. But such indicators represent a higher rationalization and systematization of quantitative data, rather than any full array of social science explanations. Thus, social indicators movement is a step toward a more expansive role for the social sciences, but it carries some severe limiting factors in the definition of such a role.

SOCIAL SCIENTISTS AND THE EXECUTIVE OFFICE

Until recently, there were two direct channels by which social scientists could provide their expertise to the president and his top advisors. The first was the general science policy advisory machinery, and the second was OMB. PSAC has had three social-scientist members; OST has also had several staff members who were social scientists. These two organizations were called upon occasionally to integrate their expertise to find technological solutions to social problems—for example, in the fields of public safety and energy utilization and supply. Both of these organizations were disbanded in January 1973.

One of the most influential organizations in the federal government is OMB. The mission of this office is to provide direct staff assistance to the president, so there is frequent interraction between the president and the OMB director. The director attends all meetings of the National Security Council and the Cabinet. In addition to continually advising and reporting to the president, OMB transmits policy, as well as management information, to the departmental level. Instructions from OMB convey "what agencies should do to accomplish the purposes of the Administration and achieve greater administrative efficiency (Bureau of the Budget 1965:21). The professional members of OMB are comprised primarily of economists. The unusually demanding assignment encompasses the entire range of federal activity. "Solutions of issues requires skillful combinations of political science, economics, sociology and other social sciences. It is at the summit of the executive branch responsibilities, within the Executive Office of the President, that issues must be and finally are resolved" (Bureau of the Budget 1965a:2).

Social scientists from academic settings are pressed into government services at the highest levels, no less than in bureaucratic-line tasks. Henry Kissinger was a Harvard professor of political science before entering the government as head of the State Department; George Schultz was at the University of Chicago before becoming Secretary of State and then Treasury. Daniel Moynihan, another Harvard professor, was an assistant to the president for urban affairs before his appointment as U.S. ambassador to India. These men often serve executive authority without respect to party labels or affiliations. It is their special attribute to be "nonpartisan" experts. Such high-level personnel serve to underwrite a view of social science as objective and value free and an orientation providing a set of interchangeable parts in a systemic context.

AUXILIARY MEASURES: INDUSTRY

Approximately 5 percent of all social scientists who have their doctoral degrees are employed in private industry. The National Science Foundation in a 1968 survey determined that 1,658 social scientists were employed in the private sector. The distribution was as follows: psychologists, 1,001; economists, 405; statisticians, 151; political scientists, 36; sociologists, 35; linguists, 20; anthropologists, 10. This figure may be slightly inflated, since some of the firms labeled as private industry are themselves service agencies dominated by social science personnel.

The distribution of social scientists across management positions was determined by Radom (1970) as shown in Table 3.1. Radom's typology classifies top management as those who report to the president or the chairman of the board of a company. Middle management is defined as those who report to a departmental head or vice-president. Bottom positions are described as those who are supervisors, staff, or technicians, or those who report to middle management personnel. As Table 3.1 reveals, social scientists, especially sociologists, are clustered in influential positions in the table of organization.

TABLE 3.1

**Field and Level of Social Scientists in Industry
(percent)**

	Position			
Field	Top	Middle	Bottom	Total
Economists	33	37	30	100
Psychologists	21	43	36	100
Sociologists	40	20	30	100
Statisticians	4	26	70	100

Source: Radom (1970, p. 9).

Those who report to the president or the chairman of the board are often in a position to have a significant impact on the policy choices and decisions of a company.

General Motors Corporation gives a sound illustration of how social scientists are deployed for policy research in industry. It has a Societal Analysis Department that makes long-range studies used in planning the future activities of General Motors. For example, the Societal Analysis Department is performing research on social indicators in order to forecast changing social values of a society-wide scale. Game-theoretic models of political behavior are also being constructed. Social justification for automotive use of fuel and materials, the social justification and impact of corporate profit, and the socio-environmental impact of automobiles are among the subjects of inquiry for this department. As pressures mount on giant corporations to curb their pollution practices, the use of social science personnel has sharply increased.

General Motors clearly prefers social scientists with a highly quantitative orientation, again reflecting a strong business tendency to consider social scientists as middle echelon personnel not unlike accountants in skill and performance. This professional staff includes a chemical engineer, a sociologist, a mathematical economist, an economist, a systems analyst, and a physicist. The department has a commitment to expand its professional staff to 50, with a total staff of 70 by 1980. In addition, General Motors has a Department of Urban Transportation that performs socioeconomic analyses. Its staff contains two economists, two psychologists, and one urban planner, as well as numerous physical scientists.

Ford Motor Company, General Electric, and Bell Laboratories also conduct social research along similar lines. In general, those corporations best described as multinational in character—that is, with a high proportion of business production and consumption taking place outside the confines of the United States—have the most social science inputs into their corporate policy and planning. In a sense, this is simply because multinationals must function with an organizational chart and a series of international obligations more akin to a nation-state than to an old-fashioned company producing a single type of product or service.

The case of Bell Laboratories is particularly instructive. Bell Laboratories employs 98 social scientists with master's or doctor's degrees in the following fields: education, 10; social studies, 5; political science, 1; psychology, 72; philosophy, 3; economics, 7. The preponderance of its social scientists are in psychology, and those are primarily concentrated in experimental psychology. Work is performed in the areas of human engineering, educational technology, evaluation of speech quality, and fundamental research in human information processing. At times, Bell Laboratories has done some work in social psychology in the areas of communications between two or more people. Its Research Center intends to expand activities in this area. However, the director indicated informally that problems in social science research are very difficult, and Bell tends to proceed cautiously in new and difficult areas. Researchers are likewise on the lookout for solvable problems relating to interpersonal relationships among the people who make up the Bell System. Its social scientists are distributed widely throughout Bell Laboratories. However, the Acoustical and Behavioral Research Center has a concentration of about 20 psychologists. As in government, so too in the private sector: first come the economists, then the psychologists, followed in quick succession by the sociologists, the political scientists, and the anthropologists.

The degree to which private social science laboratories are themselves influenced by general ideological currents remains moot. Just as the general culture of the Department of State is influenced by broad generic writings of political scientists such as Hans J. Morgenthau and Frederick L. Schuman, so too are private laboratories emphasizing psychological research influenced by outstanding individual contributors such as environmentalist J. McVicker Hunt and geneticist H. J. Eysenck. For our purposes, given the considerable amount of debate over race, education, and the nature-nurture controversy, we can confine our discussion to a consideration of H. J. Eysenck. His work should be viewed as typifying a broad spectrum of psychological opinion whose policy implications are more often drawn by agencies such as the Educational Testing Service and Bell Laboratories than by individual psychologists themselves.

There has been some recent criticism of the behavioristic emphasis in educational psychology. Specifically, the main complaint is that oversimplification of psychological theory gives rise to inappropriate hypotheses. When these hypotheses are tested, inconclusive or inconsistent results are achieved. To overcome this shortcoming, elite social scientists recommend closer collaboration between theoretical psychologists and educationists. This would allow the latter to take advantage of progress in theoretical and applied psychology. For instance, Eysenck (1972) addresses himself to the dichotomy between "state" or environmental characteristics and "trait" or hereditary characteristics in an individual. He sees as a basic issue the manipulation of habits (and, thus, the accomplishments of the individual) by influencing the drive stimuli. He sees two major areas of control: a) selectivity and fit of personality type as the individual progresses through the various 'gates' in educational achievement and b) alteration of the material so as to influence the individual's drive.

From this vantage point a general theory of academic achievement and personality type has been constructed. Such theories have a large component of hereditary and possibly racial overtones. By employing such a theory, a consistent level of educational achievement is sought across broad socioeconomic and racial groups. This consistent level would almost certainly not be maximized for the individual. Rather, it would be a necessary feature of a large-scale operation, standardizing the achievement of large disadvantaged or underprivileged groups. Such standardization would permit an adjustment in the ability among such groups to contribute to society. The level then could be set so that a particular type of contribution could be obtained from members of groups undergoing such an industry-wide educational program.

One result might be forced equity along paramilitary lines through national-service education and training. Using such a general theory of educational psychology, it would be possible for social scientists to establish a program through which untrained youth of the lower stratum could be funneled. The actual goals of such a national-service or other large-scale education program would be established by political and mass elites. It would then be left to the social scientists to fill in the bridges. Social scientists would design programs that would peg the goals to the groups and cohorts to be absorbed by such a large-scale program of training and service. Thus, we might find psychological researchers aiming at retooling the "retarded" for appropriate tasks in industry by treating cohort groups so that their "states" and hereditary "traits" could best be adapted or perhaps forcibly altered to best serve the needs of a military-industrial complex.

Such recommendations need not be limited to the industrial sector. Manipulatory concepts can be expanded to nation-wide applications. The concept of "national service" is one such example. National service is an idea that implies coercive or voluntary participation in vast public projects that could encompass any age group, but more often encompasses youthful cohorts. Social scientists' participation in such projects, and especially the nature and type of participation, helps cement the bond between social science and the power of the state. In the spring of 1971 a group of educators, public officials, executives of voluntary associations, and social scientists assembled in New York City, under the auspices of the Russell Sage Foundation, to explore the dimensions of national service for youth.

The collective statement by several eminent social scientists foreshadows a movement of social science into a state-service industry. A striking, common characteristic of many of the participants is their interest in military affairs. Morris Janowitz, chairman of the conference, is a leading authority of military sociology. Adam Yarmolinsky, a contributor and now professor of law at Harvard, served in the office of the secretary of Defense as an advisor to President Kennedy during the early stages of involvement in Southeast Asia and was a strong advocate of a nation-wide civil defense shelter program. Colonel Jack Butler, a member of the United States Army War College has performed studies of the volunteer army concept for the Defense Department. Charles Moskos is another leading military sociologist with a special emphasis on enlisted men and combat soldiers. Other participants in this typical symposium included Commander James Barber, U.S. Navy War College; Colonel H. A. Davis, Project Volunteer Headquarters, U.S. Air Force; and Paul Akst, Selective Service director, New York.

The participants represented many different professional backgrounds (for example, Margaret Mead was a participant). This underscores the fact that national identification tends to supercede professional credos at critical junctures. Significant points presented by social scientists at various gatherings on selective service are as follows: social leveling, mixing social classes, new forms in the convergence of the military and civilian sectors, pacification of the domestic population in the United States, the social control of rioting, the termination of deviant behavior, and, finally, an end to educational failure. These points add up to nothing less than an entire reconsideration of U.S. domestic policy by a significant portion of the social science community. The fundamental recommendation is that military life for all entails an equality of opportunity, but it also entails an enforced authoritarian democracy at the lowest possible denominator. The rigid suppression of individual differences advocated by experts in the area constitutes a proletarianization of American class structure in the service of the nation-state.

The distinctions between civil and military sectors, between international justice and international order, between domestic disasters and behavioral control are to be eliminated. The highest form of personal obligation and service is aiding the state to achieve whatever goals the nation chooses. National service is to be the exclusive permissible alternative to discontented youth. If a youth fails to adjust or succeed in the larger society his option can only be national service. Marginal adjustments such as "dropping out" or living "on the street" are eliminated, perhaps by a section or corps of the same national service.

In many military-sponsored conferences we find few examples of the social scientists questioning the need for a national service. The ideological underpinnings of such a system are minimized in favor of a detailing of the means and style of implementing the program. Only one commentator touched on the specific application of the talents of the national-service youth; the area mentioned was a system of teachers' aides at inner-city schools. Nowhere in the conference papers are the dangers or potential misapplications of such a program discussed. Desiring the quick implementation of a national-service program with a large social science planning element, not a few social scientists prefer to avoid such questions. Supporters of the national service program may not desire such criticism when the program is still in its postnatal stage.

The idealism of social scientists participating in the national-service program planning stems from their profound belief in the correctability of national shortcomings, as well as the perfectibility of society through the use of social science. These social scientists forget, however, that the federal government, as well as its agencies, is limited by historical and geopolitical circumstances. It is committed to managing cumbersome, overgrown committee and data-gathering agencies. It is committed to a status quo merely for the sake of rational functioning. It can only tinker with innovating ideas. Thus, federal agencies will limit national-service programs and the ancillary social scientists simply to what is immediately useful to the state—not out of choice entirely but of necessity as well. The social scientist often imagines he is a policy formulator, an innovating designer. Because of the cumbersome operations of government, he will be frustrated in realizing this self-image and be reduced to one more instrumental agent. He gets caught up in theoryless applications to immediate problems, surrenders the value of confronting men with an image of what can be and simply accepts what others declare must be.

The question various conferences on a national military service forcefully raise is not so much about the relationship between pure and applied research but concerns the character of such application. Applied research is clearly here to stay and is probably the most singular and novel element in American social science, in contrast to its European background. What is at stake is a highly refined concept of application that removes theoretical considerations of the character and balance of social forces and private interests from the purview of application. The design of the future replaces the analysis of the present in our new utopian world.

RESEARCH FUNCTIONS OF THE UNITED STATES INFORMATION AGENCY

In its role as a linkage mechanism between U.S. foreign policy and overseas publics, the United States Information Agency (USIA) can be described as having a two-fold function: a) advising the executive branch of government about the dynamics of public opinion abroad and its implications for present and contemplated U.S. foreign policies and b) disseminating scientific and propaganda materials to the publics overseas. The USIA research program, which is administered by the Research Service in the Office of Research and Assessment, has two basic functions that parallel the two major agency objectives: a) descriptions and analyses of public opinions overseas for policy advisory purposes, including opinions regarding the United States, its foreign policy, and specific issues in which the United States has an interest, and b) evaluation of program effectiveness, including analyses of local media habits and social and communications structures.

These functions are performed through several types of survey and other empirical research studies. They include basic attitudes and values, including trends and cross-country comparisons of general images of the United States and other countries; sampling of opinions on specific topics or events of current interest relating to American domestic life or foreign policy; media habits, including stylistic and thematic preferences; patterns of influence and social structure, including identification of influential groups and social communication patterns that, together with data on media habits, can be used to help designate priority audiences and prime channels of communication; program evaluation studies, including the extent of the audience attitudes (agency and local post programs); and finally, foreign media and information service studies that seek to describe the foreign information context in which the agency operates. Through its Research Service, the USIA regularly distributes copies of foreign-attitudes research studies to interested agencies. These generally include the State Department, the Arms Control and Disarmament Agency, the Commerce Department, the Defense Department, the relevant U.S. embassies abroad, the U.S. mission to the United Nations, and OECD. These research reports are compiled into monthly listings and annual bibliographies.

Within the space of approximately 12 months, in 1972, the Research Service received over 30 memoranda requesting surveys and monitoring stories for the White House staff and the National Security Council. Topics of interest included President Nixon's visits to the People's Republic of China and the Soviet Union, Japanese opinion on Japan's national security issues, foreign reaction to the mining of North Vietnamese ports and rivers, and general indicators of the United States' standing in the world. Additionally, requests have also been received from the White House Special Action Office for Drug Abuse Prevention for information for the potential evaluation of mass media campaigns against drug abuse, particularly through the use of comic books, and from the National War College on the impact of the East-West détente.

Through the use of personnel of the International Security Affairs Division of the USIA the Research Service attempts to insure that significant documents are placed in the hands of the appropriate decision makers in other governmental departments. For example, Brooks McClure, from the International Security Division, is attached to the Department of Defense. His assignment is to summarize and then target information for use within DOD. At the same time, McClure also advises USIA on DOD's needs and interests and on ways that USIA can be useful toward those ends. Abe Sirkin serves a similar function with the State Department's Planning and Coordination Staff. In addition, Sirkin serves as an "interpreter" of social science information for the State Department and as a "lobbyist" for USIA interests at the State Department.

The findings of the Research Service are mainly used in two ways: social science and public opinion information is used to guide the development of policy and for the evaluation of the impact of past decisions on the current international situation.

In the area of guidance, social science research can evaluate the general situation within a foreign country that is conducting talks or negotiations with the United States. For example, a series of foreign opinion studies is usually prepared before the president has conferences with various prime ministers and heads of foreign nations. Before a conference with West Germany's Willy Brandt, it was determined that there was no significant amount of anti-American feeling or movement towards neutralism in Germany. Before President Nixon's meeting with Premier Georges Pompidou of France, surveys revealed that although Franco-American relationships were good, the consensus of public opinion was that there were very basic differences in respective national goals that would lead to conflict between the two nations. A survey done before the president's conference with Prime Minister Andreotti of Italy discerned a noticeable turn of Italian public orientation away from the United States and towards the European community. Prior to important discussions with Prime Minister Tanaka of Japan, Japanese public opinion was seen as being quite divided on the subject of making economic concessions to the United States.

Such anticipatory information makes it possible for negotiators to be more accurately apprised of the true strengths and weaknesses of their opposite members and the current situations they are facing in their domestic politics. In international economic negotiations the Research Service attempts to determine the version of the facts that will improve the progress of negotiations. The Service attempts to find the inputs of information that are likely to be most useful in modifying or influencing foreign opinion in a direction helpful to United States objectives abroad. Increasingly, such intelligence activities are dealt with by social scientists.

As stated, the second area of interest of the Research Service is evaluating the impact of past events on the current world situation. For example, serious consideration is being given to the upcoming United States' bicentennial celebration and its international publicity. It is felt that if too much emphasis is placed on U.S. accomplishments, the United States will be seen as an old, tired country. Thus, the emphasis of the publicity is being shifted to the nation's challenges and opportunities so that it projects the image of a young, vital country. By the same token, the interpretation of U.S. power as being just past its zenith is seen as encouraging speculation against the value of the dollar on international money markets.

A further problem is the question of the advisability of candor in Voice of America broadcasts and USIA publications. Studies have found that candor heightens credibility. Yet on specific questions, such as programs depicting the true status of black people in the United States, the Voice of America has had the effect of compelling listeners to adopt a more unfavorable picture of the United States. Thus, the tension between propaganda and propaganda analysis, particularly evident in the United States, where both are in the hands of social scientists, may lead to unanticipated consequences.

The USIA surveys provide the policy maker with valuable "situational" information to deal with international affairs. The orienting features of such surveys permit the policy maker to evaluate progress or the lack of it in the pursuit of some of his specific goals. The series of pre- and post-visit surveys of President Nixon's trips to the PRC and the Soviet Union fall into the areas of both stocktaking and stockpiling of knowledge. These surveys investigated the range of expectations and reactions to the visits among a wide variety of populations in 15 nations. The purpose of the studies was to measure the impact of the visits on the general standing of the United States in the eyes of the world. A secondary purpose of the studies was to measure foreign awareness and expectations regarding the visits.

The surveys were prepared, analyzed and disseminated in record-breaking time. The findings of the PRC surveys were deemed important enough by the USIA to warrant presentation on June 20, 1972, to all the agencies, including the State Department and the White House. Interest among members of the State Department generated a series of briefings. After the findings were presented at the State Department's area directors luncheon, a long and spirited discussion of the implications of the findings was held. A copy of the study was distributed to the White House, extensively annotated in the president's own hand Documentation of the use of the study in policy making ends here, but the thorough reading and notation of the study by the president is certainly very encouraging to the staff of the Research Service.

Significantly, the USIA does not simply operate as an information clearinghouse putting American "know-how" to use in an overseas context; it also extracts basic kinds of data of a public but nonetheless sensitive nature to be used in fashioning U.S. foreign policy. This in no way implies illegal or illicit behavior on the part of USIA officials. It is to point out that the fine line between information retrieval and policy-relevant commentary is often crossed and crisscrossed. Given the fact that a considerable number of USIA officials are expressly involved in social science research and, beyond that, have social science backgrounds, the role of agencies and middle-echelon personnel in the actual conduct of U.S. foreign policy must be ranked as considerable.

As the field of psycho-history expands, with the concomitant analysis of important or famous people from afar, there can be no question that social scientists will come to perform a significant role in providing information-retrieval and attitudinal studies for policy makers, especially for those called upon to make major decisions in face-to-face diplomatic contact. The danger is that such analysis from afar may be superficial and even downright erroneous, hence leading not only to incorrect policy evaluations but to mistaken calculations of the intentions of other leaders and ultimately other nations. But in this new field, as in other areas, the answer to poor research is sound research.

SOCIAL SCIENTISTS IN OTHER NATIONAL
POLICY AREAS

Social scientists are playing an expanded role in the guidance of U.S. science policy. For example, an increased percentage of members of the prestigious National Science Board (NSB) are of a social scientific background. The NSB recommends the orientation of the NSF, which, in turn, is responsible for the support of basic research in many fields of science. Of the past 71 members of the NSB only seven were social scientists (10 percent). However, of the 24 current members of the board, five are social scientists (21 percent). Thus, the present percentage of social science members is twice that of past social science members.

The Council of Economic Advisors (CES) has taken greater interest in national policy for science and technology. Under consideration are problems of resource allocation and the general relationship among science, technology, and the economy. For example, in the annual report of the CEA of 1972 a chapter was devoted to the topic, "Effective Use of Resources: Research and Development."

The National Association of Manufacturers (NAM) has a staff for policy consisting of over 290 persons. Of this staff, 20 percent are social scientists or have a social science degree. Half of them (i.e., 10 percent) are political science specialists. They work under Wright Elliott, the executive vice-president, who serves out of the New York office. Elliott received his doctorate in political science from Cornell University.

The primary source of information concerning United States support for population policy research is the "Federal Program in Population Research" (Office of Science and Technology 1969), which is an inventory of population research supported by federal agencies. Two editions of this publication have been published. The federally supported population policy research projects that these inventories list are as follows: a) feasibility of research effects of government population policies in Eastern Europe (Henry David, American Institute for Research); b) situation reports on population problems, policies, and program (Harrison Brown, California Institute of Technology); c) goals and conditions of population control (Kingsley Davis, University of California, Berkeley); and d) population/economic growth analysis and presentation, for political and economic policy makers in developing countries (Stephen Enke, General Electric Company).

"Population Growth and America's Future," an interim report prepared by the Commission on Population Growth and the American Future, lists the following population policy research projects and papers which it plans to publish: a) congressional-executive relations in the formation of explicit population policy (Phyllis Piotrow, Johns Hopkins University); b) historical development of values in the U.S. political legal tradition bearing on population growth and distribution (Peter Brown, Institute of Society, Ethics, and the Life Sciences); c) present and future American ethical norms as limits upon possible population policies (Institute of Society, Ethics, and the Life Sciences); d) population policy making and the Constitution (Arthur S. Miller, National Law Center, George Washington University); and e) guarding against unintended consequences of possible population policies (Theodore J. Lowi, University of Chicago). Outside of government, various foundations and organizations, such as Resources for the Future and the Population Council, are becoming more active in policy research on the population problem, and the National Academy of Sciences is preparing a report on the policy implications of rapid population growth.

The Office of Emergency Preparedness (OEP), formerly in the executive office of the president, was abolished as of June 30, 1973, with its functions and pertinent records distributed to several other agencies. As a central body the OEP had employed social scientists in planning, evaluation, and consulting, and these efforts are still ongoing but dispersed to other agencies. The natural-disaster functions were transferred to HUD.

Except for energy and civil-defense functions, the General Services Administration has been assigned the other OEP functions. The development of policies, plans, and procedures for many elements of emergency-preparedness programs within the General Services Administration involves inputs from the behavioral, economic, and political science disciplines. The emphasis, however, has been mainly on inputs from economics and economists and is provided by a small in-house professional staff supported in part by a limited amount of research monies used primarily for stimulating or "piggy backing" other federal agency research allied to the General Services Administration's emergency-preparedness programs.

Social scientists and social technicians, such as Carl Kaysen, Adam Yarmolinsky, Herman Kahn, Richard Nelson, and personnel from RAND Corporation have played a significant role in the design of a civil-defense program. In the early 1960s there was a great deal of propagandizing for the adoption of extensive civil-defense measures. This militating for increased civil-defense programs included congressional testimony and hearings, government-wide briefings and policy-oriented studies, and even the support of President Kennedy. Herman Kahn (cf. 1960, 1962), an active proponent of tremendous civil defense programs states, "I believe the civil defense program as it went was almost exactly what was recommended in RAND Report R-341 [which he authored], and many people in government will tell you that the government's program of civil defense actually came directly from those briefings" (Kahn 1973). The Hudson Institute, where Kahn is currently a fellow, has produced sociotechnical reports in the emergency preparedness area, such as *Post-Attack Social Organization* for the Office of Civil Defense.

SOCIAL SCIENCE AND THE
JUDICIAL SECTOR

Social science information is becoming increasingly important to the U.S. judicial system. A central factor in this development is the role that social science information plays in providing a surrogate precedent for the courts. This surrogate is necessary when the courts probe issues that disturb public sensitivity and hence tend not to have been dealt with openly before, as in the case of *Loving* v. *Virginia* (see below).

An early advocate of the utilization of social science in the adjudication process was the American barrister (and later Supreme Court justice) Louis Brandeis. In a 1908 Oregon case he used a defense that subsequently became famous as the "Brandeis Brief." A state statute that established a ten-hour maximum work-day for women was under attack on the grounds that it was unconstitutional. Instead of stressing the tranditional approach of precedent and common law, Brandeis cited evidence from social science disciplines. Through this work, Brandeis expanded the juridical process to include materials from social inquiry.

Since the early 1960s social advocacy linked with social science has become an increasingly significant aspect of judicial decision making. The goal of this infusion is to attain social justice by altering social policy through the judicial branch of government. Three of the most visible aspects of the emphasis on social advocacy have been the American Civil Liberties Union (ACLU), the Legal Defense Fund of the National Association for the Advancement of Colored People (NAACP), and the "store-front" law firms supported (until recently) by the OEO.

With the encouragement of the OEO, activist lawyers have intervened in various legal questions involving the rights of the disadvantaged in the United States. In 1971 the Supreme Court of California reached a landmark decision striking down the tranditional means of support for local school systems, local property taxes. The conclusion of the court was that since there was regional variation in income and property values, so too there would be regional fluctuation in the quality of education. This decision is a milestone in the relationship between social advocacy and social science research in the judicial field.

The groundwork was established through a great deal of social science research devoted to analyzing the mechanisms of the school finance system as well as various consequences and available alternatives. Factors taken into account in this groundwork included the total assessed valuation of real estate in each town, the number of dollars spent for each pupil, local variations in property tax rates, and the state contributions to student costs (Coons, Clune, and Sugarman 1970).

Social science information has played a striking role in judicial decisions involving race relations (see *Brown* v. *Board of Education* in a later chapter). Until the case of *Richard Loving, et al* v. *the Commonwealth of Virginia* in 1967 the Supreme Court had not considered anthropological data in the weighing of cases dealing with racial issues. Arguments about the concept of race as used by social scientists had not been present in courtroom cross-examination. In the supporting *amicus curiae* brief on behalf of Loving, Solomon Katz, an anthropologist at the University of Pennsylvania and Eastern Pennsylvania Institute, was invited to help clarify issues and misconceptions regarding the use and meaning of the concept of race in the legal context (cf. Katz 1973).

Laws of differing clarity and age that were interfering with interracial marriage were then carried by 16 states. The laws relied upon faulty definitions of race whenever they attempted to classify individuals, depending upon nineteenth century concepts about "racial purity" that intrinsically assumed "racial superiority." Since those assumptions had to be applied to individuals, a nonspecific causal relationship was imputed between a person's intellectual or biological superiority (or inferiority) and his race. These antimiscegenation laws also relied upon standards of proof about race that were contingent upon concepts of "blood" and could not be applied objectively under the law.

It was clear to social scientists and lawyers alike that anthropology addressed questions involved in the legal issues of race, and that relevant data were available. A careful study was performed to test each legal supposition involved in the issue of race. The suppositions were tested in areas of physical anthropology such as population-variation concepts, history of the races, and biological variations inherent in race. Katz and his associates determined that most, if not all, of the basic presuppositions involved in the application of the race laws were obscure, improper, and inappropriate. A brief was then constructed on these grounds and the verbal argument before the Supreme Court was oriented along the information yielded by the anthropological inquiry.

The Supreme Court justified the striking down of the antimiscegenation laws in terms of the Fourteenth Amendment, thus basing the decision on constitutional issues. During the courtroom procedures, however, a great deal of attention was devoted to the anthropological issues. The justices demonstrated that they understood the meaning of the anthropological argument. Chief Justice Earl Warren quoted several themes from the literature of physical anthropology.

The justices addressed many pointed questions to the appellee (the Commonwealth of Virginia) lawyer as to the enforceability and meaning of race concepts. By the time the cross-examination was completed, the commonwealth lawyers abandoned their argument of biological hierarchy. When evidence as to the weakness of such concepts was introduced, the defense of antimiscegenation laws shifted to social psychological variables involved in maintaining racial purity. While this defense raised several new points that the social sciences address, no further work was undertaken along those lines (in that brief), since the law was struck down by the Supreme Court.

The most recent illustration of social science participation in legal practice concerns not judicial decision-making per se but rather the intervention of social scientists in the choice of jury selection to determine the outcomes of jury deliberation. The most outstanding illustration of this procedure involved social scientists Jay Schulman, Phillip Shaver, and their associates, acting in support of defense counsels Ramsey Clark and Leonard Boudin. The trial was the well-reported conspiracy trial of the Harrisburg Seven (Schulman et al. 1973:37-44). Their problem was deciding on prospective jurors who would be favorable to the defendants in an essentially conservative Pennsylvania area. The results, to be sure, were mixed. But the analysis provided indicates that such kinds of social science intervention are indeed a fruitful area for future activity. What makes this especially important is the radical constituency serviced by this form of social science. Whereas most forms of social science involvement in policy making service one elite or another, this participating support was clearly counter-establishment. Again, the potency of social science is just beginning to be felt at levels of "policy" often not considered part of the normal cycle of social science and public policy interaction (cf. Gordon Heinz, et al., 1973:280-335).

Interestingly, the attention that Jay Schulman and Richard Christie received in their capacity to assess potential "fair-minded" jurors extended to the Right as well as to the Left. It has been authoritatively reported that prior to the Mitchell-Stans trial the Republican National Committee sought the services of these two sociologists to repeat the "miracle" that they performed earlier for Berrigan and his co-defendants; failing that, they retained the services of a consultant, Martin Herbst (Shapley 1974, p. 1033). The two investigators adopted quite different moral postures: Schulman took the position that he would not help in the Mitchell-Stans trial because, unlike the Berrigan trial, the defense posture compelled his support neither legally or morally. Christie, for his part, took the view that he was providing an information service and was quite willing to serve in the same capacity in another case, with two provisos: first, he would help select a fair-minded jury, not one biased on behalf of the defendants; second, the fee had to be allocated by the Republican National Committee to a radical cause of Christie's choosing. It was in effect a return to the problem of the utility of social science measured over and against any special morality of the social sciences.

This chapter makes it abundantly clear that the policy implementation of the social sciences proceeds in lock-step fashion with the evolution of quantitative forms of measurement in the social sciences. When a consensus exists as to what constitutes a social problem or a social indicator, the amount of social science participation increases considerably. Therefore, the science of economics came first, because the monetary system provided a ready-at-hand set of economic measures of production and consumption that could be handled by that social science. But, as the measures became "softer," the consensus on the values of social science participation in the policy process became markedly muddled.

The quantification of valuational measures on items such as the state of the United States (whether it is one of progress or decline), the measurement of urban decay, criminality, the environment, defense and foreign aid, and governmental reform has greatly accelerated the incorporation of social science findings into policy analysis. This is not to deny the critical or reflective role of the social sciences. It is only to note that as long as such a reflexive role is predominant, social science is largely confined to an academic and university environment. But when measures for transforming qualitative materials into quantitative terms are achieved, the social sciences move beyond their academic confines and become very much a part of the larger social and political system.

Policy makers prefer the use of quantitative aspects of social science in the formation of decisions. The presumed exact and orderly nature of the quantitative approach has inherent appeal to the policy makers in their attempts to order and audit political options and the implications of their choices. The rising value of the social sciences to basic types of decisions requires its growing use at a time of internal turmoil over the essential nature and tasks of the social sciences.

REFERENCES

Bauer, Raymond A. (editor)
   1966a   *Social Indicators.* Cambridge: MIT Press.
Bauer, Raymond A.
   1966b   "Social Indicators and Sample Surveys," *Public Opinion Quarterly.* Volume 30, pp. 339-52.
Bauer, Raymond A. and Dan H. Fenn, Jr.
   1972   *The Corporate Social Audit,* New York: Russell Sage Foundations.
Bell, Daniel
   1969   "Towards a Social Report: I, The Idea of a Social Report." *The Public Interest.* Spring, Whole No. 15.
Biderman, Albert
   1970   "Information, Intelligence, Enlightened Public Policy," *Policy Science,* Vol. I, No. 3, pp. 217-30.
Bureau of the Budget
   1965   *What It Is and What It Does.* Washington, D.C.: U.S. Government Printing Office.
Cazes, Bernard
   1972   "Historical Background: A Typology of Social Indicators" in *Social Indicators and Social Policy,* edited by Andrew Shonfield and Stella Shaw. London: Heinemann Educational Books Ltd.

Commission on National Goals
1960   *Goals for Americans.* Englewood Cliffs, N.J.: Prentice Hall.
Coons, John E., William Clune and Stephen Sugarman
1970   *Private Health and Public Education.* Cambridge, Mass.: Belknap
        Press of Harvard University Press.
Eysenck, H. J.
1972   "Personality and Attainment: An application of psychological
        principles to educational objectives." *Higher Education,* Volume I,
        Number 1, pp. 39-52.
Gordon, Andrew C. and John P. Heinz, Margaret T. Gordon,
Stanley W. Divorski
1973   "Public   Information   and   Public   Access: A   Sociological
        Interpretation," *Northwestern University Law Review* May-June,
        Volume 68, Number 2.
Gross, Bertram M.
1965   "The Social State of the Union," *Transaction* 3, No. 1 (November-
        December 1965):14-17.
1966   *The State of the Nation: Social Systems Accounting.* London:
        Tavistock Publications.
1967   *Social Goals and Indicators for American Society. Annals of the
        American Academy of Political and Social Sciences* 371 (May
        1967): Philadelphia.
Henriot, Peter J.
1972   *Political Aspects of Social Indicators: Implications for Research.*
        New York: Russell Sage Foundation.
Johnson, Lyndon B.
1967   *The Public Papers of the President,* 1966. Washington, D.C.: U.S.
        Government Printing Office.
1971   *The Vantage Point: Perspectives of the Presidency, 1963-1969.*
        New York: Holt, Rinehart & Winston.
Kahn, Herman
1960   *On Thermonuclear War.* Princeton, N.J.: Princeton University
        Press.
1962   *Thinking About the Unthinkable.* New York: Horizon Press.
1973   Personal interview with the authors.
Karl, Barry Dean
1963   *Executive Reorganization and Reform in The New Deal: The
        Genesis of Administrative Management, 1900-1939.* Cambridge,
        Mass: Harvard University Press.
Katz, Solomon H.
1973   "New roles for anthropology and public policy" [unpublished
        paper]. Philadelphia: University of Pennsylvania, Department of
        Anthropology.
Lyons, Gene
1969   *The Uneasy Partnership.* New York: Russell Sage Foundation.
Morgenthau, Hans J.
1973   *Politics Among Nations: The Struggle for Power and Peace.* New
        York: Alfred A. Knopf (5th edition).

Myrdal, Gunnar
  1944   *An American Dilemma.* New York: Harper Bros.
National Goals Research Staff
  1970   *Towards Balanced Growth: Quantity with Quality.* Washington,
           D.C.: U.S. Government Printing Office.
Office of Management and Budget
  1974   *Social Indicators, 1974.* Washington, D.C., U.S. Government
           Printing Office.
Office of Science and Technology
  1969   *Federal Programs in Population Policy Research, Ad Hoc Group
           on Population Research.* Washington, D.C.: Executive Office of
           the President.
Office of Technology Assessment
  1973   *Hearings.* Washington, D.C.: U.S. Government Printing Office.
Report of the President's Research Committee on Social Trends
  1933   *Recent Social Trends in the United States.* New York: McGraw-
           Hill Book Company.
President's Science Advisory Committee
  1962   *On Strengthening the Behavioral Sciences.* Washington, D.C.:
           U.S. Government Printing Office.
Radom, Mathew
  1970   *The Social Scientist in American Industry.* New Brunswick:
           Rutgers University Press.
Schulman, Jay and Phillip Shaver, Robert Colman,
Barbara Enrich, Richard Christie
  1973   "Recipe for a Jury," *Psychology Today.* May. Volume 6, Number
           12.
Schuman, Frederick L.
  1969   *International Politics: Anarchy and Order in the World Society.*
           New York: McGraw-Hill Book Co. (7th edition).
Report of the Special Commission on the Social Sciences
of the National Science Board
  1969   *Knowledge Into Action: Improving the Nation's Use of the Social
           Sciences.* Washington, D.C.: National Science Foundation.
U.S. Department of Health, Education and Welfare
  1970   *Toward a Social Report.* Introductory commentary by Wilbur J.
           Cohen. Ann Arbor, Michigan: University of Michigan Press.
U.S. Senate, Government Operations Committee
  1968   *Full Opportunity and Social Accounting Act, Hearings.*
           Washington, D.C.: U.S. Government Printing Office.
U.S. Senate, Government Operations Committee
  1967   *National Foundation for the Social Sciences, Hearings.* Parts 1-3.
           Washington, D.C.: U.S. Government Printing Office.
Westin, Alan F. and Michael A. Baker
  1972   *Databanks in a Free Society: Computers, Record-keeping and
           Privacy.* New York: Quadrangle Books.

CHAPTER

4

DIFFERENTIAL USES
OF SOCIAL SCIENCE
IN POLICY MAKING

SOCIAL SCIENCE AND POLICY-MAKING
ESTABLISHMENTS

Social science is viewed as valuable by policy-making agencies chiefly under two circumstances: when social science organizations have provided past services in legitimating decisions and when knowledge is not extensive or exhaustive enough to justify conventional intuitive or commonsense approaches to problem solving—in short, when managerial techniques break down. For example, OMB has demonstrated its effectiveness and ability in both the areas of legitimacy and knowledge. Hence, it is a well-integrated social science establishment vis-à-vis the presidential offices. The same is true of the CEA. Particularly in areas where past experience is seen as an inadequate guide to future choices, social science agencies will be generated. General Motors doubtless expects a definite payoff from its Societal Analysis Department in terms of forecasting trends and justifying the expense of supporting social science research.

The federal government in the United States has been unwilling to establish and support a policy voice of social scientists, exclusive of economists. This is evidenced by the inability of the National Goals Research Staff, Council of Social Advisors, or a National Social Science Foundation to take firm root. The usefulness of social scientists in such intimate capacities has not been demonstrated amply enough to the satisfaction of government agencies, at least to justify the allocation of scarce resources of money and power to social scientists at the national level of decision making.

In some areas social scientists have gained an important if peripheral foothold. They are now often required personnel on projects concerned with ecology, architecture, mental health, disaster preparation, and the human factors in engineering. Neither legislation nor contracts involving federal agencies in these areas can be cleared without social science sanction. Private organizations and foundations have a significant mediating effect between the social science and policy making realms. They are useful in encouraging private work and exploring early developments that may later prove to be useful for the policy maker. Such private sources can investigate areas and make commitments that the government, being publicly accountable and politically sensitive, usually refrains from involving itself in. A good example is the Russell Sage Foundation and its sponsorship of exploration in social indicators.

At the other end of policy making—overcoming problems that arise as a result of past decisions and policy—social scientists are seen as a source of quick sociotechnical "fixes." Much work performed at the Battelle Institute is characteristic of this type of approach. NASA's concern about the second-order consequences of a titanic space program demonstrates a longer-term concern about social impacts and problems, but it is more a concern with an afterthought of "more important" technological programs than a concern with presumed intrinsic merits. The value of social science work is often seen in terms of planning and program evaluation. At the level of planning, decision makers want wider options and anticipated consequences presented, rather than specific recommendations for certain courses of action.

The danger of using social science for legitimizing purposes is always present in commissioned work. In the larger perspective, social science is almost invariably employed to rationalize decisions that are controversial and in broad public view. Social science recommendations tend to be accepted or rejected on a basis other than that of the inherent quality of the research and conclusions. Thus, in the Supreme Court desegregation decision, "separate but equal" was an ideological posture that for political reasons was no longer accepted. Social science breakthroughs on the question of race and race relations provided only supplemental, albeit necessary, information that supported and legitimized a new series of court rulings. Social science inputs are often one of a multitude of factors that go into actual decisions. As a result, it is difficult to distinguish the specific contribution of each source of influence and thus isolate the nature and extent of social science contribution.

Social science not only encourages change (when a prior consensus dissolves) but may also protect order (when a prior consensus is present). Thus, social science cannot be seen as simply a "change agent" or as an "establishment tool." The actual activities of different kinds of social scientists, often working at subnational levels, thus becomes especially illuminating in elaborating, if not entirely resolving, the multiplicity of roles performed by social scientists and the ways they are used by policy-making agencies.

Processes of change and order both provide grounds for the support of social science research. For example, many social science projects are encouraged because they allow those in power more accurately to perceive changes that are "inevitable." Social scientists show policy agencies how to prepare to take advantage of the consequences of such changes. Arthur D. Little's studies of the recursive effects of telecommunications (especially cable TV) is one example of this newer tendency. The Battelle efforts to "fine tune" the school systems to produce individuals to meet industry specifications rather than the abstract concepts of humanism, liberal education, and so on, is a further example.

Recommendations that improve public safety forces, such as specialized education for policemen, upgrading tools, and techniques of apprehension, make the police force a more effective mechanism of social control.

What we have then are three models of social science: a) a tool promoting social change—e.g., as in the school desegregation cases; b) a tool controlling change—e.g., providing support for the military or political dimension, as in the Project Camelot effort to establish mechanisms for counterinsurgency and civic action; and c) a tool for identifying change and also harnessing such change for established agencies. A fourth model of social science concerns its role in the technical improvement of agency performance, specifically its functions as an instrument in incremental improvements. While this activity—i.e., the evaluation of policy performance rather than the manufacture of new policies—probably preoccupies a considerable majority of social science talent, its very confinement to procedural details makes it unfeasible as a direct instrument of social change. We will, therefore, confine our analysis in this section to the presentation of a series of case studies that show, better than any general theory, how specific yet typical social science agencies provide services to policy makers—sometimes within all four models.

LOCAL PLANNING AND THE
URBANIZATION PROCESS

George Sternlieb and the Rutgers University Center for Urban Policy Research have made major contributions to social policy since the center was established in the early 1960s. These contributions have now ranged from city planning to federal legislation on new housing. Their efforts have touched all branches of government. For example, a study executed by Sternlieb on the housing outlook of welfare recipients in New York City has had a bearing on a number of legal suits on the exclusion of welfare recipients from private housing.

The core of a study of Plainfield, New Jersey, that focused on changing neighborhoods ("zones of emergence") was the racial composition of the community. This particular study had a significant impact on OEO programs for dealing with problems in this area and in introducing the notion of racial mix and racial balance as planned for factors in urban programming. *The Tenement Landlord,* a study of Newark, New Jersey (Sternlieb 1966), first performed in 1964 and reexamined in the early 1970's (Sternlieb and Burchell 1973) revealed that owner residence made a substantial difference in the quality of upkeep of a rented building. This study was a significant factor in the formulation and passage of the Urban Homestead Act of 1967.

The Urban Center has produced a set of position papers for the HUD. This research had an impact on the evaluation strategy of housing policy; as well as recommending various actions regarding HUD's participation in local zoning procedures, building codes and the question of the constitution of neighborhood decline. The Urban Center has worked with the New Jersey governor's Housing Task Force and played a central role in the formulation of a land-use bill which went currently before the state legislature in 1974. The bill was, in essence, written by social scientists. Beyond that, several of the governor's speeches on the subject were clearly prepared by sociologists and economists.

Sternlieb was commissioned to perform a rent-control study for the City of New York (Sternlieb 1972). The problem was to discover the dollar amount figure that determines adequate upkeep of a rented residence. Sternlieb discovered that, rather than a simple rent figure, a cluster of broad and nebulous factors determined the quality of upkeep. This study was cited in the rationale to remove rent control restrictions in New York City. Whatever the uses or misuses of their efforts, it is plain that the Urban Center is catering to both "local" and "cosmopolitan" interests and has become an authentic legitimizing factor in policies directed toward the urban dweller, especially the urban poor.

The Urban Studies Center typifies an increasing trend in the linkages between policy sectors and social scientists based at universities in the United States but fundamentally deriving their income and influence from federal, state, and local agencies. In the case of the Urban Center, its director has links with the federal government through the Housing Authority of HEW; with the New Jersey state government through associations with the Byrne administration in Trenton; with municipal governments through large-scale urban research grants on the housing authority of the cities and through countless municipalities ranging from rich suburbs such as Princeton (Sternlieb et al. 1971) to changing semiurban ghettos such as Plainfield (Sternlieb and Beaton 1972). In this way, nonuniversity funding has the consequence of producing desirable research in applied fields and at the same time results in university "pay-offs": graduate degrees for research conducted, additional fiscal support for professors and lecturers, and, perhaps the most significant element of all, bringing about a closer series of connections between social research and applied policy needs that permit autonomy as well as further integration with the university community.

The weakness of such an organizational-structural approach is that it must constantly go outside the university for funding. University organization, in the meantime, absorbs such a high proportion in its overhead that any excessive entrepreneurship is discouraged (which case may indeed be a blessing in disguise). As in all such instances, the crucial moment of truth comes when the outside funding sources begin to dry up, leaving the university the choice of either picking up an unexpected and unwanted overhead burden or discarding and dismantling these very novel agencies that are most clearly linked to social problems in the broader society. The fact that nearly every major university can lay claim to similar nondepartmental programs and centers, and hence similar volatile issues of organization, employment, and tenure is an indication that the infusion of policy demands on the social sciences has resulted in revised estimates, not simply of what the social science role at a modern university is to be in the future but what, in fact, that role means to universities here and now.

This situation also draws attention to the fact that the infusion of policy-related research into the life of social science has considerably shifted the emphasis of professionals from departmental considerations to task-oriented concerns. Interests in urban planning are particularly prone to cross-disciplinary activities, and in this very act serve to dissolve the inherited primacy of academic departments. This too creates critical cleavages between those whose primary stake is in the profession and those who center their concerns in the policy. In other words, the relationship between social science and public policy affects the inner life of the social sciences no less than the general patterns of policy making. The rise of urbanisms as an interdisciplinary structure, no less than a way of life, is indicative of this central transformation within the social structure of social science.

REGIONAL AND SYSTEMS PLANNING

The Columbus, Ohio, laboratories of Battelle comprise the original research center of a public purpose and multinational organization devoted to scientific research and development. In 1972 Batelle's staff of 5,600 people carried out more than 3,600 studies of 1,700 industrial organizations and government agencies and earned more than $71 million in fees in the process. The interests of Battelle are concentrated in materials research, engineering, and systems fields. Their work relating to social sciences has been in the departments of biology and medical sciences, technical and business planning research, environmental systems and processes, communications systems research, and most recently in the Center for Improved Education.

The Social and Systems Sciences Department is comprised of five research groups totaling about 90 professional researchers and supporting staff. The backgrounds of the researchers are heavily concentrated in the quantitative, engineering, systems, and physical science disciplines. The personnel in the department comprise a staff with over 30 degree specialties, ranging from community planning and social welfare in the "applied" fields to economics, sociology, and psychology in the "pure" fields. Although the department is organized around the experience and competence of its five component groups, rarely is a research project performed by one group alone. Usually, appropriate talent is furnished to accomplish a given task.

The major themes of the educational systems group are information, technology, educational planning and management, and educational-systems analysis. The group has had experience in applying educational technology—a systems approach to instructional development that includes, for example, behavioral specification of instructional objectives, development of evaluation techniques and instruments, and pilot testing and evaluation of instructional materials, techniques, and courses. The group has capabilities in educational network analysis, cost-effectiveness evaluation, evaluation of vocational programs and facilities, and development of differential staffing models for individualized instruction. The group also has capability and experience in job and task analysis, experimental design, psychological measurement, and development of personnel selection and placement techniques.

The Man/Systems Technology Group has a broad capability in human factors and engineering psychology, as well as in basic methodological skills that are applicable to a variety of problem areas. Studies conducted by the group involve the application of principles, techniques, and literature that relate to designing equipment, tasks, workspaces, and physical environments systematically for maximum compatibility with human characteristics. More specifically, group staff members are knowledgeable in such areas as: human capabilities and limitations, characteristics of the human operator, assessment of human performance, reduction of human error, effects of environmental factors on performance, man-machine system simulation techniques, and display/control design. This group also has the capability for planning (or assessing) the design of experiments involving human subjects. Group staff members are skilled in the specification of the procedures of data collection, methods of data analysis, computer applications, and the appropriate statistical tests. In addition, members of this group have experience in conducting large data-collection efforts involving on-site field interviews.

The primary mission of the Management Systems Group is the application of science and engineering technology to the solution of management problems, with emphasis on the development or improvement of men, facilities, equipment and other resources. The systems approach to problem solving is the basic philosophy for the Management Systems Group. This philosophy is put into practice both in problem solving and in management of large-scale multidisciplinary projects. Projects accomplished by members of the group encompass several areas of application, involving health-systems planning and analysis, law enforcement and corrections, defense logistics and support systems, salary surveys of scientific and technical personnel and social systems (cf. Steger 1973).

The Community and Economic Development Group is responsible for conducting and coordinating research and action-oriented programs in the areas of urban studies, locational analysis, regional development, minority-oriented programs, demographic analysis, and various types of modeling. The people associated with this group have backgrounds in sociology, industrial development, regional economics, urban economics, transportation, city planning, rural and small community development, manpower economics, and economic geography. Experience of the group includes socioeconomic modeling and analysis, economic development, locational analysis, urban studies, and transportation and trip behavior.

The Environmental and Land Use Planning Group is staffed with individuals of diverse backgrounds and professional experience and leads in cooperative research involving skills in ecology, landscape architecture, systems analysis, economics, political science, meteorology, engineering, chemistry, and other physical sciences. Problems have been approached on several geographic scales, including river basins, metropolitan areas, and groups of states. Problem areas include water quality, coastal development, regional air quality, solid-waste management, river-basin development, and economic growth. The group is also active in such areas as environmental-impacts assessment, economic dimensions of environmental planning, social and institutional aspects of environmental planning, and recreational elements of environmental planning.

The Center for Improved Education runs projects that have been undertaken by the center as a whole. Battelle's center has applied its knowledge of the physical and psychological needs of children in a wide variety of studies. The goal of one program was to develop and evaluate a high-quality child-care center to be operated for the preschool children of employees of a large public service company. Such a center enables working mothers to stay on the job and permits others to return to their former jobs. Further, its successful operation will make available the opportunity to work to many mothers who have never before been able to work. In another study psychologists and educational technologists researched the needs priorities and recommendations relevant to establishing a statewide policy of preschool education in a Midwestern state.

In a study of a local school district vocational-education programming and facility needs were assessed and recommendations made for an improved and expanded career-education program in the district. In a third study Center for Improved Education staff members investigated the relationship between an employee's actional criteria of employability and an employer's stated criteria. A methodology was developed to enable school systems to reduce discrepancies between employer-desired skills and curriculum-produced skills.

The objective of several Battelle Center studies has been to refine and develop education and training programs for prisoner rehabilitation. In one of these research efforts education specialists analyzed the education and training programs at two federal prisons. They developed a model prisoner education and training system and formulated recommendations for implementing their model. In 1972 Battelle initiated a major program with the Ohio Department of Rehabilitation and Corrections. The goal of this study is to develop an alcohol education and rehabilitation program directed toward the reduction of alcohol use among former inmates of correctional institutions.

There has always been a wing of social science quite close to its social engineering inheritance (Horowitz 1969:585-98). With the breakdown of classical models of historicism, functionalism, organicism, and the like, and the corresponding emergence of systems design, game theory, and decision theory as variants in the armory of the behavioral as well as the engineering sciences, the relationships between these two groups have drawn tighter. In the development of such agencies as RAND Corporation, Systems Development Corporation, and Lincoln Laboratory as well as Battelle, the connections have become intimate in application no less than in theory (cf. Boguslaw 1965). The involvement of engineering personnel in broad-scale programs, from international development at the macroscopic level to urban renewal at more intimate levels of human intervention, has meant that social scientists have been consulted on a wide array of issues. At the same time, the social sciences were making far greater use of computer technology and systems design, and in this way the bridge between behaviorism and equilibrium theory in engineering, if not entirely cemented, at least drew to a closer condition than at any time since Comte, Pareto, and Sorel were involved in the formation of social science principles.

At the same time, the practical requirements of agencies, whether federal or subnational, began to develop a common rhetoric of equilibrium, function, design, and decision theory that led to operationalism's become a general criterion for all sponsored forms of research. Perhaps as a consequence of federal research specifications no less than of the inner turmoil created by the breaking up of older social science traditions, the social sciences began to develop an isomorphic set of working premises that permitted their researches to be plugged directly into the efforts of engineering principles and made possible the sort of large-scale fiscal support that, even as a form of spinoff of master projects, such as those sponsored by NASA, meant a great deal more support than the social sciences had commanded in the past. What we witness, therefore, in research efforts of Battelle and like-minded agencies is a strong impulse to reinterpret social science data as positive human inputs into new programming on a national and world scale. The critical tradition clearly suffers in this reinterpretation. However, the actual broadening out and humanizing of engineering approaches has expanded to a commensurate degree.

MINORITY INTERESTS AND SOCIAL RESEARCH

The Metropolitan Applied Research Center (MARC) was founded in January 1967 by Kenneth B. Clark, a well-known black educator and psychologist whose book, *Dark Ghetto* (1965), was a landmark effort in making clear the inequalities in racially segregated schooling. The MARC Corporation is an independently funded consortium of people with experience, knowledge, and skills in the fields of social science, law, and municipal and public affairs, who are committed to the purpose of influencing social policy on behalf of the poor and racial minority groups. Although the number of staff members has ranged as high as 100, currently the level is 50. It is perhaps the most successful black-run social science research agency in the nation.

The MARC experiment is an attempt to determine by systematic exploration whether trained intelligence can be mobilized as an effective form of power for positive social change (MARC 1973). MARC's staff undertakes the monitoring of governmental services and programs to ensure that the rights of the economic poor and lower-status minority groups are not ignored or shortchanged and that their share of the economic and political benefits of the society is not lost or preempted by others because of their lack of power to protect themselves.

When social exploitation is made possible by lack of coherent and concrete information, MARC tries to gather and present the relevant data in a meaningful pattern. Various MARC publications and films have focused on issues such as educational deprivation, pupil transportation, residential segregation and day care in the inner city (1973a). For example, the pro-busing booklet, *Fact Book on Pupil Transportation* (1973b), allows individuals to refute commonly held misapprehensions about busing. Taking the view that busing is "as American as apple pie," the booklet distills pertinent facts on busing and seeks to present these facts so that readers can determine the validity of the arguments offered by those who seek to prohibit the transportation of children for purposes of public school desegregation.

MARC academic fellows, largely drawn from the social sciences, are encouraged to use their skills to influence social policy and to experiment with ways to narrow the gap between social science knowledge and social policy. The monitoring of public and governmental agencies is performed in order to detect and halt what are perceived as retrogressive social policy. MARC academic fellows perform watchdog services, writing critical articles in response to professional social science studies and papers that are seen as counterproductive to equitable social policy. Studies that have come under fire are James Coleman's report on education and the genetic theories advocated by Richard Hernstein, Arthur Jensen, and William Shockley, linking intelligence to race by heredity.

As a consultant to community groups and national organizations concerned with social change, MARC often works behind the scenes as a pressure agency in its own right. MARC personnel act as a catalyst in bringing together civil rights leaders of opposing views, provide coordinating and advising services for various urban planning efforts, and help to bring into existence an organization of black-elected officials.

On some issues it is felt that a lobbying appeal to the public forum will be the more effective stimulus to social change. For example, MARC is compiling an easy-to-understand textbook in social studies aimed at high school and first-year college students. The text covers, among other themes, current arguments on the connections among race, intelligence, and heredity. MARC officials anticipate that discussions engendered by this book will help expand student social consciousness and prepare the groundwork for a more active utilization of social science findings by minority groups.

Even after doing a great amount of work and research on a particular issue MARC often has difficulty in locating outlets for the implementation of its findings. For example, the Washington, D.C., school board commissioned MARC to design a plan for improving the reading and arithmetic skills of its elementary school system. In its exhaustive study, later published as a book (Clark 1972b), MARC saw the school system, rather than poor home environment, as the main causal factor in the low educational achievement of ghetto children. MARC's recommendations met with mixed response: a few points of the program, including tutoring and reading teams in certain schools were implemented, but the most central features were not; reorganization of teacher certification, teacher internships, and the involvement of parents have been steadfastly opposed by the Washington, D.C., teachers' union. Because of the vociferousness and solidarity of this opposition, the board of education felt it had little choice but to ignore the rest of MARC's recommendations. The board was, however, clearly typical of all agencies seeking revised policies in the face of established and basically content constituencies.

Clark, who is the head of MARC, is the only black member of the New York State Board of Regents. In 1966 he helped formulate plans in five East Harlem communities for the purpose of giving parents a voice in the operation of the controversial Intermediate School 201. Continuing his work for community participation in the school systems, he supported a strong school decentralization plan, aided by Ford Foundation funds, which became known as the Bundy plan. The State of New York legislature eventually passed a watered-down version of the Bundy plan, turning over educational control of school of political leaders and teachers unions as well as the community at large.

Recently, the MARC staff has become involved in the Flatbush-Canarsie school-busing controversy. Along with the New York Civil Liberties Union,

MARC is one of the organizations bringing suit over the suspension of Luis Fuentes, a teacher in the district. However, as the contours of community control have evolved to mean less funds, more racial segregation, and considerable idiosyncratic variations in educational policies, Clark and his MARC staff have increasingly questioned such local measures and have begun to reexamine large-scale instrumentalities to induce education and income equality.

After having been a champion of decentralization, Clark announced, during the course of the struggle in the Canarsie school district, that he was now "vehemently opposed" to decentralization, which he termed a "disastrous experiment" because of "racial politics" and "intimidational pressures." (Clark 1972a). In explaining this shift in his position Clark emphasized that his primary goal has always been the effective teaching of vital basic skills, especially in ghetto communities (1965). Clark earlier thought that the decentralization of school systems, with a reasonable accountability system and local community involvement, would be a means to an equitable end. As it turned out, public energy and emotion became diverted to the issue over who would control the school, away from questioning whether the schools were doing their job of teaching children properly and optimally.

The formation of MARC and the pathbreaking efforts of psychologists like Clark and sociologists like Hylan Lewis represent a large step beyond the conventional situation in which social science organizations and information alike are supplied by wealthy and powerful clientele and used exclusively by that narrow population stratum. The effort of MARC to break this cycle by involving socially conscious and often young social scientists and linking their energies to the will and the interests of the urban power, the racial minorities, and the economically underprivileged provides a unique experiment in demonstrating the possibilities of social science at the nonelitist level. That these efforts have not proven uniformly successful should surprise no one; that policy shifts have taken place among the social science policy formulators should also hardly come as a surprise. The overwhelming impression, however, is of serious work, rigorous concern with factual presentation, and public service in areas rarely serviced in the past by either federal, industrial, or university agencies. Perhaps the most serendipitous finding is that those social scientists who seriously wish to advise makers of political and social policy not infrequently end up by entering the political process themselves in active, change-producing roles.

PUBLIC CITIZEN RESEARCH

Ralph Nader is an institution no less than an individual. As a public-interest lawyer he is responsible for many changes and improvements in the functioning of public policy in the United States. He first won national attention by his efforts in improving automotive safety and technology. His book, *Unsafe at Any Speed* (Nader 1965), attacked the irresponsibility of Detroit automobile manufacturers. This was followed up by a more recent study on European automobiles (Cox, et al. 1972). And despite their initial animosity and even harrassment, the automobile industry has finally become "safety conscious." His work, and that of his many supporters, his staff, and part-time volunteers, is directed towards closing the citizen gap that exists, according to Nader, when business or governmental abuses occur without public knowledge and without mechanisms to correct them.

Public Citizen is a foundation established by Nader and his associates to solicit funds and supervise a wide variety of operations held to be in the public interest (Public Citizen 1972). It serves as an umbrella institution for the Tax Reform Research Group, the Health Research Group, the Retired Professionals Action Group, the Citizen Action Group, the Litigation Group, and the Public Interest Research Group, all of which are Nader-supported research agencies for bringing about specific social reforms (Esposito 1970; and Green 1972).

One of the most active has been the Public Interest Research Group [PIRG]. Its staff-size varies; it presently consists of five people: two lawyers, one physicist, one political scientist, and a receptionist-secretary. PIRG uses government documents, industrial reports, and various informants as sources of information in its work. Industries themselves, usually inadvertently, provide critical information to PIRG investigators, who have become masters in the art of secondary data analysis, showing the vast possibilities for social scientists to use already-existing first-class data rather than waste precious time and funds generating second-class information.

PIRG investigators have given important study materials to congressional staffs and have provided significant testimony in hearings held by the Environmental Protection Agency and the Traffic Safety Administration. PIRG was also a force in the passage of the Retirement Security Benefit Act and in work for the pension bill that at this writing has passed the Senate and is now in the House.

Another committee operating under the Public Citizen umbrella is the Health Research Group (HRG), which is currently involved in activities centering around health and safety problems (Page and O'Brien 1973). Three of the areas are health problems of foods and drugs, occupational health and safety, and health-care delivery systems (Nader, et al. 1973d).

Present activities concerned with food and drug health problems include the preparation of congressional oversight testimony and/or the recommending of changes in legislation and the preparation of formal comments on proposed regulations (Nader 1973c). An example is the HRG review of enforcement of the Radiation Safety acts and its comments on the federal nutritional guidelines for foods. Long-range activities include the establishment of a technical advisory committee review meeting that would work to put Public Citizen committees on greater public display. This move would be important in diminishing private industry domination of decisions made by food and drug groups and in preventing secret agreements made with government regulatory agencies.

Under the category of occupational health and safety, HRG performs ongoing analyses of Occupational Health and Safety acts, considering the roles of the departments of Labor and Health, Education and Welfare. Site visits are also conducted by HRG to meet and discuss with workers the Occupational Safety and Health Act and their rights under it, and to aid workers in acting to eliminate hazardous conditions in their work place. HRG is working to institutionalize accountability of government, industry, and private organizations to the public health. Its activities include improving legal and medical education and encouraging public interest in the activities of social scientists, physical scientists, and other professionals in the area of occupational health.

The scrutiny of health-care delivery systems includes the preparation of consumer manuals of hospital evaluation, a study of indications, alternatives, risks, and benefits for common surgical procedures, and a consumer guide to doctors in the Washington area (Nader and Blackwell 1973a). Professional standards review organizations to evaluate medical practices as per House Bill No. 1 will be monitored closely to forestall built-in conflicts of interests (Nader, et al. 1972). These activities are designed to increase the accountability of the medical establishment to the consumer. Particular emphasis is placed on the quality of medical care.

Social science is ubiquitous enough to be performed, and ably, by those who are not social scientists. Thus, in groupings such as the Nader Raiders all sorts of projects—from housing for the poor to congressional reform to special care for the aged—are dealt with by young attorneys and public-interest personnel who perform as surrogate social scientists, preparing reports on everything from rest homes for the aged (Townsend 1971) to special congressional reports on each member of Congress (Nader et al. 1973). Whatever the quality of these reports may be, the plain fact is that social science as a handmaiden to public policy is not confined to those with formal training in the social sciences. The Nader collectivities are a clear indication that those with strong attachments to legal training are probably more likely to catch the attention of legislative or executive-reform groups, precisely because of the isomorphism between researchers concerned with legal limits and politicians concerned with legal possibilities (Nader 1971a; Nader 1971b).

One of the more intriguing aspects of the Nader groups is that the more they mature over time, the deeper their penetration of major U.S. institutions, the more they act and perform like any other social science formation in terms of canons of evidence, concern for explicit statement of experimental controls, and closer scrutiny to quantitative as well as qualitative aspects of research. The most controversial of the Nader activities, involving a person-by-person profile and examination of congressional performance, is a good indication of this new concern for detail and data (Nader 1973c). That such an approach has met with hostility and even vilification from orthodox political science groups is indicative of the way policy-related social research often leads to a reexamination of scientific premises and creates new directions in social science as such. The idea of individual profiles is certainly now implausible, and yet the largely variable-oriented, rather than person-oriented, research of standard political science has led to a neglect of the possibilities of such kinds of political psychology. In any event, we again see the phenomenon of change-oriented groups adopting social science techniques to bring about social reforms and in that very process providing theoretical inputs that have the potential in the long run, for changing the structure of scientific paradigms.

The social science base of the Nader congressional studies is vouchsafed by a number of elements: first, the utilization of specific social indicators to which all congressmen were subjected; second, an attempt to avoid simplified background information as an explanatory device for congressional voting behavior; third, each congressman was afforded the opportunity to comment in either written or verbal form on the validity of the profile. In short, although journalistic elements were clearly in evidence, the core of the Nader reports represented a social science attempt to link social history with personal biography.

SOCIAL SCIENCE AND URBAN POLICY MAKING

Anticipating federal government initiatives to implement fair hiring practices in municipal agencies, Robert Wagner, former mayor of New York City, implemented a survey of the racial composition of the city's work force. The survey was completed in 1963, and annual reports have been issued since then. By 1971 the need was clear for revised, up-to-date data. Requests for employment statistics were received from various federal agencies, elected officials, and concerned citizens. Individual agencies were hard pressed to provide raw statistical material on their own. The chairman of the New York City Commission on Human Rights, Eleanor Holmes Norton, advised the mayor that raw statistics collected and published by individual agencies were insufficient. They could easily be unscientific, misleading, inaccurate, and of little value in determining whether there had been discrimination. She recommended that the city take its census in the manner of many other cities and states, including New York State, employing a uniform system that used professional standards. Accordingly, at the urging of Commissioner Norton, on October 1, 1971, Mayor John V. Lindsay issued Executive Order No. 49, regarding the "conduct of census concerning the composition of the work force of city agencies."

In order to protect the privacy and identity of individual employees while at the same time maintaining scientific accuracy and uniformity, the method of "sight survey by supervisors" was utilized. This method, widely used throughout the country, achieves identification through observation (cf. Norton 1972). The commission must investigate any complaint of discrimination that could be validated through an investigative (not a social science) technique. As a result, a legal methodology is used to determine infractions of equal-opportunity legislation.

The post of director of research was formerly filled by social scientists holding advanced degrees; however, there are none on the commission staff at the present time. The research staff, however, does produce informational studies of a social scientific nature. Statistical studies, such as the *Employment of Minorities* (1973), are aimed specifically at changing urban policy. The *Employment of Minorities* report came up with definite recommendations.

Eleanor Holmes Norton is an attorney with a master's degree in international law. But, increasingly, as part of her activities as chairman of the New York City Commission on Human Rights, she has relied on the work of social science researchers. In an article on the selection of teachers and community control (Norton 1971:29-31) she makes direct reference to the work of Marilyn Gittell, director of the Institute for Community Studies at Queens

College, and to the parallel efforts of the Center for Community Studies at Columbia Teachers College. The research efforts of these groups on the superiority of community screening of teaching staffs and the essentially universalistic criterion parents use in the choice of principals have a direct bearing on New York City's support of community control. The bitter opposition to this approach by the teachers' unions and by white middle-class sectors of the city are indicative, once again, of the grave and serious issues involved in social policy making based on social science premises and researches. The further support of community educational control by the Ford Foundation provided yet another element in the dramaturgy, indicating that social science research sponsored by agencies can be perceived by community sectors as representative of power elites, even though the ostensible purpose of the research is a furtherance of social equity.

The activities of the New York Commission on Human Rights also invaded domains of other agencies—a not infrequent practice encouraged by the ecumenical nature of much social research. Arguing strongly against the approaches taken by the Rutgers Center for Urban Policy Studies, which had been commissioned by the City of New York to do housing studies and, in fact, tended to accept the end of urban center cities as de facto, Norton claimed that housing "represents the singlemost resistant civil rights issue today," and that upon its solution "hands the key to a myriad of other American problems" (Norton 1972:8-12). She starkly poses the consequences of enforced segregation and voluntary integration by contrasting Newark and New York. Segregation, far from encouraging even growth in the Newark community, heightened tensions and hastened the flight to suburbia. Segregation left the city with 70 percent of the population made up of minority groups and poor, and led to disastrous economic consequences, in which one of every three citizens is on welfare. In New York City, where the pattern has been to encourage multi-racial and multi-ethnic co-participation in housing projects and new homes programs, the diverse economic class base of New York has largely been kept intact.

The approach as well as the conclusions of Norton and the New York City group are clearly at variance with the position taken by Sternlieb and the New Jersey research effort. For the former, New York and urban life generally remains viable; whereas for the New Jersey group, which is, perhaps, responding to the tragedy and failure of Newark in the 1960s, the city becomes a "sandbox," doomed to inevitable failure. What makes this contrast in research orientations particularly interesting is that it illustrates that social science research may not always come up with uniform answers, but rather, like the policy-making sector as such, it is subject to the sort of local pressures and state contours that invite certain kinds of results. In the larger sense, policy planners and politicians tend to gravitate to the kind of social science results that buttress their initial persuasions, rather than to be persuaded by new research findings. Thus, we find the legal aspects of social science performing a client-related role, prevailing over universalistic criteria for social science to be a general science.

In an agency such as the City Commission for Human Rights one can find an intermediary use of social scientists and lawyers for the promulgation of new social legislation or the enforcement of existing legislation. Indeed, in that New

York City grouping the relationship between agency enforcement and agency sponsorship of social research is quite plain. Brooke Aronson, director of research at the city commission, is trained in political science. She performs a central role of checking the percentages of minority groups in the city work force, supervises the investigation of complaints when they arise, and synthesizes material to be transmitted to the commission itself. In addition, the directors of this group are close to a New York University-based group of social scientists, such as psychologist Frank Riessman, editor of *Social Policy*, that has evolved sophisticated programs in paraprofessionalism precisely to insure equity in municipal hiring practices. In this situation one sees a fusion of activist and social scientist types—a fusion based on a clear notion of goals in common and, beyond that, a distribution of work tasks to achieve these goals, which basically reduce to equal hiring practices and the upgrading of minorities to existing positions.

INTERGOVERNMENTAL SOCIAL SCIENCE

There is a growing use of social science in policy planning and evaluation in the intergovernmental nexus. An institutionalized form of this contribution is the NSF's Intergovernmental Science and Research Utilization Office. Several social scientists, such as Bruce Reiss, serve at the program management level, but the thrust of the program and office activities is toward the development and funding of projects outside the foundation.

Social science inputs have been considerable in the development of the office. In its early days political scientists conducted a series of studies on the nature of science and technology activities in individual states. Similarly, studies were conducted by public administrators and economists. These studies and resulting recommendations have served as the basis for program strategies as the intergovernmental science program has unfolded. As part of the basic study activities there were a number of conferences conducted to begin the dialogue in this area and to develop a community of interest. Social scientists have had considerable involvement in this activity as well.

In an effort to establish an academic center of policy competence in intergovernmental science activities, M. Frank Hersman, director of the office and founder of the intergovernmental science program, awarded a grant to Pennsylvania State University that provided for the establishment of a policy-oriented research center to develop suggested criteria in federal, state, and local roles in fostering national science policy. The center is directed by Irwin Feller, an economist, and has turned out several landmark studies in such areas as intergovernmental relations in the determination of air-pollution research and the development of a science and technology capability in state legislatures. In the evolution of this program a series of policy development studies were undertaken by public-administration experts for the most part, based in the RAND Corporation, Abt Associates, Inc., the International City Management Association, and the National League of Cities/United States Conference of

Mayors. In this way federal policy studies were undertaken by largely private research agencies—a not uncommon practice which may itself be indicative of the absence of uniform standards and enforcement mechanisms at the national level (cf. Palley and Palley 1972:681-95).

A general review of the activities undertaken by various federal programs indicate that social science inputs are scattered throughout the federal establishment. Demonstration projects in state government, executive and legislative branches, local government, academic public service, and technology transfer normally include elements of social science participation on an equal footing with the "hard" or physical sciences. For example, nine studies have been funded in the area of citizen feedback systems (content, components, and competence), 14 in legislative body assistance (primarily in California), and a like number oriented toward the assistance of science by local government.

One area of social science activity supported at the state level is the State Council of Economic Advisors for the State of Minnesota. Starting as a pilot project in 1972, the Council of Economic Advisors has received nearly $60,000 in NSF support. The program of advisors is under the direction of A. Edward Hunter and Francis M. Boddy, members of the Minnesota State Planning Agency. We see, thus, that federal styles of social-science-based policy are often replicated at state levels.

A second project under the Intergovernmental Science Office's jurisdiction, and solely social science in nature, is being investigated by Division of Behavioral Sciences of the National Academy of Sciences (NAS). The project provides for a conference to bring together social and behavioral scientists interested in the application of research to policy making, as well as public officials who would be appropriately called upon to support or participate in the performance of systematic field demonstrations growing out of the project. The title of the proposal is "Study Conference on Social and Behavioral Science Demonstration Projects Related to the Policy and Program Responsibilities of State and Local Governments."

One curious fact about special federal subagencies such as the Office of Intergovernmental Science is that they seem to prefer nonacademic to academic institutions in the conduct of their researches. It is difficult to ascertain whether this is a consequence of tighter controls exercised over private agencies or simply because those in agencies think that there is greater cost efficiency in nonacademic research. Yet it is evident that university-based social science no longer has an iron-clad monopoly over vital researches or policy inputs. The main advantage of this sort of relationship between the federal government and private research agencies is the opportunity offered for circumventing the customary conservitizing influence of university departments. On the other hand, this advantage holds out a risk: the research performed might become too "pragmatic" and hence far removed from the normal controls of scientific method and acceptable general theory. In societies in which the entrepreneurial spirit still ranks as a high element in research assignments, this increasing tendency to lodge policy-oriented research in private social science agencies must be considered both an intriguing and risky tendency that bears careful scrutiny.

PRIVATE ENTERPRISE POLICY MAKING

Perhaps the most fascinating example of directly private-enterprise and entrepreneurial tendencies is in the area of urban affairs. We repeatedly return to that field because there, in the overlap among private builders, social planners, and constantly-revised policy recommendations all link up with each other. In the case of Morris Milgram and "M-Reit" the three roles of entrepreneur, social scientist, and policy planner are linked into a single individual and corporate identity.

Milgram became a builder in 1947. He joined the firm of William M. Smelo to learn the housing business so that he could help end what he called the unwritten law that all new and decent housing is for white people only. After learning the business for four and a half years, during which time he supervised construction of 152 apartments for The Sylvester Company and built small residential and commercial jobs in the greater Philadelphia area, he retooled in 1952 to develop only interracial communities. Milgram was the first recipient, in 1968, of the Congress-established National Human Rights Award from HUD. Articles about his work appeared in the major mass media, and a national educational television show, *Seven Who Dared* (in 1964), featured him as a civil rights pioneer. The major ventures that he organized are as follows (Milgram 1973):

1. 1954-57. Concord Park Homes: 139 single-family houses in Trevose, Bucks County, Pennsylvania, selling for $12,000 and up. Greenbelt Knoll, Inc.: 19 contemporary single-family houses in Northeast Philadelphia selling for $20,000 to $35,000 and up. The ventures together paid 6 percent a year to the investors, who got back their original $15,000. At Concord 45 percent of the buyers were black. At Greenbelt Knoll, where Milgram lives, 42 percent were black.

2. 1957-59. Princeton Housing Associates: with a capital of about $135,000, two developments totalling 40 houses were built. Glen Acres: just outside of Princeton, 15 houses selling at $18,000 to $26,000. Maple Crest: 25 houses in Princeton, New Jersey, selling for $22,000 to $35,000. Of the 40 buyers 25 percent were black. Investors received 7 percent a year as a capital gain, and their funds were returned.

3. 1958-present. In 1958, Modern Community Developers formed to build multiracial housing nationally, raising $1 million through public offerings of MCD and a subsidiary. MCD struck a major road block in 1959 in Deerfield, Illinois, where its two separate improved sites and model houses were taken away by that Chicago suburb for public parks, in order to keep blacks out (that same community had voted twice that year that it wanted no more parks). The late Adlai Stevenson was counsel for MCD but the company lost more than $250,000 when the United States Supreme Court declined, in 1963, to review an unfavorable lower court decision. While the Deerfield case was being fought, MCD organized a partially-owned subsidiary, Planned Communities, Inc. (with

which it later merged), whose board included Eleanor Roosevelt, Willard Wirtz, Chester Carlson (the inventor of Xerox), James Farmer of CORE, Dorothy Height of the National Council of Negro Women, Eliot Pratt (publisher of *Current*), and Irving Fain (Providence, Rhode Island, industrialist). To avoid Deerfields, the board decided to stop building and to buy good-quality apartment buildings in good neighborhoods far from the ghettos. Three were purchased in 1962-64, with Milgram as general partner.

The Mutual Real Estate Investment Trust (M-Reit) was organized by Morris Milgram and Planned Communities, Inc. (PC), which also managed M-Reit. In 1966 it registered a $4-million dollar stock issue. By mid-1969, when PC ceased managing M-Reit, about 9,000 people had invested $12 million to buy $32 million of apartment buildings in six states. Integration proceeded without incident. All the buildings remained a majority white and a minority black (Milgram 1973a).

M-Reit's rapid growth to about 100 times the assets of PC caused M-Reit to run itself. PC ceased to be its manager and advisor in June 1969. PC's shareholders then voted to liquidate. Milgram lost control of M-Reit after its rapid growth. An informal merger between M-Reit and PC was arranged. PC agreed to liquidate, and this liquidation is now in process. In the same year Milgram reactivated his old family firm as New Hope Housing, Inc., with him the owner; the firm manages housing. In 1969, too, he formed Partners in Housing, which has invested in more than 1,000 units in construction or planning stages in Massachusetts, Virginia, and Pennsylvania and is registering a $5-million offering of limited partnership shares. He owns the common stock of Choice Communities, Inc., which manages Partners in Housing.

More than $17 million has been invested by 10,000 individuals and institutions in housing bought or developed under Milgram's leadership. This housing, costing $50,000, serves 4,500 families. All of Milgram's communities remain well integrated, except for the very first one, Concord Park. There, before the fair-housing laws became effective, heavy demand from black families pushed the bidding for resale houses far higher than in nearby communities, where the whites were able to purchase houses easily. Concord Park became largely a minority community. Partners in Housing is now registering a $5-million offering of limited partnership shares to increase the supply of truly multiracial housing for families of modest means. Four developments are under construction in Massachusetts and Virginia; families have started moving into two or these. In addition, developments are owned or under agreement in Texas, California, Pennsylvania, and Virginia.

Founding investors in Partners in Housing subscribed $786,000, of which $731,000 is paid. Indications of interest totalling more than $1,000 have been received from over 400 investors, most of whom also invested in Milgram's earlier ventures. The general partners of the partnership are Morris Milgram, Charles N. Mason, Jr., and Choice Communities, Inc. (Choice), a Pennsylvania corporation controlled by Milgram; they believe that there is a need for private investment in multiracial housing for the following five reasons:

- Residential segregation has transformed many inner cities into islands of minority-group populations, causing segregated school and major social problems.

- While some black people may be unwilling to move alone into a white neighborhood, the general partners believe a substantial number would live outside the urban ghettos in an interracial setting; similarly, many whites would be willing to live in racially integrated areas.

- In the opinion of the general partners, marketing techniques specially designed to induce both blacks and whites to live in interracial housing, especially low- and moderate-income housing, may help to convince others in the housing industry that there is a worthwhile potential market for integrated housing and lend support to the recent activities of the federal government directed toward reducing discrimination and segregation in housing.

- In voluntary multiracial neighborhoods black and white children can get equal educational opportunities as mandated by the United States Supreme Court in 1954. In the view of the general partners, ending economic and racial segregation in housing will eliminate much of the need for lengthy debates over neighborhood schools and busing.

- The recent moratorium on subsidized housing programs makes more urgent the need for additional private investment to increase the supply of multiracial housing.

The legal prohibition of racial discrimination in education, voting, access to public accommodations, and housing has been achieved during the past 25 years. The general partners believe that the elimination of black ghettos can be achieved too, if enough people thoughtfully use their investment funds and entrepreneurial energies. In order to help advance these goals, the partnership intends to invest in properties that in its judgment will increase racial and economic integration in housing and to encourage the managing agents of such properties to use affirmative marketing techniques designed to achieve multiracial housing. The general partners intend to develop and review the rental policies of each project and to advise each occupant of such rentals with a view of facilitating racial and economic integration (Milgram et al. 1973).

Milgram and his associates have always been quite close to the latest findings in the social sciences. Their efforts have been carefully and critically informed by the latest findings in demographic patterns among the urban blacks, new styles of inner-city housing, and class mobility within and out of urban regions. In fact, his work is singularly informed in the sophisticated techniques of the social sciences, and he himself attributes part of his admittedly modest success to a clear-eyed utilization of social science. Too often, when the relationship between social science and policy making in the United States is discussed, there is a strong tendency to ignore the private sector. In this regard, a close examination of the ways that private enterprise is dedicated to the public good is a matter of profound importance, especially in a leading private-sector economy.

In this Chapter we have sought to provide a selective view of the ways that policy processes are aided and abetted by national and subnational levels, by private and public sectors of the economy, and by huge institutions acting as umbrellas for a myriad of research tasks involving individuals who focus their attention exclusively on one part of the policy-making forest. Seen in this light, one can better ascertain the social science element—an element that in the past was largely confined to university surroundings and that for the most part eschewed policy *pronunciamentos* as such. Attention must be drawn to the fact that so much of this policy-related activity is extremely recent. Indeed, for the most part we have been describing activities and agencies that came into being during the last decade of the 1960s, a period that must be seen in retrospect as a remarkable era of experimentation in the public uses of the social sciences.

REFERENCES

Boguslaw, Robert
      1965   *The New Utopians.* New York: Wiley and Sons.
Clark, Kenneth B.
      1965   *Dark Ghetto: Dilemmas of Social Power.* New York: Harper & Row.
Clark, Kenneth B. et al.
      1972a   *The Educationally Deprived: the Potential for Change.* New York: Metropolitan Applied Research Center.
Clark, Kenneth B.
      1972b   *A Possible Reality: A Design for the Attainment of High Academic Achievement for Inner-City Students.* Prepared with the assistance of the MARC Corporation. New York: Emerson Hall, distributed by D. White.
Council of Economic Advisors
      1973   *Economic Report of the President,* Washington, D.C.: U.S. Government Printing Office.
Cox, Edward et al. (project directors)
      1972   *Small-On Safety: The Designed-In Dangers of the Volkswagen.* Center for Auto Safety. New York: Grossman Publishers.
Esposito, John (project director)
      1970   *Vanishing Air: The Ralph Nader Study Group on Air Pollution.* New York: Grossman Publishers.
Green, Mark
      1972   *The Closed Enterprise System; Ralph Nader's Study Group on Antitrust Enforcement.* New York: Grossman Publishers.
Horowitz, Irving Louis
      1969   "Engineering, Sociology, and Economic Development," *International Social Science Journal.* 21, no. 4. UNESCO.
Metropolitan Applied Research Center
      1973a   *The MARC Experiment.* New York: MARC Corporation.
      1973b   *Fact Book on Pupil Transportation.* New York: MARC Corporation.
Milgram, Morris
      1973a   *Housing Background of Morris Milgram.* May (mimeo)
      1973b   *Biographical Brief of Morris Milgram.* July (mimeo)

Milgram, Morris et al.
1973c   *Prospectus: Partners In Housing.* March 21 (privately printed)
Nader, Ralph
1965   *Unsafe at Any Speed; The Designed-In Dangers of the American Automobile.* New York: Grossman Publishers.
Nader, Ralph et al.
1971a   *The Rape of the Powerless: A Symposium at the Atlanta University Center.* New York: Gordon and Breach.
Nader, Ralph
1971b   *Beware.* New York: Law-Arts Publishers.
Nader, Ralph et al.
1972   *Whistle Blowing; The Report of the Conference on Professional Responsibility.* New York: Grossman Publishers.
Nader, Ralph and Kate Blackwell
1973a   *You and Your Pension.* New York: Grossman Publishers.
Nader, Ralph et al.
1973b   *The Ralph Nader Congress Project: Analysis of the Promises and Performances of 484 U.S. Senators and Representatives.* Washington, D.C.: Grossman Publishers.
Nader, Ralph and Mark Green
1973c   *Corporate Power in America: Ralph Nader's Conference on Corporate Accountability,* Washington, D.C., 1971. New York: Grossman Publishers.
Nader, Ralph
1973d   *The Consumer and Corporate Accountability.* New York: Harcourt Brace Jovanovich.
New York City Commission on Human Rights
1973   *The Employment of Minorities, Women and the Handicapped in City Government.* New York City: Commission on Human Rights.
Norton, Eleanor Holmes
1971   "How to Select Good Teachers." *Social Policy* (July/August):27-31.
1972   "The Most Irresponsible Industry in New York City." *Integrated Education.* 10 (March-Arpil):8-12.
Page, Joseph and Mary W. O'Brien
1973   *Bitter Wages: Ralph Nader's Study Group Report on Disease and Injury.* New York: Grossman Publishers.
Palley, Marian Lief and Howard A. Palley
1972   "A Call for a National Welfare Policy" in *American Behavioral Scientist.* Vol. 15, No. 5 (May-June).
Steger, William
1973   *Consad Activities and Projects* (mimeographed). Consad Corp.
Sternlieb, George
1966   *The Tenement Landlord.* New Brunswick, New Jersey: Rutgers University Press.
Sternlieb, George, Robert W. Burchell and Lynne Sagalyn
1971   *The Affluent Suburb*: Princeton. New Brunswick, New Jersey: Transaction Books—E. P. Dutton & Company.

Sternlieb, George
   1972   *The Urban Housing Dilemma: The Dynamics of New York City's Rent Controlled Housing.* New Brunswick, New Jersey: Center for Urban Policy Research, Rutgers University.
Sternlieb, George and W. Patrick Beaton
   1972   *The Zone of Emergence: A Case Study of Plainfield.* New Brunswick, New Jersey: Transaction Books—E. P. Dutton & Company.
Sternlieb, George and Robert W. Burchell
   1973   *Residential Abandonment.* New Brunswick, New Jersey: Center for Urban Policy Research.
Townsend, Claire (project director)
   1971   *Old Age: The Last Segregation. Ralph Nader's Study Group on Nursing Homes.* New York: Grossman Publishers.

CHAPTER
5

SOCIAL SCIENCE
DISCIPLINES AND
NATIONAL POLICY
AGENCIES

The demand for social science research findings among government agencies continues unabated, despite reticence on the part of some sectors of the social science community to supply such information, and beyond that, the relatively desultory results thus far obtained in the areas of applied social research. In a recent report before the American Association for Public Opinion Research, Nathan Caplan (1974: 172-73) notes that a) there is a need felt among most federal officials for finding better ways of plugging research into the decision-making process; b) top officials get most of their social science news from newspapers; and c) policy makers see the need for more large-scale, community-based social experiments, such as the negative income tax study, along with a widening interest in developing noneconomic measures of social well-being.

Social science research is used about as much as hard science data. Problems of use are generic and cut across the board, but top bureaucrats may be more suspicious about the validity and reliability of social science data. Even when policy makers cite physical science research, they are likely to notice social consequences first. For the money, the government probably gets its best use-payoff from social science research. While there is a "motherhood" effect in support for getting information about noneconomic social indicators (94 percent of the respondents said that information was needed), policymakers make a distinction between survey research (valuable) and public opinion (not so reliable). *Survey research* was the *third*-most-frequently mentioned area of information needed from social science, following *social experiments* and *quality of life*. In terms of usefulness of science input, physics is at the top of the scale and psychiatry at the low end. Economics, psychology, and sociology share the middle ground. When asked whether it is necessary to be familiar with the scientist in order to evaluate a set of findings, almost half the users said *yes* for social science.

Despite this increased demand for policy-related social science, the teaching and learning of social science (both inside and outside of the university) and its relationship to public policy are still drastically underdeveloped in the United States. Since the collapse of the "policy science" approach in the 1950s there has been a widespread suspicion that "policy scientist" is simply a code word for a poorly trained social scientist—a scholar in search of a lost or never-to-be-found field. The social indicators and futurology movements of the 1960s, while giving real impetus to policy science, are beset by their own problems: crossdisciplinary research lacking specific focus and the infusion into the area of social forecasting by rank amateurs who cloud up science with astrology. In any event, whatever the exact causes, the condition of the teaching of social science with a policy orientation still leaves a great deal to be desired.

In response to an enquiry Pio Uliassi (1973), officer in charge of academic relations in the external research section at the Department of State, indicated that few universities with active social science sections seem to be offering major courses, much less concentrations on public policy. Special programs do exist at Yale, Syracuse, Chicago, Wisconsin, and Michigan State universities. In addition, course offerings with a social science concentration can be found in specialized parts of such universities as Rutgers, Harvard, California (Berkeley), and a number of other major centers. At undergraduate institutions there are hardly any concentrations in public policy under the auspices of the social sciences; indeed, there are still quite a few colleges where the basic core offerings in the social sciences are still often noticeable by their paucity. The quality of these courses is obviously indeterminate, and their departmental auspices vary.

For the most part, such courses, when they do exist, are sponsored by the political science departments and are marginal activities rather than central-core curriculum. Nevertheless, the efforts at some of the leading universities do provide a notable "secular" effort to reach out and train a new generation that might well be directly involved in policy formulation and execution. In basic courses of international relations, economic development, political parties of the Third World, comparative political systems, and so on, portions of the work are directly dedicated to policy components. But again, these are largely peripheral, rather than core, framework.

Curiously, course instruction in policy matters seems highest in the military war colleges or under the rubric of the Reserve Officers Training Corps. Course outlines for many of their programs indicate a very high use of literature on policy making written by social scientists. The writings of Morgenthau, Henkin, Kaufmann, Boulding, Kahn, Rapaport, Schelling, and so on, proliferate in courses having direct military interest. This stems largely from the proximity of foreign affairs to foreign policy, as well as to a well-evolved "science" of military strategy. The same set of considerations do not obtain with respect to domestic or subnational policy making.

The most extensive interdisciplinary programming has taken place under the rubric of "national security studies." These have been defined by Trager (1973:3) as those courses concerned with the pursuit of vital national goals in international politics and concerned primarily with the interaction between the national security system and the larger political and social systems of which they are a part. Trager's survey excluded ROTC policy-oriented courses or simple military science courses taught under military academies; still, it is the most ambitious

TABLE 5.1

Breakdown of National Security Courses

Course Type	Undergraduate	Graduate	Total
National security policy; defense; strategy; military power	130	69	199
Civil-military relations; military-industrial complex	15	2	17
Comparative defense or security policies	12	5	17
Arms control; disarmanent	6	4	10
Military history	40	17	57
Sociology of the military; sociology of war	9	3	12
Defense economics	6	1	7
Miscellaneous	4	7	11
Total	222	108	330

Source: Trager (1973).

survey to date and indicates that the ties that bind national security to public policy are firmly rooted in university social science departments. For example, of 230 national security courses, 185 were taught within the political science departments. The breakdown of such course offerings is significant for the insight it provides into those areas covered by social science programming in national policy areas (see Table 5.1). In addition to full-time courses, there were considerable numbers of offerings with a strong policy segment (again, it must be remembered that the survey was confined to largely military or security-type orientations). To the extent that these segments become larger and more numerous, one can anticipate an ever-greater concentration in directly policy-related courses in the 1970s (see Table 5.2).

The International Studies Association Section on Military Studies (SOMS) was organized in April 1970. John Lovell was elected chairman and corresponding secretary of the group in 1972. His first task was to try to get a profile of SOMS membership by sending a questionnaire on research and teaching to each person who joined. A special report summarizing the questionnaire responses was prepared and mailed in May 1972. Financial support for preparing and mailing the report was provided by the National Strategy Information Center. The report classified the research-writing and teaching activities of SOMS members by name, under substantive categories; no cumulative totals were provided (see Table 5.3).

In the absence of comparable firm data on the civilian side of public policy offerings, one can only conclude either such offerings are, as claimed by the State Department (which has been the only agency to have systematically surveyed both academic and nonacademic sources), far less numerous or that they are less

TABLE 5.2

Percent of Time Devoted to, and Number of, Courses with a National Security Segment

Percent of Time	Number of Courses
1-15	154
16-25	162
26-50	89
51-75	8
Above 75	0
No percent indicated on questionnaire	210
Total	623

Note: Many, if not most, of these teachers (total number, 335) also have a full course in a national security subject and are included in the national security course tabulation.

Source: Trager (1973).

TABLE 5.3

Teaching Activities of ISA/SOMS Members

Lovell Report Categories	Number of Courses
U.S. national security policy; civil-military policy; strategy	62
U.S. foreign policy; public policy	20
International relations	20
Comparative foreign and defense policy	13
Comparative politics (role of military; revolutionary war)	17
Arms control and disarmament; conflict and conflict resolution; peace keeping; science and technology	19
Diplomatic and military history	15
Other	6
Total	172

Note: There were 107 ISA/SOMS members, representing 78 schools, teaching courses in the national security field.

Source: Lovell (1972).

systematically taught, with a higher proportion of segments and a lower percentage of courses dedicated to full-time scientific study of public policy. It is especially intriguing that "interdisciplinary" efforts simply have not caught on. The situation is one in which the "policy sciences" simply do not exist—at least in course form. What does exist is the teaching of policy within the conventional rubrics of economics, sociology, psychology, and especially political science. Thus, the analysis of public policy must turn its attention to the ways in which each discipline has impact on or influences select portions of the policy-making establishment.

Immediately noteworthy is how each of the major social sciences— psychology, political science, sociology, and so on—maintains its head offices in Washington, D.C., functioning as a lobby for its own special professional interests. But quite beyond that, they serve to recommend key personnel for special projects, provide raw material for urgent policy proposals, and generally act as political bodies unto themselves. This concentration of professional social science headquarters in the Capitol is a clear indication that the federal policy-making potentials of the social sciences are widely understood. And as the limits of academic hiring of social scientists are reached, the area of personnel expansion into policy-related matters becomes not simply an issue of ideological persuasion but practical necessity: an area of growth that warrants the utility as well as practicality of each field of social science. Thus, we turn now to a select, case-by-case study of the ways that each of the social sciences makes a special appeal and impact on an area of public policy.

THE COUNCIL OF ECONOMIC ADVISORS (CEA)

The CEA represents continual and high-level utilization of social scientists and social science knowledge in a highly quantitative form. The central responsibility of the council is to inject economic analysis to policy decision-making mechanisms at the level of the executive office of the president. The CEA was created by the Employment Act of 1946, which set as a primary goal "to promote maximum employment, production and purchasing power." The focal point of the council's activity is to furnish the president with analyses and recommendations directed toward the attainment of these goals. The CEA provides the president with periodic analyses of current economic conditions and forecasts future directions of the economy. In-depth economic studies supply the president with information to make appropriate policy choices to achieve greater price stability, in order to expand employment and economic growth and to reach a balance of external payments position. Recently, the CEA scope has expanded to incorporate emphasis on the optimum evolution of aggregate demand management, the operation and impact of the wage-price control system of the Economic Stabilization Program, and the creation of proposals for international economic reform.

The CEA's professional staff is drawn from universities and research institutions, and these economists serve a normal tour of duty for one or two years. There is a high degree of permeability between the CEA and the ranks of economists. Economists move directly from the academic setting to the CEA and as easily return to the academic setting, and there is a high degree of interaction between the groups. The council's annual economic report has become required reading for economics courses across the nation. Schools such as the University of Minnesota and the University of Chicago have had a marked impact upon the CEA.

The professional staff contains 13 senior staff economists, two statisticians, and eight members in the junior research staff. The professional staff produces the economic analyses and policy recommendations. Beyond these functions, staff economists are involved in many different interagency and council assignments that demand broad-based knowledge and analytical abilities.

The CEA's role has diversified well beyond the initial goal of macroeconomic policy promulgated in the Employment Act. Economic analysis has been proven valuable in handling the issues involving the economy that go well beyond employment and price stability. As the council's role has become diversified, its role of advising the president has been elaborated to include advising many other agencies, departments, and offices in the federal government.

Currently, the CEA covers a broad spectrum of economic issues. The council involves itself in areas of developing prominence, such as the structure of national science policy, the nature of programs to improve the environment, studies of foodstuff production, and especially the U.S. energy situation. Other areas include the evaluation of the problems confronting regulated industries, especially the transportation sector, and the analysis of central policy aspects of the promotion of national growth. Work in the area of human resources deals with manpower programs and many aspects of health and education policy. At times, the council supervises interagency work dealing with these areas. The CEA contributes to the formulation of administration policy on overall international trade policy as well as the resolution of specific trade issues. The council makes inputs on the decisions regarding import-export policy, trade legislation, and negotiations and studies on the effect of direct foreign investment and technology-transfer abroad. Thus, the original narrow concept for a council of economic advisors has been considerably broadened into a full-scale operation at the policy-making level.

The CEA, then, constitutes one of the most widely-accepted forms of the institutionalization of social scientists in a policy-making and advisory capacity. So great is the gap between the relatively sophisticated and advanced role played by economists and the still-underdeveloped stage reached by the other social scientists that in this broad survey, where the tendency is to level all social scientific performance, a special point must be made about the thoroughly special status of the economics profession. So widely accepted are its policy-making and advisory roles that perhaps the critical issue (one which falls quite beyond the scope of this survey) becomes the capacity of the other social science disciplines to have their views and perspectives acted upon with equal alacrity and sobriety.

There is considerable interpenetration between academic economists and the CEA. Indeed, the council is a prototype for the federal involvement of social scientists. Economists move directly from their university positions into the council and then return to the universities when their term of service is completed. Often an economist may accept a position at a quasi-academic institution such as the Brookings Institution after his tenure of service in the CEA expires. In this way he continues to perform ancillary policy and advisory roles. Recruitment patterns on the council tend to follow fashionable ideological currents as well as personal networks of prior associations. Hence, economists from the University of Chicago, in addition to their representation on the council, also form a significant element in the Department of the Treasury and in OMB.

THE AMERICAN PSYCHOLOGICAL
ASSOCIATION (APA)

The APA is the umbrella organization of the psychological profession. It is perhaps the largest single such professional society with an acknowledged crucial role in setting forth the policy guidelines and even ethical framework within which psychological research is to be conducted. Since the psychological profession ranks second only to economics in influence, members, and power in the policy-making area, it is perhaps significant to focus attention on those activities fostered or at least encouraged by the APA.

The APA has taken an organizational interest in the many public-policy questions that affect professional psychology. This "shaping" of policy, as it is called by the APA, is carried forward by four formal and informal units: the APA council, a network of noted psychologists, the Washington D.C., staff of the APA and the APA membership.

In the international-affairs arena psychologists have constructed a wide variety of simulations and other heuristic devices that train individuals to cope with various situations that either have arisen or might arise. Role-playing games include the JCS "political-military desk" games (McDonald 1964) and Harold Guetzkow's pioneering work in environmental simulation known as "internation simulation" (1963). Osgood's "graduated and reciprocated initiative in tension-reduction strategy" (GRIT) and Abt's man-machine simulations have pioneered in exploring behavioral influences on international affairs, especially on peaceful alternatives in conflict resolution and settlement (Davis 1966).

The APA Council passes general resolutions on transcendental questions effecting psychology both as a profession and as a science. These resolutions provide a perspective from which a point of view on many particular issues may be derived. For example, an APA resolution advocating liberalized abortion restrictions led the APA to support groups opposing the "right to life" lobby on Capitol Hill. Other issues upon which the APA council has passed resolutions include ethical standards, conflict of interest, behavior modification for police and correctional use, the insanity-defense plea, community mental health, and juvenile delinquency causes and treatment.

By employing the letters and testimony of "great individuals" of psychology, professional psychologists influence the formulation of public policy. For example, the APA maintains a pool of noted individuals who are willing to testify on specific issues that call upon their expertise. One recent example is the testimony of J. McVicker Hunt, who submitted a letter in support of the Child and Family Services Act (S 3754 in the Senate, and a companion bill, HR 15882, in the House). Although this bill was vetoed by President Nixon, it was subsequently reintroduced by Senator Walter Mondale. In late April 1974 Albert Bandura, the president of the APA, appeared before the House Ways and Means Committee to argue that psychologists be included in any form of national health insurance. Citing studies by several health insurance groups, Bandura concluded that mental disorder is the "single largest disabling factor" in the work force. He forcefully argued that "psychological factors be a major concern of national health programming" (American Psychological Association 1974:4).

Noted members of the APA have been called upon to play a policy-advising role in other areas as well. Several individuals are consultants on HEW's Panel on Aging. The panel report, "Toward a National Policy on Aging," is to be released shortly. APA attention has been drawn to the Hungate bill (HR 5463), which is aimed at eliminating the privileged relationship governing the rules of evidence for certain courts and proceedings. Included in this measure is a section calling for the abolition of the privileged relationship between doctor and patient, priest and parishioner, and therapist and client. Understandably, the APA leadership is opposed to a reduction of common-law status of the special relationships in this area and is actively campaigning to impede its passage.

The APA staff works continually to provide pertinent information for the process of policy formation. One of the most significant access points for the APA staff is in Congress. Inputs range from formal letters to informal telephone calls to panel participation to marking up a bill for scrutiny by a congressional committee. This process is furthered by the close relationship between the APA staff and congressional staff members with a background in psychology, such as Senators Vance Hartke, Daniel Inouye, and Walter Mondale. APA input has been significant in the area of American Indian health policy through the auspices of the Internal and Insular Affairs Committee. Other areas of APA leverage include the Alcohol, Drug Abuse and Mental Health Administration (ADAMHA), the Office of Education, the Child Health and Human Development Institute, and various segments of HEW.

The APA strives to keep its members aware of policy developments affecting the status of psychologists, so that the support of the large membership can be drawn on and used as leverage in support of the APA position. One channel for this activity is the monthly newsletter, the *APA Monitor*, which contains a one-page "Washington Report" on policy matters germane to psychologists, a "Legislative Notebook" noting the type and status of various legislative proposals in the psychological field, and occasional articles devoted to policy relating to psychology, such as "Influencing the Shaping of Public Policy" by Harry Seymour (American Psychological Association 1974b:2).

The APA is unable to lobby directly for the profession since it is chartered as a tax-exempt "educational" organization. To serve the need for a lobby, the APA recently created the Association for the Advancement of Psychology (AAP). Independent of the APA but working in close association with it, the AAP is set up as a lobbying organization (with the proper tax status; it has notified Congress of its willingness to serve in a research and advisory capacity). The AAP made its first appearance to testify before the House Ways and Means Committee in June 1974.

The APA is well-funded and well-organized and represents the most highly developed means for professional social science to come to bear independently on the formulation of public policy. This professional organization thus serves a range of purposes that includes the protection of the psychologists' interests in its capacity as pressure and (through the AAP) a lobbying group. The APA also represents the centralized source of psychological knowledge on policy-relevant questions.

Within DOD there has been the most successful adoption of psychologists' inputs into policy. For example, Donald Michael discovered that a source of anxiety that impaired the performance of nuclear submarine crews was the sailor's concern about his family. Part of this anxiety was caused because the sailor was out of touch with his family for long stretches at a time. The navy changed its personal and family support policies to relieve this problem. The policy adopted was that the navy would care for the families in the event of any type of emergency, thus lifting the burden of concern off the shoulders of the individual sailor. Indeed, the Office of Naval Research (ONR) has been noted for working closely with psychologists on a wide variety of shared concerns. John Dunlop, a psychologist from Norwalk, Connecticut, influenced the human-engineering aspects of contracting for equipment within DOD. Because of his policy influence the Defense Department requires that new equipment also include a training package that can efficiently teach the operators their tasks.

The Society for the Psychological Study of Social Issues has been very active in peace research. For example, Herbert Kelman has clarified attitude-changes in the conformity process (attitude changes occur because of fear, self-interest, and logical appeals) and has thus helped bridge the gap between international behavior and psychological theory. Psychologists were also active in militating against the civil defense policies of the early 1960s (Waskow 1962; see also Oppenheimer 1964).

The psychology profession was actively engaged in developing programs for the War on Poverty. For example, Milton Kutler of the Institute for Policy Studies developed a method for funneling OEO funds around the local governments in order to strengthen the Community Action Program. Martin Deutsch helped establish Project Headstart by determining the effects of differential exposure to environments on school and preschool children. Leonard Duhl of the University of California developed techniques and programs that gave psychological support and means of adjustment to Peace Corps volunteers, both while in the field and upon return to the United States. William Medina has helped to develop an in-house small-group training for highly placed personnel within the Civil Service Commission.

Corporations have used psychologists and psychological programs in order to develop the capacities of their own personnel. General Electric and IBM are two examples of corporations that have extensively employed such techniques. Rensis Likert has worked in the area of management training and management problem solving. Herbert Sheperd and Warren Bennis have worked on organizational-development techniques. Psychologists have also evaluated the impact of building design and structure on work organization and human relations. Understandably, too, psychologists have done work with mental institutions, determining, among other things, the impact of physical space on mental health and on mental-health rehabilitation. Other areas have included decision-making processes and the impact on individual mental-health perceptions and small-group pathologies.

Two critical areas of support for psychology within the government are the National Institute of Health (NIH) and the National Institute of Mental Health (NIMH). They operate on a $500-million budget that includes approximately $49 million for research fellowships, grants, and training. The dismantling of OEO has weakened the influence of psychologists in federal policy making. There can be little doubt that the major support for a federal role for psychology stems from "liberal" Senators such as Edward Kennedy and from psychologist John Gardner, former secretary of HEW, whereas the strongest opposition derives from "conservative" Senators such as Ted Stevens and from the presidential office itself (Moore 1973). The size of the budget allocations for NIH- and OEO-related programs makes support for the institutes a real political football, and the portion of those funds supervised by psychologists places them in a central role.

The successful adaptation of the medical imagery by the profession of psychology has meant a great deal to the policy-making potentials of the APA. For if economists can boast that theirs is the "hardest" of the soft sciences, psychologists can claim a role in the "healing" sciences. The connection of both with scientism as an ideology (mathematics in the case of economics, biology in the case of psychology) has increased their credibility as policy agents capable of supplying objective information devoid of bias or special pleading. If the criterion used is simply numerical, this strategy has paid huge dividends, but if the judgment is to be based on the quality of policy recommendations or even on the results of such' policies, this same strategy would have to be considered problematic.

ANTHROPOLOGY AND THE BUREAU OF
INDIAN AFFAIRS

The handling of the "Indian Problem" by the Indian Office of the United States in the nineteenth century can simply and succinctly be described as a combination of seizure of the red man's land and suppression of the Indian culture (Danziger, 1974:198-214). If in the early twentieth century an infusion of the anthropological perspective into Indian policy did not change matters much, it did make clear the monumental nature of the grievances of Indian peoples against the federal government.

Anthropological contributions to policy commenced with John Wesley Powell's Bureau of Ethnology in the late nineteenth century. James Mooney's study, *The Ghost Dance Religion and the Sioux Outbreak of 1890*, was done in conjunction with the military investigation of the massacre at Wounded Knee in 1891. In the years after World War II anthropologists served as advisors to the military governments and occupation forces of conquered U.S. territories and occupied Japan and Germany. Anthropological advice ameliorated many problems for U.S. navy administrators in Malaya. At the same time, dozens of anthropologists worked as consultants for U.S. diplomatic representatives in Allied nations.

During World War II anthropologists were called in to consult with the military about the handling of native populations and the behavioral patterns of the cultures of the Axis powers. Ruth Benedict and Clyde Kluckhohn influenced War Department approaches to capturing and interrogating Japanese prisoners of war. The War Department's policy prior to Benedict's and Kluckhohn's advice had been that the Japanese soldier would not surrender to U.S. forces and, even if he were captured, would be of little intelligence value to the Allies. Kluckhohn and Benedict maintained that the Japanese soldier would indeed be willing to surrender (and not commit suicide after his capture) and that U.S. forces in the field should modify their operations accordingly. Not only was the anthropologists' advice correct, but the Japanese soldier was even more useful to intelligence gathering than his German counterpart. At the conclusion of World War II Kluckhohn and Benedict were central in advocating that the occupation forces in Japan permit the emperor to continue as figurehead of the government. Because of the great success Kluckhohn and Benedict enjoyed in the utility of their previous advice, their recommendations were heeded and the powerful legitimating institution—the emperor—remained (Stoetzel 1955: 11-63).

Since 1950 anthropologists have been consulted by various agencies, such as the National Research Council, National Science Foundation, National Institute of Mental Health, Office of Education, Social Science Research Council, and the Ford Foundation. Anthropological work with policy implications has been performed in psychiatric hospitals, evaluating the fit between care and patient need, and anthropologists have advised state commissions on mental-health systems. Anthropologists have served as witnesses before American Indian land-claims commissions and were a central force in convincing the federal government to permit the Native American (Indian) Church to use peyote in its religious rites.

Anthropological contributions have been solicited by municipal agencies. For example, Anthony Wallace of the University of Pennsylvania (and the Eastern Pennsylvania Psychiatric Institute) was commissioned by the Philadelphia Housing Association in the late 1950s to prepare a report on the relative human-engineering merits of high-rise and low-rise housing. The report on the subject was later published by the Philadelphia Housing Authority itself. The state hospital system is another government agency that uses anthropological insights and research. For instance, as a result of a miscellany of new information and viewpoints, including the introduction of psychotropic drugs, the realization was made that changes in milieu often improve the condition of psychotic patients. Because of general research emphases on chemical and situation factors in disturbed behavior, some state systems are now undertaking the policy of emptying the state hospitals of most of their patients and of maintaining them in out-patient status in contact with community clinics and specially-prepared housing situations.

Anthropologists made notable contributions to the National Research Council's Committee on Disaster Studies, which in turn influenced civil-defense programs of the United States. These studies, undertaken in the late 1950s and early 1960s, no doubt added to a policy decision *not* to embark the nation on a program of deep-shelter building or civil-defense evacuation plans.

The most intriguing and singular contribution of anthropology in the federal-policy apparatus is its role in the Bureau of Indian Affairs. The continuing unsettled nature of the "Indian question" in the United States provides a good test case for the potentials, and even more, the limitations of anthropology in a policy role only partially supported by the federal establishment.

John Collier was appointed commissioner of the Bureau of Indian Affairs in 1933. From the beginning of his tenure in office Collier tried to introduce a greater use of social research in the formulation of bureau policy and in the reform of previous bureau policy. By 1934, under his leadership, many of the more destructive and abusive policies of the bureau had been rethought and revised on the basis of social science research inputs. In 1933, too, an anthropological research unit was established as part of the Indian bureau. One of its first missions was to undertake studies of Indian organizational patterns as a basis for developing self-governing arrangements.

The research work of anthropologists in this area was not completed when new arrangements for the conduct of tribal affairs were made and put into motion by other officials in the bureau. It was thus a classic case of lack of coordination in the production and use of social science information. It was suggested in an earlier analysis of applied anthropology in the federal government that at the time "the anthropologists . . . were more interested in the still functioning Indian patterns and trends of social groupings than the new social values that were developing. The Indian administration was envisaged as an agency of American culture directly involved in a clash with Indian cultures, rather than as an integral part of the social universe of the Indian on the reservation" (Kennard and MacGregor 1953:833). Because of this and other problems, the research unit was disbanded in 1938 (Lyons 1969:115-17). Collier blamed its end solely on cuts in federal appropriations. However, the last director of the research unit, anthropologist Scudder McKeel, felt strongly that the regular Indian service had exerted pressure to end the research program because of the inherent conflict between "the professional administrator with little or no social science training and the 'theorist' " (McKeel 1944:209).

Despite the formal demise of the research unit, some research was conducted intermittently. In conjunction with the Soil Conservation Bureau of the Department of Agriculture, social scientists studied land use and served as advisors in the bureau's education program. The bureau also sponsored several long-range studies of Indian life that provided a foundation for future changes in policy.

Collier was not uncritical both of social science techniques and of social scientists. His response to a special anthropological report written by staff anthropologists is an example of his approach:

. . . the report does not prepossess me either as social philosophy or as factual reporting. . . As a recorder of atomized facts, one may put in years of time among a population and his atomized recording, or photography, may be accurate and even useful. But in determining Indian Service policies and in attempting to evaluate human beings and to chart the future of human spirits, there are needed some endowments of enthusiasm, confidence in the human nature one is dealing with and social philosophy. . . . This is another case showing that achievement in a special science, anthropology or any other, provides no assurance to deal with social problems [Collier 1936].

The social scientist is forced to justify in hard cold facts and statistics his value to the policy maker. Just as the anthropologists considered themselves experts on charting human behaviors, the officials of the bureau believed strongly in their own "common sense" or "experiential" angle on human affairs, especially in comparison to the abstract "theoretical" approach of social scientists. Further, if the social scientists were not sensitive to political currents, they were abused or bypassed in the course of bureaucratic in-fighting.

Cohen (1937) has identified some of the many areas in which there has been practical application of anthropological information to the construction of policy by the Bureau of Indian Affairs. These areas include education, the problems of administrative areas, economic activities, land tenure, inheritance, health conditions, and art and recreation. He points out that impact of the social science approach to policy-making has had a particularly important impact on Indian administrators. Except during the Collier years, the bureau has not set up positions or job descriptions at the policy level that would attract anthropologists and historians. At a lower quasi-policy level the bureau has utilized individuals with professional social science training: Robert Young, an acknowledged expert in linguistic anthropology (Navajo); D'Arcy McNickle, who has years of experience in the bureau and has made important contributions in the field of ethnohistory; Stephen Feraca, an anthropologist; and Robert Pennington, who studied with Ray Allen Billington in frontier history, serving as chief of the Special Projects Section, Division of Tribal Government Services (Pennington 1973).

The number of anthropologists is much smaller than that of either economics or psychology. Anthropology's influence has thus been far more confined and selective than theirs. Yet, by virtue of the intimate connection of anthropology to overseas research and to ministering to the needs of underdeveloped peoples, it has been more widely subject to both internal and external professional and political criticism than the other social sciences. Since it works in areas of wide dissensus rather than of consensus, its support base is much weaker politically as well as financially. Be that as the case may be, the role of anthropology—from occupied Japan to the occupied Indian Reservations— has placed it in the forefront of the disciplines involved in the formulations of national and local policies affecting large numbers of people.

THE RUSSELL SAGE FOUNDATION

The Russell Sage Foundation, established in 1907, is dedicated to the "improvement of social and living conditions in the United States of America." This phrase is usually interpreted as meaning support for social scientists, and more specifically sociologists, on work with broad-based social implications. The foundation further operates on the premise that social science knowledge and methods can be used in the planning, development, and implementation of social-action efforts. Beyond that, Russell Sage assumes that the social sciences can provide an understanding of the dynamics that facilitate or impede social change.

The foundation maintains a professional staff of social scientists who advise researchers on a wide range of projects and engage in their own research. The staff participates in the planning of each program supported by the foundation and remains an active partner in the operation of research and evaluation. One area of particular attention for the foundation is the application of the findings of its research projects. This interest is manifested by monitoring a project at least into the early stages of practical use.

One-fourth of the foundation's roughly $2 million in expenditures supports research projects conducted by its staff members, who spend part of their time on foundation administration and the remainder on their own social science research projects. Recent staff members have included Raymond Bauer, Edgar F. Borgatta, Raymond Mack, James S. Coleman, Kenneth C. Land, and Harriet A. Zuckerman. Foundation interest has been focused on studies of social change; human resources and education; developing the social sciences; and the social sciences and mass media, law, and human biology.

Within the area of social change the foundation has given particular attention to improving the methodology and techniques of the measurement of social change. For example, work is proceeding in conjunction with the University of Chicago's National Opinion Research Center (NORC) on the development of social indicators. Five annual surveys—the first in 1972—will monitor facial attitudes, marriage and family concerns, socioeconomic status, morale, family characteristics, and family composition. Useful comparative and longitudinal data will hopefully be generated through this study. Other projects include studies on technological shortcuts to social change; the evaluation of social change; developing a report, *On the Future State of the Union*, a study of U.S. population distribution, in conjunction with the National Planning Association; generating a macrosociological model of the United States; monitoring the quality of American life and the human meaning of social change: in short, projects that emphasize social science in social policies directly bearing on the United States. The foundation does little in the way of sponsoring overseas activities (Russell Sage Foundation 1972).

The domestic mandate behind Russell Sage Foundation support for social research is a broad one, extending from the gathering of primary information in sensitive areas (ranging from the occupational role of women to the dangers in maintaining secret files on prominent persons) to the forceful presentation of social action and social reform policies (ranging from the use of social indicators in federal policy making to the wider involvement of foundations in minority-rights activities). Toward this end Russell Sage has a unique internal setup—one that involves in-house sociologists doing applied research on a rotating project or per annum basis—and an organizational structure in which sociologists are crucially involved in deciding to allocate funds.

In recent years, Russell Sage has come under increasing criticism from radical sociologists for not being sufficiently involved in the practical needs of the poor and the exploited and, beyond that, for taking a thoroughly meliorative attitude to social change. In part, this criticism is acknowledged by foundation authorities; in part the policy stems from an original grant charge that mandates funds for social reform but not for social revolution and that encourages research with possible policy payoffs but not partisan involvement in the political process. The foundation has definitely shifted emphasis by encouraging research in such major applied areas as media application of social science, educational reform among minorities, policy guidelines for the social sciences, and generally assisting projects that have a potential for wide public appeal and increasing public awareness of social science.

Russell Sage is a clear illustration of a foundation with a special mission: one in which social welfare intersects with social research. But as the century wears on and the social-work "profession" distinguishes itself from the sociological "science," the foundation's efforts to bridge the gap between the informational role and the action role have become somewhat more difficult. In general, it is the "harder" wing of the sociological profession that has carried the day, with sociologists rather than social-work personnel becoming increasingly pivotal. Yet, within that framework, the foundation has served to provide an intense lobby for the wider policy uses of the social sciences. In the main, it has done so by providing support for basic research in areas of deep sensitivity and widespread ignorance, such as the problems of aging and dying in American society, or in support of fundamental theoretical and methodological work that could eventually lead to a uniform set of standards for judging sociological products. Whatever the prospects are for such standardization of concerns and procedures, the fact remains that in its more than 65 years of operation the Russell Sage Foundation has not only seen sociology grow immensely as a profession, but it has also substantially contributed to the character of that growth by the careful and selective investment of its roughly $40-million portfolio. If its work has been done quietly and in a low-risk context, it has, through its publications as well as its sponsorship of crucial research, served to underwrite the theory of much policy practice in areas of health, welfare, education, sex, and race. And in its forthright support of social indicators it has further served to tighten the relationship between social science and public policy in domestic areas—those areas in which the greatest degree of consensus among selective elites presently obtains.

In 1961 the Russell Sage Foundation began exhibiting interest in questions concerned with the conflict between personal rights to privacy and society's (or an organization's) need to know. The first program was directed toward investigating the implications of standardized achievement testing in the United States. That study found that despite growing use of record-keeping on all aspects of a student's life, there was no standard policy—and often a lack of any policy whatsoever—regarding the dissemination of such records (Goslin 1963). As a result of this study the foundation convened a conference to probe the ethical and legal issues involved in the management of records. The report of this conference (Russell Sage Foundation 1970), which included guidelines on this matter, was distributed to over 100,000 educators and educational policy makers. It provoked widespread discussion about record-keeping policy at the local level. The foundation has since extended its interest to the analysis of student records at colleges and universities. The foundation's concern over the power an organization holds over its members became focused in a collection of original papers edited by a staff member of the foundation, Stanton Wheeler (1970), who is also on the faculty of Yale University Law School. The study focused on reports of record keeping by the business, government, educational, professional, and welfare structures.

Human experimentation, another aspect of personal privacy, generated Russell Sage Foundation interest in 1964. A landmark study produced by the chairman of the board of trustees and the president of the foundation (Ruebhausen and Brim 1965) dealt directly with guidelines for such research. These guidelines have subsequently been used by HEW and have been included in the codes of ethics of various social science professional societies. In related studies Bernard Barber (1972) has examined the practices for review and the approval procedures of peer committees with control over projects dealing with human subjects used in experimentation. Jay Katz (1972) has produced for the foundation the most extensive case-book approach to the utilization of human experimental subjects in all areas of endeavor. This case book includes the disciplines of medicine, psychology, sociology, biology, and law and the perspectives of the state, investigator, subjects, and the professions.

The process of developing social indicators, an area in which the foundation has consistently demonstrated interest, necessitates the large-scale collection and analysis of data from all segments of society. The effect on privacy of the comingling of broad-based data files was broached in a foundation study by Alan Westin (1972). The Westin study originated as a result of the initiative the quasi-official National Academy of Science, which established the Computer Science and Engineering Board in July 1968. The board wished to discuss questions of due process and privacy within the framework of increasing technological processing of individual records (cf. Brim 1972:xiii-xviii). The most satisfactory approach, the board determined, was to undertake a broad-based case-study attack on the problem of computer recording, retrieving, and communication of individual data files. The study included an emphasis on social and policy features of factors shaping individual file use, as well as a scrutiny of the harder technical linkages. Original research seemed the most feasible approach to the subject matter in order to insure and strengthen reliability.

Because of its long-standing interest in technology, law and their relationship with the social sciences, the foundation was receptive to the proposed Westin study. Westin, a professor of public law and government at Columbia University, proceeded to draw together a staff for the study. The staff included specialists in computer science, economics, journalism, law, political science, psychology and sociology. The staff made over 50 site visits of computer-file facilities. From these visits 14 in-depth analyses were undertaken. The report of the study included an extended discussion of the implications of the findings and a prognostication of developments in this area.

The study report, issued in 1972, provoked a flurry of discussion. The federal government, which served as a major focus of the study, had several areas of record keeping and exchange on individual files carefully scrutinized. More recently, the Twentieth Century Fund, another social-science-oriented philanthropic organization, has pursued this area. Howard A. Latin of the Earl Warren Legal Institute at the University of California, Berkeley, commenced a study in June 1973, focusing on specific aspects of computer information processing practices and the individual's right to privacy.

POLITICAL SCIENCE AND THE STATE DEPARTMENT

One area of significant policy impact for the political science discipline has been in the Department of State (DOS). As early as 1952 the American Council on Education issued a report on sponsored research policy of colleges and universities (1954), recommending the development of linkages between the political scientist and the State Department. In April 1964 the Fascell subcommittee of the House Committee on Foreign Affairs urged improved use of social science research reports (U.S. Department of State 1971a:1-3).

DOS sponsored an NAS conference in 1966 that recommended "full and effective use of social science research for policy and operations." Two types of in-house courses are now offered by DOS that are oriented toward social science: a) courses on the techniques, concepts, and theories of social science disciplines and b) courses having, as a major component, materials relating to social science. In addition, there are a number of extended training opportunities in academic institutions for DOS personnel at the policy-input level (U.S. Department of State 1968:11). The Foreign Area Research Coordinating Group found relatively few in-house courses dealing directly and primarily with research methods and concepts of the social sciences. However, many courses offered by the government draw heavily on the behavioral and social sciences. Chief examples are the course offerings of the National War College and the Foreign Service Institute. Lecturers in DOS programs include political scientists such as Joseph La Polombara and A. James Gregor, but these lecturers are in no way bound by department policies. More often than not, they provide general orientation and briefing services.

DOS encourages the "brokerage" concept of ideas between suppliers and users of social science information. For example, in 1970, the department held a conference on social research and foreign affairs where Edwin Fogelman presented a paper on "The Relevance of Social Science Research to Foreign Policy Making" (U.S. Department of State 1970:1-3). In addition to conducting social science research under contract arrangements, academic social science consultants complement DOS's research capabilities by working directly with department officers on a variety of policy-related problems (U.S. Department of State 1969:2). DOS sometimes issues invitations to private researchers to perform contract research on social science topics. However, the department does not desire "detailed, formal, unsolicited proposals" from the private social scientists, especially since such research must be let out on a competitive-bid basis. The overall purpose, then, is to have a free flow of ideas between department officers and qualified outside researchers (U.S. Department of State 1971b:2).

DOS's political science heart is the Bureau of Intelligence and Research (INR). At this writing, the staff of INR consists of about 330 individuals, of whom 200 or so are professional foreign-policy affairs and intelligence analysts, trained in the social sciences. But political scientists compose the overwhelming majority of the social science disciplines represented. There are also economists and a limited number of sociologists and historians. These social scientists work primarily on applied problems. INR has displayed less interest in advancing the methodology or the theory of the social scientists than in application (Platig 1968; and Platig 1973). Depending on the assumptions used, INR favors applied over basic research in the ratio of 58:42 or 69:31.

INR has two primary responsibilities: a) to provide raw and finished intelligence to the State Department from the intelligence community, to produce finished intelligence of its own for the department, and to participate in certain community-wide intelligence production efforts; b) to serve as the coordinator, within the department, for U.S. government intelligence activities abroad that have operational significance for the department. In the substantive intelligence field the focus is on timely "policy-oriented" or "issue-oriented" research. Thus, INR is the organization specially assigned within DOS to supply information tailored to specific needs, to provide the professional researcher's view of developments abroad and to insure that the department benefits from and contributes to the workings of the Bureau of Intelligence and Research (Uliassi 1971:309-42). INR produces a biannual "consolidated plan" that analyzes foreign-affairs research expenditures and guides future research efforts.

An assessment of the 1974-75 budget will give some idea of the size and magnitude of DOS's research effort in foreign-affairs external research. The total amount allocated for fiscal year 1975/76—$54,600,000—constitutes an increase in the external-research effort of 11.5 percent. The Agency for International Development (AID) and DOS both show planned research funding increases; DOD and the AVMS Control and Disarmament Agency (ACDA) show decreases; USIA remains essentially the same.

Leaving aside global or multiregional studies (47.6 percent of the total foreign area research effort) and those focusing on the United States (0.7 percent), allocations in the First Plan for the remaining eight regions rank as follows: Africa (28.4 percent), Latin America (9.4 percent), East Asia (5.4 percent), USSR (2.3 percent), Western Europe (2.0 percent), China (1.8 percent), Australia (1.5 percent), and Eastern Europe (0.8 percent). This order remains similar in the Second Plan. It reflects the large role played by AID in the total USC/FAR funding picture. Between them, the USSR and China will receive 4.1 percent of foreign-affairs research attention, up from about 3 percent in the Second Plan, in which foreign area research objectives called for various actions to improve research on these countries. The study of affairs within foreign nations will receive 84.3 percent of FAR's research attention; the study of relations between and among nations will receive the remaining 15.7 percent.

Between the Second and Third plans there is an absolute as well as relative decline in research on international relations, whereas research on international sociopolitical and military relations each show a steep decline (43.1 percent and 37.2 percent respectively) and that on international economic relations shows a small (3.4 percent) increase. DOS, USIA, and the NSC staff are the three member agencies that devote more of their resources to the study of international relations than to national affairs. AID's program is heavily weighted (93.3 percent) toward the study of national affairs. Concerning studies that focus on the national affairs of foreign countries, economic, sociopolitical, and military affairs will receive attention roughly in the ration of 11:10:1, not very different from the Second Plan, where the ration was 13:11:1. As for research on international relations, economic, sociopolitical, and military relations will receive attention roughly in the ratio of 2:1:2, a substantial shift from the Second Plan, where the ratio was 2:2:3. Across all regions, science-technology matters—both national and international—receive only 0.4 percent of the USC/FAR's planned research effort.

In the Second Plan the member agencies agreed on six USC/FAR research objectives; in the intervening year, steps have been taken in pursuit of them. In preparing the Third Plan the member agencies have agreed on three new objectives. These, along with a status report on the six original objectives, are presented in Part 2 of the plan. The three new USC/FAR research objectives are listed below with action responsibilities indicated:

1. Assess the state of research on the political, social, economic, military, and foreign-policy dynamics of the countries of the Near East and South Asia and develop recommendations in this field for the USC/FAR agencies. Action: USC/FAR Consultative Group on Near East and South Asia.

2. Explore the need and, as appropriate, recommend steps for advancing knowledge about the evolution, dynamics, and long-range implications of emergent international society (societies) as manifested in multinational public and private institutions, areas of interdependence among nations, and various trans-national phenomena. Action: USC/FAR Consultative Group of International Political-Social Relations.

3. Assist ACDA in assessing the priority research needs in the field of arms control and disarmament, and develop recommendations in this field for the USC/FAR agencies. Action: USC/FAR Consultative Group on International Military Relations.

Those examples are illustrative of principles that hold true generally. In comparing and contrasting sociologists and political scientists, it is evident that the former are concentrated in domestic affairs with considerable private-sector support, and emphasizing tasks for the least-advantaged sectors of society, and the latter are concentrated in foreign affairs with considerable public-sector support, emphasizing tasks for the powerful and even dominant sectors of society. Undoubtedly, this helps to explain differences in the overall posture of the two disciplines: the "liberalism" of much sociology and the "conservatism" of much political science. Even in their respective revolts against empiricism and functionalisms, these sorts of differences are manifest. For the most part sociologists moved into "critical" postures with respect to the American society, while the political scientists moved into "normative" postures. While no clear causal chain can be established between funding conditions and inner disciplinary structures (certainly not within the confines of this report), it is more than accidental that those who service the lower portions of society should often be found among the most critical segments of the intelligentsia, while those who service the elite sectors in their research efforts are found with equal frequency to be most supportive of establishment sectors. This entire area of the support basis of social science and the character of the professional ideologies involved needs considerably more work, but it certainly points up more than accidental relationships that can have great importance in the future history of the autonomy of the social sciences.

REFERENCES

American Council on Education
    1954   *Sponsored Research Policy of Colleges and Universities.*
American Psychological Association
    1974a   "Bandura calls for inclusion of psychology in National Health Insurance." *APA Monitor.* Vol. 5 (June).
    1974b   "Influencing the Shaping of Public Policy." *APA Monitor.* Vol. 5 (July).
Barber, Bernard
    1972   2Experimenting with Humans. New York: Russell Sage Foundation.
Brim, Orville G.
    1972   "Foreword." in Alan F. Westin, *Databanks in a Free Society.* New York: Quadrangle Books—NYT Publishers.
Caplan, Nathan
    1974   Research cited in *Behavior Today* 5, no. 24 (June 17, 1974):172-73.
Collier, John
    1936   Cited in Robert Pennington, Chief, Special Projects Section, Division of Tribal Government Services, Bureau of Indian Affairs, U.S. Department of the Interior, personal correspondence with the authors. (November 1973).
Danziger, Jr., Edmund Jefferson
    1974   *Indians and Bureaucrats: Administering the Reservation Policy during the Civil War.* Urbana and Chicago: University of Illinois Press.
Davis, Robert
    1966   "International Influence Process: How Relevant is the

Contribution of Psychologists?" *American Psychologist.* 21 (March):236-43.

Far Horizons
1973   Third USC/FAR Consolidated Plan for Foreign Affairs Research, FY 1974-75. November 1973.

Goslin, David A.
1963   *The Search for Ability: Standardized Testing in Social Perspective.* New York: Russell Sage Foundation.

Guetzkow, Harold et al.
1963   *Simulation in Inter-Nation Relations.* Englewood Cliffs, N.J.: Prentice-Hall.

Katz, Jay
1972   *Experimenting with Human Beings: The Authority of the Investigator, Subject, Profession, and State in the Human Experimentation Process.* New York: Russell Sage Foundation.

Kennard, Edward and Gordon MacGregor
1953   "Applied Anthropology in Government: United States," in *Anthropology Today,* edited by A. L. Kroeber. Chicago: University of Chicago Press, pp. 832-40.

Lovell, John
1972   Profile of Section on Military Studies of the International Studies Association. Bloomington, Indiana (mimeograph) May 1, 1972.

Lyons, Gene
1969   *The Uneasy Partnership.* New York: Russell Sage Foundation.

Mckeel, Scudder
1944   "An Appraisal of the Indian Reorganization Act, *American Anthropologist* 46, no. 2, Part I (April-June 1944):209-17.

McDonald, Thomas J.
1964   "JCS Politico-Military Desk Games," in *Second War Gaming Symposium Proceedings* ed. Murray Greyson. Washington, D.C.: Washington Operations Council, 63-74.

Moore, Pamela
1973   "A Behavioral Guide to Congress." *Behavior Today.* 4, No. 23 (June 4).

Oppenheimer, Martin
1964   "The Peace Research Game" *Dissent.* 11 (January):44-48.

Pennington, Robert
1973   Personal correspondence with the authors.

Pilisuk, Marc and Phyllis Pilisuk
1973   *How We Lost the War on Poverty.* New Brunswick, N.J.: Transaction Books—E. P. Dutton.

Platig, Raymond
1968   "Research and Analysis," *Annals of American Academy of Political and Social Scientists* 380 (November 1968).
1973   Personal interview with the authors.

Ruebhausen, Oscar M. and Orville G. Brim
1965   "Privacy and Behavioral Research": Columbia Law Review 65:1184-1211.

Russell Sage Foundation
  1970   *Guidelines for the Collection, Maintenance and Dissemination of Pupil Records.* New York: Russell Sage Foundation.
  1972   *Annual Report 71-72* New York: Russell Sage Foundation.
Stoetzel, Jean   .
  1955   *Without the Chrysanthemum and the Sword: A Study of the Attitudes of Youth in Post-War Japan.* New York: Columbia University Press (A UNESCO Publication).
Trager, Frank
  1973   *National Security Studies Survey: A Summary of Results.* New York: New York University in Cooperation with the National Strategy Information Center (Mimeo) February 1, 1973.
Uliassi, Pio D.
  1971   "Government Sponsored Research on International and Foreign Affairs," in *The Use and Abuse of Social Science,* ed. Irving Louis Horowitz. New Brunswick, N.J.: Transaction Books.
  1973   Correspondence with the authors, December 15, 1973.
U.S. Department of State
Foreign Area Research Coordination Group
  1968   *Horizons* (January 1968): Washington, D.C.
  1969   *Horizons* (March 1969): Washington, D.C.
  1970   *Horizons* (November 1970): Washington, D.C.
  1971a   *Horizons* (May 1971): Washington, D.C.
  1971b   *Horizons* (July 1971): Washington, D.C.
Waskow, Arthur
  1962   *The Shelter Centered Society.* Washington, D.C.: Peace Research Institute.
Westin, Alan F.
  1972   *Databanks in a Free Society.* New York: Quadrangle Books— NYT Publishers.
Wheeler, Stanton (ed.)
  1970   *On Record: Files and Dossiers in American Life.* New York: Russell Sage Foundation.

6

SOCIAL SCIENCE
PARTICIPATION IN U.S.
FOREIGN POLICY

SUCCESS AND FAILURE OF SOCIAL SCIENCE
PARTICIPATION IN DECISION MAKING

Events have lives of their own. They compel the use of whatever tools available in the arsenal of knowledge to resolve problems are considered to be of major national and international standing. The Bay of Pigs and the Cuban missile crisis, the program of "civic action" to frustrate guerrilla movements in the Third World, the process of "Vietnamization" to pacify revolutionary movements in Southeast Asia—all of these are not simply newspaper headlines of the past decade or forms of basic international geopolitics (although they are indeed that, too). Each in its own way also elicited a use of the social sciences that both amazed and shocked the scientific communities involved. No longer was the old question about the scientific status of the social sciences being asked in mock seriousness. Rather, now that the social sciences had come of age, it was questioned whether they served the universal interests of humanity any better than the physical or biological sciences. At the same time—less well-known on an international scale—there were a series of internal, quite American events: the desegregation of the armed forces; the evolution of the doctrine of equal opportunity and equal access to public education in place of the older legal doctrine of separate-but-equal status; and the rise of affirmative action programs and war-on-poverty programs that also had an ultimate aim of reducing structural inequality. There, too, the weight and authority of the social sciences were solicited and called upon to legitimize the national goals of equality and democracy.

One found the social sciences, very much like the presidency, called upon to defend U.S. interests overseas without respect to their lack of popular and democratic content at the same time that social sciences were called upon to expand U.S. citizens' horizons within a nation that did indeed have a popular and democratic content. This underscores several points. First, the social sciences do not create a consensus or a dissensus so much as they respond to the presence or absence of such public opinion as it already has been shaped in the crucible of political and economic struggles. Second, when a dissensus exists, the infusion of social science neither bails out poor strategic decisions nor serves to turn the tide of battle. (The converse is also true: when a consensus does exist, the likelihood of successful use of social science is considerably heightened.) Third, if one employs a mandarin model of the social sciences (i.e., a service model), it is simpler to postulate outcomes in keeping with general political conditions than if one expects from the social sciences a turning about of basic political premises and principles. These outer limits of applied social science understood, it is possible to proceed to a brief consideration of cases in which social science operated in areas of international dissensus (with disastrous effects) and of national consensus (with dramatically successful outcomes).

THE CUBAN MISSILE CRISIS

Doubtless, the Cuban missile crisis fits a general definition of war-game strategy. The U.S. government had at the time of the missile crisis, and still has, three basic national aims with respect to Cuba. Those main goals were intended to prevent the spread of communism in Cuba and were expressed in a joint resolution of Congress passed on September 20 and 26, 1962. The substance of this resolution noted that:

The United States is determined a) to prevent by whatever means may be necessary, including the use of arms, the Marxist-Leninist regime in Cuba from extending, by force or by the threat of force, its aggressive or subversive activities to any part of this hemisphere; b) to prevent in Cuba the creation or use of an externally supported military capability endangering the security of the United States; and c) to work with the Organization of American States (OAS) and with freedom-loving Cubans to support the aspirations of the Cuban people for self-determination [Pachter 1963:179].

By military power and by other instruments of national power, such as trade discrimination, Cuba was to be isolated in order to make the maintenance of communism there costly to the Soviet Union (McNamara 1963:274). The missile crisis provided a test case for hemispheric containment (Posvar 1964). The next question became, how was game-strategy policy to be formulated in the Cuban case? In formal terms the answer was simple: An executive committee of the National Security Council, appointed ad hoc by President Kennedy, formulated and recommended a course of action, and the president approved it. But the real issue was, how did game strategy come to be implemented, if it was, in the actual policy followed? This is the crux of the problem and a much more difficult question to answer.

There are several modes of influence to be considered. The first is the assembly and use of specific recommendations or studies dealing with the introduction of offensive weapons into Cuba. Whether the analysis was solicited by higher or lower government offices makes a difference only after the recommendations exist; the first problem is to establish their existence. Bruce Smith (1966:231) pointed out, however, that the effective advisory group usually goes to great pains to conceal its impact on policy. For example, the RAND strategic bases study, "Selection and Use of Strategic Air Bases," was put into effect in 1953 but remained classified until 1962, nine years later. In establishing his case for the influence of this study over air-force policy, Smith relied extensively on personal interviews that might have been difficult to obtain if his dissertation adviser, Don K. Price, had not been both a member of RAND's board of trustees and a Harvard University dean. The RAND Corporation made a number of studies after the crisis, but if any studies were made before it, they are still classified (cf. Graham and Brease 1967). Because any such study would be extremely sensitive politically, its classification in the near future would be unlikely. Second, specific policy recommendations are atypical: most RAND strategy analysis deals with more abstract questions. Information analysis directed toward specific policy is the responsibility of the intelligence branch. Although on the Cuban question the theoretical distinction between research and intelligence fades, the institutional distinction remains clear: research and intelligence functions are performed by different bureaus. By all accounts, only the intelligence experts were involved in the executive-committee council of war. According to Wohlstetter (1965), no one thought the Cubans and Soviets would install the missiles. One must infer, lacking any other evidence, that no specific policy recommendations relating to the Cuban situation were produced by the RAND Corporation. Since RAND's influence seems out of the question in this case, there is no point in speculating about methodological problems, such as communication and distortion of policy recommendations or the merits of systems analysis.

The other mode of influence is the pervasive frame of reference contained in the "massive outpouring of scholarship" in support of the new politics based on behavioral psychology. In addition to the significant effort devoted to systems analysis, the early 1960s were characterized by the emergence of war-game theory as the basic form of macroscopic social science. This occurred, in part, as a metaphorical displacement of the "historical" orientations of previous periods, characterized by the writings of such men as Hans Morgenthau and Arnold J. Toynbee, and, in part, as a commonly held belief that the results of experimental psychology—particularly of reinforcement, exchange, and balance theories— could be extended to cover political behavior between nations. The concurrence of circumstance—that is, the emergence of a group of war gamers, such as Alain Enthoven and Adam Yarmolinsky, in positions of advisory power; the professional demands by men, such as Bernard Brodie and Ithiel de Sola Pool, to "test" behaviorist assumptions in a broadened context; the coalescence of "systems" designers with engineering backgrounds, such as Seymour J. Deitchman, and "social" designers with political science backgrounds, such as

Henry A. Kissinger—served as a fulcrum for organizing a new view of "relevance," a new faith in a social science of political "meaning."

At the same time that the inner organizational requisites of war-game theory were being met, the outer political requisites of real conflict were also being met in the Cuban missile crisis. This crisis had the perfect scenario dimensions: it was a simple two-person struggle between major powers (or so it seemed to the protagonists at the time); it had a stage setting of showdown proportions that revealed relatively clearcut and unambiguous dimensions; it was a situation in which victor and vanquished would be readily determined by the behavior shown. That all of these assumptions were radically in error was either disbelieved or discounted at the time. It was not a simple two-person struggle but, as interpreted by Cuba (and much of the Third World), a struggle between big powers acting arrogantly and a small power acting with principles to preserve its autonomy and sovereignty. There was nothing unambiguous about the showdown, since the nature of the resolution convinced all combatants and parties to the dispute that they had, in fact, been the winner; it was a showdown without losers. Indeed, this ambiguity really made peace possible under the circumstances, because no party was willing to accept responsibilities for defeat or for any outcome perceived by any party as a defeat.

According to the New York *Times'* account of the committee's October 19 meeting, there were some second thoughts about the blockade, some renewed interest in an air attack: "The reason was what the group called a 'scenario' (a phrase originating in the strategy community)—a paper indicating in detail all the possible consequences of an action" (New York *Times* 1962). Elie Abel (1966:86) pointed out that "Bundy prepared the air-strike argument; and Alexis Johnson with Paul Nitze's assistance, drafted what came to be called the blockade scenario," indicating that the frame of reference of the executive committee was game-strategy analysis.

Smith (1966:112) noted that "gaming and simulation had important uses as a training device for government officials to help them understand what kinds of behavior to be prepared for in various crisis situations. Crisis games became widely used by high State and Defense Department officials early in the Kennedy Administration." In addition, many high-level civilian executives were formerly members of the game strategy community: Charles Hitch, assistant secretary of Defense (comptroller); Henry Rowen and Alain Enthoven, deputy assistant secretaries of Defense; Walt W. Rostow, assistant secretary of State, and Paul Nitze, secretary of the Navy (Posvar 1964:48). At the time of the crisis Paul Nitze was assistant secretary of Defense for international security affairs and a member of Kennedy's ad hoc crisis committee.

Political gaming as a special subfunction of military policy is a procedure that the RAND Corporation began developing in 1954 for the study of foreign affairs. A RAND report, referring to DOS' interest in gaming, noted: "Even before the first four games had been completed RAND began to receive requests for information about its political gaming procedures, and staff members have by now taken part in a substantial number of discussions about it" (Speier and Goldhammer 1959:80). As witness to this interest, "three senior Foreign Service officers from the Department of State participated in the fourth political game, along with specialists from RAND's Social Science, Economics and Physics Divisions" (Speier and Goldhammer 1959:74).

There is scant doubt that gaming and simulation were widely used by the president's executive committee. Nearly all higher-echelon figures knew immediately what games were referred to. Although DOS officers such as George W. Ball may have doubted that political games were of greater value than a similar amount of involvement in ordinary reading and study, many senior officers even of the "traditional" State Department, no less than the "modern" Defense Department, participated in the fourth round. Although only a minority of Kennedy's war council came from the departments of State and Defense, the rest were seemingly also familiar with strategy analysis.

The chilling degree to which a game of showdown proportions had been created around the Cuban missile crisis is reported by Schlesinger (1965:830): "Saturday night was almost the blackest of all. Unless Khrushchev came through in a few hours the meeting of the Executive Committee on Sunday night might well face the most terrible decisions." In a revealing metaphor Schlesinger then notes: "At nine in the morning Khrushchev's answer began to come in. By the fifth sentence it was clear that he had thrown in the hand." And it became finally clear that this unwillingness to risk all-out war on the Soviet Union's part came "barely in time." Schlesinger concludes by drawing out the option: "If word had not come that Sunday, if work had continued on the bases, the United States would have had no real choice but to take action against Cuba the next week. No one could discern what lay darkly beyond an air strike or invasion, what measures and countermeasures, actions and reactions might have driven the hapless world to the ghastly consummation." It should be noted that this account comes not simply from a writer but from a member of the president's inner group of advisors, and that the differences between hard-liners and soft-liners over the missile crisis concerned the character of the response, not the necessity for playing the game of showdown poker. Thus, at a critical point in U.S. foreign policy traditional methods of accommodations were abandoned in favor of a military definition of the situation—a definition made intellectually palatable by the "science" of game theory.

Game-strategy analysis also played an influential role through the Joint Chiefs of Staff. Although Senator John Sparkman (1962:75) of Alabama remembered in the September hearings "General LeMay, Chief of Staff of the Air Force, stating that there would be no difficulty in knocking out those missile sites," among the military leaders, only the chairman of the Joint Chiefs, Maxwell Taylor, actually sat in on the executive committee. When Kennedy met separately with the Joint Chiefs they would not guarantee that a so-called "surgical strike"—one that would destroy all the missiles and bombers yet inflict few casualties on the general population—was feasible (cf. Sorenson 1965). In any case, such feasibility studies are the proper responsibility of the military profession and are not farmed out to research corporations. Under the circumstances, the war game posture about the dominant influence of strategy analysis had little empirical validation value. The final executive-committee recommendations actually emerged from a political bargaining process that involved not only the military factors and strategic analysis but also considerations of morality (for example, Robert F. Kennedy argued against the air-strike position, saying it would be another Pearl Harbor) and international political consequences.

Many questions arose to make even the hardiest political man uneasy over this concept of "surgical strike." For people like Wohlstetter and Kahn, the problem of defense begins with the military issues surrounding a first-strike strategy and proceeds to conditions for a second strike situation. The uses of war-game theory thus serve to limit options and to deepen ambiguity in the military situation as well. Under such circumstances it is small wonder that even those who in the past were close to the systems design would raise serious questions as to the efficacy of war gaming.

Given the general context of the political situation of the defense establishment, it is time to examine the Cuban missile crisis in its specifics. The services and DOD expressed different strategic interpretations of the Cuban crisis in the congressional appropriations hearings in 1965. Curtis LeMay (Senate Armed Services Committee 1963:888-96), air force chief of staff, expressed the air force position:

> We must maintain a credible general war force so that lesser options may be exercised under the protection of this general war deterrent. It is the general war strength of aircraft and missile forces which place an upper limit on the risks an aggressor is willing to take and which deter escalation into an all-out conflict. In the Cuban crisis this limit was tested. . . . I am convinced that superior U.S. strategic power, coupled with obvious will and ability to apply this power, was the major factor that forced the Soviets to back down. Under the shelter of strategic power, which the Soviets did not dare challenge, the other elements of military power were free to exercise their full potential.

This version of strategic theory is clearly beneficial to the long-run interests of the air force. The air force answer to the problem of deterring minor "aggression" is to play "chicken" with the air-force-delivered general war force. Posvar's comments on the Cuban crisis, given above, though brief, seem quite consonant with their force position. Earle Wheeler (Senate Armed Services Committee 1963:507), army chief of staff, expressed the army position in his statement:

> In my opinion, the major lesson for the Army in the Cuban situation lies in the demonstrated value of maintaining ready Army forces at a high state of alert in order to equip national security policy with the military power to permit a direct confrontation of Soviet power. As Secretary McNamara pointed out to the NATO ministers recently, ". . . the forces that were the cutting edge of the action were the non-nuclear ones. Nuclear force was not irrelevant but it was in the background. Non-nuclear forces were our sword, our nuclear forces were our shield." I wholeheartedly agree with this statement. In the Cuban situation, the Army forces were alerted, brought up to strength in personnel and equipment, moved and made ready for the operations as part of the largest U.S. invasion force prepared since World War II.

The air force interpreted limited war and limited "aggression" as capable of being deterred by strategic nuclear forces and the credibility of its threatened use, while the army viewed strategic nuclear forces alone as insufficient.

A circumstantial argument for the influence of strategy expertise could be made, if the position of the RAND Corporation coincided with the strategic interpretation of the air force, its sponsor. However, as early as 1957 a staff-initiated RAND study noted that "in the case of a sharply limited war in Europe, tactical forces have renewed utility, with strategic air forces complementing tactical forces as the necessary enforcers of weapons limitations" (Hoag 1957:13; also see 1961:26). In at least a dozen other studies of limited war before the crisis the RAND Corporation developed the same theme: because of the strategic balance of power, "neither side could expect to use its strategic capabilities to enforce a level of violence in the local area favorable to itself"; a limited war capability was needed because "we shall not be able to rely on our strategic forces to deal with limited aggressions" (DeWeerd 1961:17). These studies clearly supported the army doctrine on limited warfare and contributed to the above-mentioned estrangement of RAND and the air force. DOD, however, became quite interested. In early 1962 a large contract was consummated between the RAND Corporation and the office of the assistant secretary of Defense for International Security Affairs. This particular contract involved analytic studies of a variety of defense problems, including counterinsurgency and limited-war questions, and the annual funding under the ISA contract for a two-year period amounted to over $1 million. The ISA contract frightened the air force, because many air force officers felt that some of the civilians in the ISA were contemptuous of military professionalism (Smith 1966:127).

The standard interpretation of this complaint by the new civilian militarists (NCMs) is the masking of a lack of understanding and competence in strategic theory. However, the air force officers correctly perceived a threat to their position in the defense establishment—a more plausible explanation. The NCM theory would similarly attribute the air force's failure to implement the RAND-generated expertise on limited war to a lack of understanding. This theory would not explain why bureaucratic incompetence was limited to the air force and was not also a fault of the army or DOD. The NCM theory of expertise equates lack of enthusiasm with ignorance and incompetence. One might argue that the air force neglected RAND's contribution out of ignorance; Smith's account of the implementation of the strategic-bases study shows that the communication of research findings is a long and complicated process. Furthermore, the NCM objection does not explain how the army's and DOD's positions coincided with RAND's, since both knew about RAND's work. The air force refused to understand because RAND's expert judgment benefited the army to the detriment of the air force.

Implementation of policy depends not only on the validity of game theory but also on the party that benefits. The above discussion emphasizing conflicts within the defense establishment neglects the consensus on two articles of faith: ideological anticommunism, which divides the world into Communists and anti-Communists, and coercion as the only mode of intercourse between the two antagonists.

The careful perusal of the military definition of game theory reveals that gaming strategy is the "science" of coercion. Anything that is not coercive is irrational from a strategic frame of reference. Anticommunism, too, is deeply rooted in strategic analysis. A RAND study notes that if limited wars occur, "they should be looked at as a local and limited manifestation of the global struggle between Communism and the Non-Communist World" (De Weerd 1961:17). These two articles of faith pervade not only the strategy community and the defense establishment but also the rest of the government involved in the crisis, so that even if the strategy community had no influence over anyone else, it is questionable whether there would be any substantial difference in policy (cf. Commager 1968:15-18).

While this analysis has emphasized the political and sociological aspects of gaming analogies, experts themselves often emphasize the truth and rationality of war games. As Ithiel de Sola Pool (1967:268) puts matters: "That is essentially policy based on social science. Traditional political concerns vanish in this hygienic version of social science." The claim of truth is a powerful way to legitimize authority, but it is also an exclusive way. The claim to social science expertise illegitimizes other decision criteria. The illegitimization inherent in the recommendations is a function of ignorance and bureaucratic incompetence. Further, it is claimed that the failure to perceive the role of expertise as a weapon in the political conflict within the defense establishment and between the defense establishment and civilian groups against militarism weakens the U.S. military "posture" abroad. Thus, game theory serves as an organizational weapon of overseas military activities, even when its strategies may go awry, as in the Cuban missile crisis.

One might conclude by noting that the United States used war-game strategies while the Soviet Union used conventional rhetoric of Marxism, and yet the Soviets managed to walk away with a stalemate at the very least—and in some interpretations with a full victory. In exchange for the withdrawal of long-range missiles, the Soviet Union guaranteed the long-range survival of Cuba's socialist regime and, no less, a long-term Soviet presence in the Western Hemisphere. It might be argued that conventional diplomacy might have netted the United States far greater results: the maintenance of diplomatic ties between Cuba and the United States. Direct negotiations with Castro rather than negotiations with the Soviets *about* Castro would have prevented the Soviets from maintaining a long-range presence and would not have strengthened Cuba's sense of sovereignty any more than it already was. But, of course, this would make the military subject to pressures of a historical, geographic, and cultural variety that they reject almost instinctively. War-game theory is a model of simplicity. It supplies a two-person situation, even if it does sometimes select the wrong players. It structures outcomes, even if it does leave out the reckoning of the optimal sort of outcome. It resolves problems, even if it does so by raising the ante of the problem beyond its initial worth.

The sociological explanation of the functional role of war-game theory for the military is still in its infancy (cf. Green 1966; Horowitz 1967: 339-76). Only a final word needs to be said about the symbol role of war game theory; namely, the comfort it provides is that of a world of psychological neatness, a world in which the behavior of large-scale nations is reducible to the decisions of a single man or small group of men. In this sense, war-game theory is the ultimate expression not only of the military ethic but also of the elitist and statist mentality. But it remains the case that the management of political crisis is made more complex, not more simple, by the new military technology. The danger is that military leaders have chosen to ignore this development and respond simplistically, precisely as the world of politics and ideology grows more problematic and complicated.

It is important to appreciate the fact that we have been describing a conventional war game built on coercion and threat and not a model of a game premised on a mechanism of positivist reinforcement built on consensus and compromise. Nor are we prepared to argue the merits of the claim that ultimately-consensual game models reduce to conflictual models anyhow, thus eliminating the need to study "milder" forms of game theory. Indeed, one might point out that the consensual models only seem to have penetrated the literature when some sort of equilibrium was, in fact, reached between the Soviet Union and the United States in the post-missile-crisis period. Hence, war-game theory is not so much an independent input in decision making as it is a sophisticated rationalization of decisions already taken.

Beyond the clear sets of objections that analysts of war game theory have pointed out over the years, there is one that has seemingly escaped everyone's attention in the past: namely, the role of war-game theory as a legitimization device for whatever crude military strategy has been decided upon. A tautological aspect thus emerges: if the decision to blockade Cuba is taken, war game theory is appealed to as ultimate arbiter; if the decision to lift the blockade is taken, the same appeal to war gaming is made. Since any complete holocaust would "terminate the game" and "eliminate the players," there is no real possibility of disconfirming the "theory on which the decision is ostensibly reached."

Under such a wonderful protective covering of post hoc legitimization, and with every strategic decision confirming anew the worth of war-game theory, it is extremely difficult to reach any final estimate of the theory as such. For this reason, the examination of real events—particularly of military retaliations—may be the clearest way open to analysts for evaluating the potency, or as is more usually the case, the paucity of war-game strategies. When a particular strategy becomes elevated to the level of military theology, the clear and present danger to human survival soon becomes apparent. And in the shock surrounding the Cuban missile crisis—the delayed awareness that the world stood still for a week while games of strategy were permitted to run their course—war-game theory had its proudest and yet its last moment.

It was not long after the missile crisis that the "game of chicken" was abandoned in favor of conventional forms of political accommodation. This came about through the mutual realization of the Soviet Union and the United States (and especially the latter) that Cuba was not a pawn or an ace in the hole but a sovereign power in its own right. The Castro revolution was both national and hemispheric; it evolved its own brand of socialism to meet the challenges of a single-crop island economy. Thus, the Cuban regime was a system that had to be dealt with in the traditional political terms by which sovereign states with differing social structures relate to each other. When this dawning took place, the

Cuban "crisis" was really solved, precisely by surrendering the notion that the situation was a behavioral one, reducible to the moves and countermoves of the world's two big military powers. Yet, as long as such repudiation of strategic thinking remains informal and unthinking, the dangers in a repetition of such forms of crisis management through games of chance remain ever present. What first appeared as tragedy may return not so much as comedy but as absurdity—in this instance the absurdity of total mutual annihilation.

PROJECT CAMELOT

Project Camelot was a project for measuring and forecasting the causes of revolutions and insurgency in underdeveloped areas of the world. It also aimed to find ways of eliminating the causes, or coping with the revolutions and insurgencies. Camelot was sponsored by the United States Army on a $4- to 6-million contract, spaced out over three to four years, with the Special Operations Research Organization (SORO). That agency is nominally under the aegis of American University in Washington, D.C., and does a variety of research for the army. Projects include making analytical surveys of foreign areas; keeping up-to-date information on the military, political, and social complexes of those areas; and maintaining a "rapid response" file for getting immediate information, upon army request, on any situation deemed militarily important.

Latin America was the first area chosen for concentrated study, but countries on Camelot's four-year list included some in Asia, Africa, and Europe. In a working paper issued on December 5, 1964, at the request of the office of the chief of research and development, Department of the Army, it was recommended that "comparative historical studies" be made in these countries: Argentina, Bolivia, Brazil, Colombia, Cuba, Dominican Republic, El Salvador, Guatemala, Mexico, Paraguay, Peru, and Venezuela (Latin America); Egypt, Iran, and Turkey (Middle East); Korea, Indonesia, Malaysia, and Thailand (Far East); and France, Greece, and Nigeria. "Survey research and other field studies" were recommended for Bolivia, Colombia, Ecuador, Paraguay, Peru, Venezuela, Iran, and Thailand. Preliminary consideration was also being given to a study of the separatist movement in French Canada (it, too, had a code name: Project Revolt).

In a recruiting letter sent to selected scholars all over the world at the end of 1964 Project Camelot's aims were defined as a study to "make it possible to predict and influence politically significant aspects of social change in the developing nations of the world." This would include devising procedures for "assessing the potential for internal war within national societies" and "identifying with increased degrees of confidence, those actions which a government might take to relieve conditions which are assessed as giving rise to a potential for internal war." The letter further states that the United States Army has an important mission in the positive and constructive aspects of nation building in less-developed countries, as well as a responsibility to assist friendly governments in dealing with active insurgency problems. Such activities by the army were described as "insurgency prophylaxis"—preferable to the "sometimes misleading label of counter-insurgency."

Project Camelot was conceived in late 1963 by a group of high-ranking army officers connected with the Army Research Office of the Department of Defense. They were concerned about new types of warfare springing up around the world. Revolutions in Cuba and Yemen and insurgency movements in Vietnam and the Congo were a far cry from the battles of World War II and also different from the envisioned—and planned for—apocalypse of nuclear war. For the first time in modern warfare, military establishments were not in a position to use the immense arsenals at their disposal but were, instead, compelled by force of a geopolitical statemate to engage increasingly in primitive forms of armed combat. The questions of moment for the army were: *Why can't the "hardware" be used? What alternatives can social science "software" provide?*

A well-known Latin American area specialist, Rex Hopper, was chosen as director of Project Camelot. Hopper was a professor of sociology and chairman of the department at Brooklyn College and had been to Latin America many times over a 30-year span on research projects and lecture tours, including some under government sponsorship. He was highly recommended for the position by his professional associates in the Capitol and elsewhere. Hopper had a long-standing interest in problems of revolution and saw in this multimillion dollar contract the possible realization of a lifelong scientific ambition.

Were the Camelot participants critical of any aspects of the project? Some had doubts from the outset about the character of the work they would be doing and about the conditions under which it would be done. It was pointed out, for example, that the U.S. Army tends to exercise a far more stringent intellectual control of research findings than does the United States Air Force. As evidence for this, it was stated that SORO generally had fewer "free-wheeling" aspects to its research designs than did RAND (the air-force-supported research organization). One critic inside SORO went so far as to say that he knew of no SORO research that had a "playful" or unregimented quality, such as one finds at RAND (where, for example, computers are used to plan invasions but also to play chess). One staff member said that "the self-conscious seriousness gets to you after a while." "It was all grim stuff," said another.

Another line of criticism was that pressures on the "reformers" (as the participants engaged in Camelot research spoke of themselves) to come up with ideas were much stronger than the pressures on the military to actually bring off any policy changes recommended. The social scientists were expected to be social reformers, while the military adjutants were expected to be conservative. It was further felt that the relationship between sponsors and researchers was not one of equals but rather one of superordinate military needs and subordinate academic roles. On the other hand, some officials were impressed by the disinterestedness of the military and thought that, far from exercising undue influence, the army personnel were loath to offer opinions.

Another objection was that if one had to work on policy matters (if research is to have international ramifications), it might better be conducted under conventional DOS sponsorship. "After all," one man said, "they are at least nominally committed to civilian political norms." In other words, there was a considerable reluctance to believe that DOD, despite its superior organization, greater financial affluence, and executive influence would actually improve upon DOS styles of work or accept recommendations at variance with Pentagon policies.

There seemed to be few, if any, expressions of disrespect for the intrinsic merit of the work contemplated by Camelot, or of disdain for policy-oriented work in general. The scholars engaged in the Camelot effort used two distinct vocabularies. The various Camelot documents reveal a military vocabulary provided with an array of military justifications, often followed (within the same document) by a social science vocabulary offering social science justifications and rationalizations. The dilemma in the Camelot literature from the preliminary report issued in August 1964 until the more advanced document issued in April 1965 remains the same: an incomplete amalgamation of the military and sociological vocabularies. (At an early date the project had the code name SPEARPOINT.)

The directors of SORO were concerned that the cancellation of Camelot might mean the end of SORO as well as a wholesale slash of research funds. For while more than $1 million was allotted to Camelot each year, the annual budget of SORO, its parent organization, was a good deal less. Although no such action has taken place, SORO's future is being examined. For example, the Senate and House Appropriations Committee blocked a move by the army to transfer unused Camelot funds to SORO.

However, the end of Project Camelot does not necessarily imply the end of SORO, nor does it imply an end to research designs that are similar in character to Project Camelot. In fact, the termination of the contract does not even imply an intellectual change of heart on the part of the originating sponsors or key figures of the project.

One of the characteristics of Project Camelot was the number of antagonistic forces it set in motion on grounds of strategy and timing rather than from what may be called consideration of scientific principles. DOS grounded its opposition to Camelot on the basis of the ultimate authority it has in the area of foreign affairs. There is no published report showing serious criticism of the projected research itself. Congressional opposition seemed to be generated by a concern not to rock any foreign alliances, especially in Latin America. Again, there was no statement about the project's scientific or intellectual grounds. A third ground of skeptics—academic social scientists—generally thought that Project Camelot and studies of the processes of revolution and war in general were better left in the control of major university centers and, in that way, kept free of direct military supervision. The army, creator of the project, did nothing to contradict McNamara's order cancelling Project Camelot. Army influentials not only felt that they had to execute DOD's orders, but they have been traditionally dubious of the value of "software" research to support "hardware" systems.

A number of issues did not so much hinge upon as swim about Project Camelot. In particular, the "jurisdictional" dispute between Defense and State loomed largest. In substance, the debate between the Defense and State Departments is not unlike that between electricians and bricklayers in the construction of a new apartment house. What "union" is responsible for which process? Less generously, the issue is over who controls what. At the policy level Camelot was a tool tossed about in a larger power struggle that has been going on in government circles since the end of World War II when DOD emerged as a competitor for honors as the most powerful bureau of the administrative branch of government.

The divisions between Defense and State are outcomes of the rise of ambiguous conflicts, such as Korea and Vietnam, in contrast to the more precise and diplomatically controlled "classical" world wars. What are the lines dividing political policy from military posture? Who is the most important representative of the United States abroad: the ambassador or the military attaché in charge of the military mission? When soldiers from foreign lands are sent to the United States for political orientation, should such orientation be within the province of DOS or DOD? When undercover activities are conducted, should the direction of such activities belong to military or political authorities? Each of these is a strategic question with little pragmatic or historic precedent. Each of these was entwined in the Project Camelot explosion.

It should be plain that DOS was not simply responding to the recommendations of Chilean left-wingers in urging the cancellation of Camelot. It merely employed the Chilean hostility to "interventionist" projects as an opportunity to redefine the balance of forces and power with DOD. This resistance to such projects is not so much a defense of the sovereignty of the nations where ambassadors are stationed as it is a contention that conventional political channels are sufficient to yield the information desired or deemed necessary.

In the main, congressional reaction seems to be that Project Camelot was bad because it rocked the diplomatic boat in a sensitive area. Underlying most congressional criticisms is the plain fact that most congressmen are more sympathetic to DOS control of foreign affairs than they are to DOD control. In other words, despite military-sponsored world junkets, National Guard and State Guard pressures from the home state, and military training in the backgrounds of many congressmen, the sentiment is greater for political rather than military control. In addition, there is a mounting suspicion in Congress of varying kinds of behavioral science research, stemming from hearings into such matters as wire tapping, uses of lie detectors, and truth in packaging.

One reason for the violent response to Project Camelot, especially among Latin American scholars, is its sponsorship by DOD. The fact is that Latin Americans have become quite accustomed to DOS involvements in the internal affairs of various nations. DOD is a newcomer, and a dangerous one, inside the Latin American orbit. The train of thought connected to its activities is in terms of international warfare, spying missions, military manipulations, and so on. DOS for its part is often a consultative party to shifts in government and has played an enormous part in either fending off or bringing about coups d'état. This State Department role has by now been accepted and even taken for granted—but not so the Defense Department's role. It is interesting to conjecture on how matter-of-factly Camelot might have been accepted if it had had DOS sponsorship.

Social scientists in the United States have, for the most part, been publicly silent on the matter of Camelot. The reasons for this are not hard to find. First, many "giants of the field" are involved in government contract work in one capacity or another, and few souls are in a position to tamper with the gods. Second, most information on Project Camelot has thus far been of a newspaper variety, and professional men are not in a habit of criticizing colleagues on the basis of such information. Third, there is no doubt that many social scientists see nothing wrong or immoral in the Project Camelot designs. They are therefore most likely to be either confused or angered at the Latin American response than at the directors of Project Camelot (at the time of the blowup Camelot poeple spoke about the "Chilean mess" rather than the "Camelot mess").

So that there would be no stigma of secrecy, the directors of Project Camelot did not "classify" research materials. They also tried to hire, and even did hire away from academic positions, people well known and respected for their independence of mind. The difficulty was that even though the stigma of secrecy was formally erased, it remained in the attitudes of many of the employees and would-be employees of Project Camelot. They unfortunately thought in terms of secrecy, clearance, missions, and the rest of the professional nonsense that so powerfully afflicts the Washington scientific as well as political ambience. Project Camelot had much greater difficulty hiring a full-time staff of high professional competence than in getting part-time, summertime, weekend, and sundry assistance. Few established figures in academic life were willing to surrender the advantages of their positions for the risks of the project.

One of the cloudiest aspects of Project Camelot is the role of American University. Its actual supervision of the contract appears to have begun and ended with the 25 percent overhead on those parts of the contract that a university receives on most federal grants. Thus, while there can be no question as to the "concern and disappointment" of President Hurst R. Anderson of the American University over the demise of Project Camelot, the reasons for this regret do not seem to extend beyond the formal and the financial. No official at American University appears to have been willing to make any statement of responsibility, support, chagrin, opposition, or anything else related to the project. The issues are indeed momentous and must be faced by all universities at which government-sponsored research is conducted: What amount of control should a university have over contract work? What is the role of university officials in the distribution of funds from grants? And what are the relationships that ought to be established once a grant is issued? There is also a major question concerning project directors: Are they members of the faculty, and, if so, do they have necessary teaching responsibilities and opportunities for tenure as do other faculty members?

The difficulty is that American University seems remarkably unlike other U.S. universities in its administrative permissiveness. SORO received neither guidance nor support from university officials. It seems that from the outset there was a "gentleman's agreement" not to inquire or interfere in Project Camelot but simply to serve as some sort of camouflage. If American University were genuinely autonomous it might have been able to lend highly supportive aid to Project Camelot during the crisis months. As it was, American University maintained an official silence that preserved it from more congressional or executive criticism. This situation points up some serious flaws in American University's administrative and financial policies.

The relationship of Camelot to SORO represented a similarly muddled organizational picture. The director of Project Camelot was nominally autonomous and in charge of an organization surpassing in size and importance the overall SORO operation. Yet at the critical point the organizational blueprint served to protect SORO, sacrificing what was nominally its limb. The fact that Camelot happened to be a vital organ may have hurt, especially when Congress blocked the transfer of unused Camelot funds to SORO.

Military reaction to the cancellation of Camelot varied. It should be borne in mind that expenditures on Camelot were minimal in the army's overall budget and that most military leaders are skeptical to begin with about the worth of social science research. So there was no open protest about the demise of the project. Those officers who have a positive attitude toward social science materials, or are themselves trained in the social sciences were dismayed. Some had hoped to find "software" alternatives to the "hardware" approach applied by the Secretary of Defense to every military-political contingency. These officers saw the attack on Camelot as a double attack: on their role as officers and on their professional standards. But the army was so clearly treading in new waters that it could scarcely jeopardize the entire structure of military research to preserve one project. This very inability or impotence to preserve Camelot—a situation threatening to other governmental contracts with social scientists—no doubt impressed many armed-forces officers.

The claim is made by the Camelot staff (and various military aides) that the critics of the project played into the hands of those sections of the military predisposed to veto any social science recommendations. To the question as to the military's motives in offering such huge support to a social science project to begin with, the response is that $6 million is actually a trifling sum for the army in an age of a multibillion-dollar military establishment; the amount is significantly more important for the social sciences where such contract awards remain relatively scarce. Thus, there were different perspectives of the importance of Camelot: an army view that considered the contract as one of several forms of "software" investment; a social science perception of Project Camelot as the equivalent of the Manhattan Project.

While most public opposition to Project Camelot focused on its strategy and timing, a considerable amount of private opposition centered on more basic, though theoretical, questions: Was Camelot scientifically feasible and ethically correct? No public document or statement contested the possibility that, given the successful completion of the data gathering, Camelot could have indeed established basic criteria for measuring the level and potential for internal war in a given nation. Thus, by never challenging the feasibility of the work, the political critics of Project Camelot were providing backhanded compliments to the efficacy of the project.

Some of the most critical problems presented by Project Camelot are scientific. Although for an extensive analysis of Camelot the reader would, in fairness, have to be familiar with all its documents, salient general criticisms can be made without a full reading. The research design of Camelot was, from the outset, plagued by ambiguities. It was never quite settled whether the purpose was to study counterinsurgency possibilities or the revolutionary process. Similarly, it was difficult to determine whether the project was to be a study of comparative social structures, a set of "in depth" case studies of single nations, or a study of social structure with particular emphasis on the military. In addition, there was a lack of treatment of the indicators that were to be used and of questioning whether a given social system in Nation A could be as stable in Nation B.

In one Camelot document there is a general critique of social science for failing to deal with social conflict and social control. While this attitude in itself is admirable, the tenor and context of Camelot's documents make it plain that a "stable society" is considered the norm no less than the desired outcome. The "breakdown of social order" is spoken of accusatively. Stabilizing agencies in developing areas are presumed to be absent. There is no critique of U.S. Army policy in developing areas, because the army is presumed to be a stabilizing agency. The research formulations always assume the legitimacy of army tasks: ". . . if the U.S. Army is to perform effectively its parts in the U.S. mission of counterinsurgency it must recognize that insurgency represents a breakdown of social order. . . ." (SORO 1964:53-54). But such a proposition has never been doubted—neither by Army officials nor by anyone else. The issue is whether such breakdowns are in the nature of the existing system or a product of conspiratorial movements.

The use of "hygienic" language disguises the antirevolutionary assumptions under a cloud of aesopian declarations. For example, studies of Paraguay are recommended "because trends in this situation [the Stroessner regime] may also render it 'unique' when analyzed in terms of the transition from 'dictatorship' to political stability" (SORO 1964:31-32). In this case it is a tactic to disguise the fact that Paraguay is one of the most vicious and undemocratic (and, like most dictatorships, stable) societies in the Western Hemisphere. These typify the sort of sterile premises that do not have scientific purposes. They illustrate the confusion of commitments within Project Camelot. Indeed, the very absence of emotive words such as "revolutionary masses," "communism," "socialism," and "capitalism" only serves to intensify the discomfort one must feel on examination of the documents, since the abstract vocabulary disguises rather than resolves the problems of international revolution. The use of clearly political rather than military language would not have "justified" governmental support. Furthermore, shabby assumptions of academic conventionalism replaced innovative orientations. By adopting a systems approach, the problematic, open-ended aspects of the study of revolutions were largely omitted, and the design of the study became an oppressive curb on the study of the problems inspected.

This points up a critical implication for Camelot (as well as other projects). The importance of the subject being researched does not per se determine the importance of the project. A sociology of large-scale relevance and reference is all to the good. It is important that scholars be willing to risk something of their shaky reputations in helping to resolve major world social problems. But it is no less urgent that in the process of addressing major problems the autonomous character of the social science disciplines—their own criteria of worthwhile scholarship—should not be abandoned. Project Camelot lost sight of the "autonomous" social science character.

It never seemed to occur to its personnel to inquire into the desirability for successful revolution. This is just as solid a line of inquiry as the one stressed, concerning the conditions under which revolutionary movements will be able to overthrow a government. Furthermore, the researchers seem not to have thought about inquiring into the role of the United States in these countries. This points up the lack of symmetry: the problem should have been phrased to include the study of "us" as well as "them." It is not possible to make a decent analysis of a situation unless one takes into account the role of all the different people and groups involved in it; and there was no room in the design for such contingency analysis.

In discussing the policy impact on a social science research project we should not overlook the difference between "contract" work and "grants." Project Camelot commenced with the U.S. army; that is, it was initiated for a practical purpose determined by the client. This differs markedly from the typical academic grant in that its sponsorship had "built-in" ends. The scholar usually seeks a grant; in this case the donor, the army, promoted its own aims. In some measure the hostility for Project Camelot may be an unconscious reflection of this distinction—a dim feeling that there was something "nonacademic" and certainly not disinterested about Project Camelot, irrespective of the quality of the scholars associated with it.

The issue of "scientific rights" versus "social myths" is perennial. Some maintain that the scientist ought not penetrate beyond legally or morally sanctioned limits, and others argue that such limits cannot exist for science. In treading on the sensitive issue of national sovereignty, Project Camelot reflects the generalized dilemma. In deference to intelligent researchers, in recognition of them as scholars, they should have been invited by Camelot to air their misgivings and qualms about government (and especially army-sponsored) research, to declare their moral conscience. Instead, they were mistakenly approached as skillful, useful, potential employees of a higher body, subject to an authority higher than their scientific calling.

What is central is not the political motives of the sponsor, for social scientists were not being enlisted in an intelligence system for "spying" purposes. But given their professional standing, their great sense of intellectual honor and pride, they could not be "employed" without proper deference for their stature. Professional authority should have prevailed from beginning to end with complete command of the right to thrash out the moral and political dilemmas as researchers saw them. The army, however respectful and protective of free expression, was "hiring help" and not openly and honestly submitting a problem to the higher professional and scientific authority of social science.

The propriety of the army to define and delimit all questions that Camelot should have had a right to examine was never placed in doubt. This is a tragic precedent; it reflects the arrogance of a consumer of intellectual merchandise. And this relationship of inequality corrupted the lines of authority and profoundly limited the autonomy of the social scientists involved. It became clear that the social scientist savant was not so much functioning as an applied social scientist as he was supplying information to a powerful client.

The question concerning the proper sponsors of research is not nearly so decisive as the question regarding the correct ultimate use of such information.

The sponsorship of a project, whether by the United States Army or the Boy Scouts of America, is by itself neither good nor bad. Sponsorship is good or bad only insofar as the intended outcomes can be predetermined and the parameters of those intended outcomes tailored to the sponsor's expectations. Those social scientists critical of the project never really denied its freedom and independence but questioned instead the purpose and character of its intended results.

It would be a gross oversimplification, if not an outright error, to assume that the theoretical problems of Project Camelot derive from any reactionary character of the project designers. The director went far and wide to select a group of men for the advisory board, the core planning group, the summer study group, and the various conference groupings who, in fact, were more liberal in their orientation than any random sampling of the sociological profession would be likely to turn up.

In nearly every page of the various working papers there are assertions that clearly derive from U.S. military policy objectives rather than from scientific method. The steady assumption that internal warfare is damaging disregards the possibility that a government may not be in a position to take actions either to relieve or to improve mass conditions, or that such actions as are contemplated may be more concerned with reducing conflict than with improving conditions. The added statements about the United States Army and its "important mission in the positive and constructive aspects of nation building" assume the reality of such a function in an utterly unquestioning and unconvincing form. The first rule of the scientific game is not to make assumptions about friends and enemies in such a way as to promote the use of different criteria for the former and the latter.

THE PENTAGON PAPERS

The publication of the Pentagon Papers is of central importance to the social science community in at least two respects: social scientists participated in the development of a posture and position toward the Vietnam involvement; and, at a more abstract level, the publication of these papers provides lessons about political participation and policy making for the social sciences.

We live in an age in which the social sciences perform a special and unique role in the lives of men and in the fates of government, whatever the status of social science theory. And because the questions of laymen are no longer concerned with whether social science is scientific but with the kinds of recommendations that are offered in the name of social science, it is important that social scientists inquire as to any special meaning of the Pentagon Papers and documents, over and above the general and broad-ranging discussions that take place in the mass media. Thus, what follows is not to be construed as a general discussion of issues but rather a specific discussion of results.

The Pentagon's project director for a *History of United States Decision-Making Process on Vietnam Policy* (now known as "The Pentagon Papers"), political scientist Leslie H. Gelb, now of Brookings, remarked: "Writing history, especially where it blends into current events, especially where the current event is

Vietnam, is a treacherous exercise" (Gelb 1971). Former Secretary of Defense Robert S. McNamara authorized this historical and social survey of this Vietnam conflict in 1967. In initiation and execution this was to be "encyclopedic and objective." The actual compilation runs to 2.5 million words and 47 volumes of narrative and documents. And from what has thus far been made public, it is evident that this project was prepared with the same bloodless, bureaucratic approach that characterizes so much federally-inspired social science and history. The Pentagon Papers attempt no original hypothesis, provide no insights into the behavior of the "other side," make scant effort to select important from trivial factors in the escalation process; they present no real continuity with past U.S. foreign policy and in general eschew any sort of systematic survey research or interview of the participants and proponents. Yet, with all these shortcomings, these materials offer a fascinating and unique account of how peace-keeping agencies can be transformed into policy-making agencies. That this record was prepared by 36 political scientists, economists, systems analysts, inside dopesters, and outside social science research agencies provides an additional fascination: the government has learned very well to entrust its official records to mandarin types who in exchange for the cloak of anonymity are willing to prepare an official record of events. An alarming oddity is that, in part at least, the chronicle was prepared by analysts who were formerly participants.

For those who have neither the time nor the patience to examine every document thus far released it might be worthwhile simply to summarize what the documents contain. Through a review of the papers it becomes clear that the Vietnam War was neither the Democrats' nor the Republicans' war but one conducted by the political elite, often without regard to basic technical advice and considerations, and for reasons that had far less to do with curbing communism than with the failure of the other arms of government in their responsibility to curb executive egotism. The publication of these papers has chronicled this country's overseas involvement with a precision never before available to the American public. Indeed, we now know more about decision making in Vietnam than about the processes by which we became involved in the Korean War. For instance, we have learned that:

1. The United States ignored eight direct appeals for aid from Ho Chi Minh in the first half-year following World War II. Underlying the U.S. refusal to deal with the Vietnamese leader was the growth of the cold war and the opposition to assisting a Communist leadership.

2. By 1949 the Truman administration had already accepted the "domino principle," before the National Security Council was told, early in 1950, that the neighboring countries of Thailand and Burma could be expected to fall under commuist control if Vietnam were controlled by a communist-dominated regime.

3. The Eisenhower administration, particularly under the leadership of Secretary of State John Foster Dulles, refused to accept the Geneva accords ending the French-Indochina war on the grounds that if permitted the United States "only a limited influence" in the affairs of the fledgling South Vietnam. Indeed, the Joint Chiefs of Staff opted in favor of displacing France as the key influence, rather than assisting the termination of hostilities.

4. The final years of the Eisenhower administration were characterized by a decision to commit a relatively small number of U.S. military personnel to maintain the Diem regime in Saigon and to prevent a détente between Hanoi and Saigon.

5. The Kennedy administration transformed the limited-risk gamble into an unlimited commitment. Although the troop levels were indeed still quite limited, the Kennedy administration moved special-forces units into Vietnam, Laos, and Cambodia, thus broadening the conflict to the area as a whole.

6. The Kennedy administration knew about and approved of plans for the military coup d'état that overthrew President Diem. The United States gave its support to an army group committed to military dictatorship and no compromise with the Hanoi regime.

7. The Johnson administration extended the unlimited commitment to the military regime of Saigon. Under this administration, between 1965 and 1968, troop levels surpassed 500,000 and U.S. participation was to include the management of the conflict and the training of the ARVN.

8. After the Tet offensive began in January 1968, Johnson, under strong prodding from the military chiefs of staff and from his field commanders, moved toward full-scale mobilization, including the calling up of reserves. By the termination of the Johnson administration the United States had been placed on a full-scale war footing.

Among the most important facts revealed by the papers is that the United States first opposed a settlement based on the Geneva accords, signed by all belligerents; that the United States had escalated the conflict far in advance of the Gulf of Tonkin incident and had used congressional approval for legitimating commitments already undertaken, rather than as a response to new communist provocations; and, finally, that, in the face of internal opposition from the same Department of Defense that had at first sanctioned the war, the executive decided to disregard its own policy advisors and plunge ahead in a war already lost.

Impressive in the enumeration of policy decisions is the clinical way decisions were made. The substitution of war-game thinking for any real political thinking; the total submission of DOS to DOD in the making of foreign policy; the utter collapse of any faith in compromise, consensus, or cooperation between nations; and the ludicrous pursuit of victory (or at least nondefeat) in Vietnam— all are so forcefully illustrated in these Pentagon Papers, that the vigor with which their release was opposed by the attorney general's office and the executive branch of government generally can well be appreciated.

A major difficulty with the thinking of the new civilian militarists is that they study war while ignoring politics (Horowitz 1963). The recent disclosure of the Pentagon Papers bears out this contention with a vengeance: a kind of hot-house scientology emerges in which the ends of foreign policy are neatly separated from the instruments of immediate destruction. That a certain shock and cynicism have emerged as a result of the revelations in these papers is more attributable to the loss of a war than to the novelty of the revelations. The cast of characters who dragged the United States through the mire of a bloody conflict in Southeast Asia—from Rostow to Kissinger—remains to haunt and taunt us. They move in and out of administrations with an ease that belies political party differences and underscores the existence of more than a set of "experts"; rather, there is a well-defined ruling class dedicated to manufacturing and manipulating political formulas.

The great volume of materials thus far revealed is characterized by few obvious themes, but one of the more evident is the utter separation of the purposes of devastation from comprehension of the effects of such devastation. A kind of Howard Johnson's, sanitized vision of conflict emerges that reveals a gulf between the policy makers and battlefield soldiers that is even wider and longer than the distance between Saigon and Washington. If the concept of war gaming is shocking in retrospect, this is probably due more to its utter and contemptible failure to provide battlefield victories than to any real development in social and behavioral science beyond the shibboleths of decision theory and game theory.

A number of researchers as well as analysts of the Pentagon Papers were themselves social scientists. There were political scientists of considerable distinction, such as Morton Halperin and Melvin Gurtov; economists of great renown, such as Walt W. Rostow and Daniel Ellsberg; and systems analysts, such as Alain C. Enthoven. And then there was an assorted group of people, often trained in law, such as Roger Fisher and Carl Kaysen, weaving in and out of the papers, providing both point and counterpoint. There are the thoroughly hawkish views of Rostow, the cautionary perspective of Enthoven, and the more liberal recommendations of people like Fisher. But it is clear that social scientists descend in importance as they move from hawk to dove. Rostow is a central figure; people like Kaysen and Fisher are at most peripheral consultants (and they, in fact, seem to have been more often conservatized and impressed by the pressurized Washington atmosphere than to have had an impact on the liberalization or softening of the Vietnam posture).

Those of the social science contingency in the Pentagon were by no means uniform in their reactions to the quagmire that Vietnam had become. Political scientists such as Halperin and economists such as Enthoven did provide cautionary responses, if not outright criticisms of the repeated and incessant requests for troop buildups. The Tet offensive, which made incontrovertible the vulnerability of the U.S. posture, called forth demands from General William C. Westmoreland and Maxwell Taylor for higher troop levels. Enthoven, in particular, opposed this emphatically and courageously:

> Our strategy of attrition has not worked. Adding 206,000 more U.S. men to a force of 525,000, gaining only 27 additional maneuver battalions and 270 tactical fighters at an added cost to the U.S. of $10 billion per year, raises the question of who is making it costly for whom. . . . We know that despite a massive influx of 500,000 U.S. troops, 1.2 million tons of bombs a year, 200,000 enemy killed in action in three years, 200,000 U.S. wounded in action, etc., out control of the countryside and the defense of the urban areas is now essentially at pre-August 1965 levels. We have achieved stalemate at a high commitment. A new strategy must be sought. [cf. Gelb 1971:542-49).]

In the same month, March of 1968, that Enthoven prepared this critical and balanced report he wrote a curious paper on "Thomism and the Concept of Just and Unjust Warfare," which, in retrospect, seemed to be his way of letting people know that he was a dissenting voice despite his earlier commitment to war-game ideology and whiz-kid strategy.

As a result of these memoranda, Assistant Defense Secretary Paul Warnke argued against increased bombing and for a bombing pause. He and Assistant Secretary of Defense for Public Affairs Phil G. Goulding were then simply directed to write a draft that "would deal only with the troop issue," hence forcing them to abandon the internal fight against an "expansion of the air war." And as it finally went to the White House, the report was bleached of any criticism. The mandarin role of the social scientists was reaffirmed. President Johnson's commitments went unchallenged. The final memo advocated deployment of 22,000 more troops, reserved judgment on the deployments of the remaining 185,000 troops, and approved a 262,000 troop reserve buildup; it urged no new peace initiatives and simply declared that a division of opinion existed on the bombing policy, making it appear that the division in opinion was only tactical in nature. As the Pentagon Papers declared:

> Faced with a fork in the road of our Vietnam policy, the working group failed to seize the opportunity to change directions. Indeed, they seemed to recommend that we continue, rather haltingly down the same road, meanwhile, consulting the map more frequently and in greater detail to insure that we were still on the right road.

One strange aspect of this war game-strategy is how little the moves and motives of the so-called "other side" were taken into account. There was no real appreciation of the distinction between North Vietnam and the National Liberation Front (NLF) of South Vietnam. There is not the slightest account taken of the actual decisions made by General Giap or Chairman Ho. The Tet offensive seems to have taken our grand strategists as much by surprise as it did the political elites for whom they were planning (cf. Gelb 1971:589-623). While they were beginning to recognize the actual balance of military forces, Wilfred Burchett had already declared (in 1967 to be exact) that the consequences of the war were no longer in doubt: U.S. involvement could not forestall a victory of the Communist factions North and South. Thus, the Pentagon Papers reveal not only the usual ignorance of the customs, languages, and habits of the people being so brutally treated but also the unanticipatory arrogance of assuming throughout that logistics would conquer all. Even the doves such as George W. Ball never doubted that an influx of a certain number of U.S. troops would in fact swing the tide of battle the way that General Westmoreland said it would. The argument was rather over tactics: whether such a heavy investment was worth the end-results. In fact, not one inner circle "wise man" raised the issue that the size of the troop commitment might be basically irrelevant to the negative (from a U.S.-policy viewpoint) outcome of the Southeast Asian operations. One no longer expects good history or decent ethnography from those who advise the rulers, but when poor understanding is compounded with a heavy dose of impoverished war gaming and strategic thinking in a vacuum, then the question of "science for whom" might well be converted into a question of "what science and by whom."

All of this points up a tragic flaw in policy making by social science experts. Their failure to generate or to reflect a larger constituency outside of themselves made them continually vulnerable to assaults from the military and from the more conservative sectors of the Pentagon. This vulnerability was so great that throughout the Pentagon Papers one senses that the hawk position is always and uniformly outspoken and direct while the dove position is merely an undercurrent of indirect sentiments. The basis of democratic politics has always been the mass participation of an informed electorate. Yet it was precisely this informed public, where a consensus against the war had been building, that was cut off from the policy planners and recommenders. Consequently, they were left in pristine isolation to pit their logic against the crackpot realism of their military adversaries within the decision-making units of government.

Certain serious problems arose precisely because of the secrecy tag. For example, former Vice-President Hubert Humphrey and Secretary of State Dean Rusk have both denied having any knowledge whatsoever of these papers. Rusk went so far as to say that the research methodology was handled poorly: "I'm rather curious about why the analysts who put this study together did not interview us, particularly when they were attributing attitudes and motives to us" (cf. Gelb 1971:648-49). Perhaps more telling is Rusk's suggestion that the Pentagon Papers have the characteristics of an anonymous letter. Along with Rusk, others also believe that the names of the roughly 40 scholars connected with the production of these papers should be published. To do otherwise would not only prevent the people involved from checking the veracity of the stories attributed to them but, more important, would keep the social science community from gaining a clearer insight into the multiple roles of scholars, researchers, professors, and government analysts and policy makers. The nature of science requires that the human authorities behind this multivolume work be identified, as in the precedent established by the identification of the authors of the various bombing surveys done after World War II and the Korean War.

One serendipitous consequence of the Pentagon Papers has been the more meaningful perspective provided toward the proposed code of ethics being advanced by so many social science professional associations. All of these codes deal with the sanctity of the "subject's rights." All sorts of words guarding privacy are used: "rights of privacy and dignity," "protection of subjects from personal harm," "preservation of confidentiality of research data." The American Sociological Association proposals for example, are typical:

> Confidential information provided by a research subject must be treated as such by the sociologist. Even though research information is not a privileged communication under the law, the sociologist must, as far as possible, protect subjects and informants. Any promises made to such persons must be honored. . . . If an informant or other subject should wish, however, he can formally release the promise of confidentiality.

While the purpose of this code of ethics is sincerely geared to the protection of individuals under study, if taken literally, a man like Daniel Ellsberg would be subject to penalty, if not outright expulsion, on the grounds that he was never allowed by the individuals concerned to make his information public. What so many professional societies forget is that the right to full disclosure is also a principle, just as significant as the right of the private subject to confidentiality and far more germane to the tasks of a social science learned society. The truly difficult ethical question comes not with the idea of maintaining confidentiality but with determining what would be confidential and when such confidentiality should be violated in terms of a higher principle. All social science codes of ethics presume an ethical standpoint that limits scientific endeavor, but when it is expedient to ignore or forget this ethical code, as in the case of the Pentagon Papers, the profession embarrassingly chooses to exhibit a memory lapse. The publication of the Pentagon Papers should once again point the way to the highest obligation of social science organizations: to the truth, plain and simple, rather than the preservation of confidentiality, high and mighty. And unless this lesson is fully drawn, there will remain a dichotomous arrangement between making public the documents of public servants of whose policies they disapprove and keeping private the documentation on deviants whom, supposedly, the social scientists are concerned with protecting. This is not an ethical approach but an opportunistic approach. It rests on politcal and professional expediency. The need, therefore, is to reassert the requisites of science for full disclosure and the ethics of full disclosure as the only possible ethics for any group of professional scientists. If the release of the Pentagon Papers has done nothing else, it has reaffirmed the highest principle of all science: full disclosure, full review of the data, and full responsibility for what is done, accounted by those who do the research.

Another area that deeply concerns the social scientist and that is highlighted in the Pentagon Papers is the government's established norms of secrecy. While most officials in government have a series of work norms with which to guide their behavior, few forms of anticipatory socialization have applied to social scientists who advise government agencies. The professionalism of social scientists has normally been directed toward publicity rather than secrecy. This fosters sharp differences in opinion and attitudes between the polity and the academy, since the reward systems for career advancement are so clearly polarized.

The question of secrecy is intimately connected with matters of policy because the standing assumption of policy makers (particularly in the field of foreign affairs) is that they should not reveal themselves entirely. No government in the game of international politics feels that its policies can be candidly revealed for full public review; therefore, operational research done in connection with policy considerations is customarily bound by the canons of government privacy. But while scientists have a fetish for publicizing their information as a mechanism for professional advancement no less than as a definition of their essential role in the society, the political branches of society have as their fetish the protection of private documents and privileged information. Therefore, the polity places a premium not only on acquiring vital information but also on maintaining silence about such information, precisely to the degree that the data might be of high decisional value. This norm leads to differing premiums between analysts and policy makers and to tensions between them.

Social scientists complain that the norm of secrecy often involves their yielding their own essential work premises. A critical factor reinforcing an unwilling acceptance of the norm of secrecy by social scientists is the allocation of most government research funds for military or semimilitary purposes. Senate testimony has shown that 70 percent of the federal funds targeted for the social sciences involves such restrictions.

The real wonder turns out to be not the existence of the secrecy norm but the relative availability of large chunks of information. Indeed, the classification of materials is so inept that documents (such as the Pax Americana research) designated as confidential or secret by one agency may often be made available as a public service by another agency. There are also occasions when documents placed in a classified category by sponsoring government agencies can be secured without charge from the private research institute doing the work. But the main point is that the norm of secrecy makes it extremely difficult to separate science from patriotism and hence makes it that much more difficult to question the research itself. Social scientists often express the nagging fear that accepting the first stage—the right of the government to maintain secrecy—often carried with it acquiescence in a later stage—the necessity for silence on the part of social researchers who may disagree with the political uses of their efforts.

The demand for government secrecy has a telling impact on the methodology of the social sciences. Presumably, social scientists are employed because they, as a group, represent objectivity and honesty. Social scientists like to envision themselves as a wall of truth off which policy makers can bounce their premises. They also like to think that they provide information that cannot be derived from sheer public opinion. Thus, to some degree, social scientists consider that they are hired or used by government agencies because they will say things that may be unpopular but nonetheless significant. However, since secrecy exists, the premises upon which most social scientists seek to work are strained by the very agencies that contract out their need to know. The terms of research and conditions of work tend to demand an initial compromise with social science methodology. The social scientist is placed in a cognitive bind: he is conditioned not to reveal maximum information lest he become victimized by the federal agencies that employ his services, yet he is employed precisely because of his presumed thoroughness, impartiality, and candor. The social scientist who survives in government service becomes circumspect or learns to play the game; his value to social science becomes seriously jeopardized. On the other hand, once he raises these considerations, his usefulness to the policy-making sector is likewise jeopardized.

Social scientists believe that openness is more than the meeting of the formal requirements of scientific canons; it is also a matter of making information universally available. The norm of secrecy leads to selective presentation of data. The social scientist is impeded by the policy maker because of contrasting notions about the significance of data and the general need for replication elsewhere and by others. The policy maker who demands differential access to findings considers this a normal return for the initial expenditure of risk capital. Since this utilitarian concept of data is alien to the scientific standpoint, the schism between the social scientist and the policy maker becomes pronounced precisely at the level of openness of information and accessibility to the work achieved. The social scientist's general attitude is that sponsorship of research does not entitle any one sector to benefit unduly from the findings, that sponsorship by federal agencies ought not place greater limitations on the use of work than sponsorship by either private agencies or universities.

A major area that deeply concerns social scientists is that of dual allegiance. The Pentagon Papers have such specific requirements and goal-oriented tasks that they intrude upon the autonomy of the social scientist by forcing upon him choices between dual allegiances. The researcher is compelled to choose between participating fully in the world of the federal bureaucracy or remaining in more familiar academic confines. He does not want the former to create isolation in the latter. Thus, he often criticizes the federal bureaucracy's unwillingness to recognize his basic needs: the need to teach and retain full academic identity, the need to publicize information, and above all, the need to place scientific responsibility above the call of patriotic obligation—when they may happen to clash. In short, he does not want to be plagued by dual or competing allegiances. The norm of secrecy exacerbates this problem. Although many of the social scientists who become involved with federal research are intrigued by the opportunity to address important issues, they are confronted by bureaucracies that often do not share their passion for resolving social problems. For example, federal obligations commit the bureaucracy to assign high priority to items having military potential and effectiveness and low priorities to many supposedly idealistic and far-fetched themes in which social scientists are interested.

Social scientists acting either as employees or as consultants connected with the government are hamstrung by federal agencies that are, in turn, limited by political circumstances beyond their control. A federal bureaucracy must manage cumbersome, overgrown committees and data-gathering agencies. Federal agencies often protect a status quo merely for the sake of rational functioning. They must conceive of academicians in their midst as a standard bureaucratic type entitled to rise to certain federal ranks. Federal agencies limit innovating concepts to what is immediately useful, not out of choice and certainly not out of resentment of the social sciences but from what is deemed as impersonal necessity. This has the effect of reducing the social scientist's role in the government to that of ally or advocate rather than of innovator or designer. Social scientists begin to feel that their enthusiasm for rapid change is unrealistic, considering how little can be done by the government bureaucracy. They come to resent the involvement in theoryless application to immediacy that is foisted on them by the "new utopians," surrendering in the process the value of confronting men with the wide range of choices of what might be done. The schism then between autonomy and involvement is as thorough as that between secrecy and publicity, for it cuts to the quick well-intentioned pretensions at human engineering.

The problem of competing allegiances is not made simpler by the fact that many high-ranking federal bureaucrats have strong nationalistic and conservative political ideologies. Their views contrast markedly with those of the social scientist who comes to Washington not only with a belief in the primacy of science over patriotism but also with a definition of patriotism that is more open-ended and consciously liberal than that of most appointed officials. Such a social scientist often perceives the conflict to extend beyond research design and social applicability, becoming one of incompatible ideologies, and he comes to resent the proprietary attitude of the bureaucrat toward "his" government processes. The social scientist is likely to consider his social science biases a necessary buffer against the federal bureaucracy.

The publication of the Pentagon Papers sheds new light on political-pluralist and power-concentrationist hypotheses. When push finally did come to shove, President Nixon and the government officials behaved as members of a ruling class and not as leaders of their political party. Nixon might easily have chosen to let the Democratic party take the burn and bear the brunt of the assaults for the betrayal of a public trust. Indeed, the Nixon administration might have chosen to join the chorus of those arguing that the Democratic party is indeed revealed in the documents to have been the war party, whereas the Republican party emerges as the party of restraint—if not exactly of principle. There was a stunning opportunity for Nixon to make political capital on a no-risk basis, simply by drawing attention to the fact that the war was constantly escalated by his Democratic predecessors. They refused to bargain in good faith with Ho Chi Minh despite repeated requests. President Kennedy himself moved far beyond anything President Eisenhower had in mind for the area, not merely by making the fatal commitments to land troops, but by adopting a domino theory of winning the war. This was taken up by President Johnson, whose role can well be considered as nefarious: coming before the American people as a peace candidate when he had already made the fatal series of commitments to continue escalation and warfare. That Nixon chose not to change policies earlier illustrates the sense of class solidarity held by the political elites in this country: there was a collective sense of betrayal of the "priesthood," rather than one of an obligation to score political points and gain political trophies. His reaction should also provide a lesson in terms of the actual power within the political structure of a small ruling elite. Surely this must be considered a fascinating episode in its own right: the reasons for his behavior are complex, but among them must rank the fact that Nixon behaved as a member of a ruling elite that had transcendent obligations far beyond the call of party—that is, to the call of class.

One fact made clear by the Pentagon Papers is the extent to which presidentialism has become the ideology and the style in American political life. The infrequency of any reference to the judicial situation with respect to the war in Southeast Asia and the virtual absence of any reference to congressional sentiments are startling confirmations of an utter change in the American political style. If any proof was needed of the emerging imbalance between the executive and other branches of government, these papers should provide such proof. The theory of checks and balances works only when there are, in fact, groups, such as Senators or stubborn judges, who believe in the responsibility of the judicial and legislative branches to establish check and balance. In the absence of such vigor, the war in Southeast Asia became very much a series of executive actions. This itself should give pause to the advocates of consensus theory in political science.

The failure of the Vietnam episode has resulted in a reconsideration of presidentialism as the specific contemporary variant of power-elite theory. The renewed vigor of Congress and the willingness, albeit cautionary willingness, of the Supreme Court to rule on fundamental points of constitutional law are indicative of the resurgence of pluralism. In this sense, the darkest hour of liberalism as a political style has witnessed a liberal regrouping around the theme of mass politics. Even the domestic notions of community organization and states' rights are indicative of the limits of presidentialism, so that Nixon, at one and the same time, was reluctantly presiding over the swan song of presidentialism in foreign affairs while celebrating its demise in domestic affairs. The collapse of the Vietnam War and the trends toward neoisolationism are in fact simply the reappearance of political pluralism in a context in which a further concentration of political power in the presidency may mean the upsurge of fascism, American style. If the concept of a power elite was reconfirmed in the Pentagon Papers so, too, strangely, was the concept of political pluralism in the public response to them. The countervailing influence of the Supreme Court was clearly manifested in the ringing affirmation of the First Amendment: in the denial of the concept of prior restraint and prior punitive actions, and in the very rapidity of the decision itself. This action by the judiciary, coupled with a show of muscle on the part of the Senate and House concerning the conduct of the war, military appropriations, boondoggles, and special privileges for a select handful of aircraft industries served in their own way to underscore the continued importance of the open society and the pluralistic basis of power. Even executives, such as Hubert H. Humphrey, have declared in favor of full disclosure and reiterated the principles guiding the publication of the Pentagon Papers.

Power elites operate behind a cloak of anonymity. When that cloak is lifted, an obvious impairment in the operational efficiency of elites occurs. What has happened with the release of the Pentagon Papers is precisely this collapse of anonymity, no less than of secrecy. As a result, the formal apparatus of government can assert its prerogatives. This does not mean that the executive branch of government will be unable to recover from this blow to its prestige or that it will no longer attempt to play its trump card, decision making by executive fiat. It does mean, however, that the optimal conditions under which power elites operate have been seriously hampered. The degree of this impairment and the length of time it will obtain depend exclusively on the politics of awareness and participation, no less than the continuing pressures for lowering the secrecy levels in high-level international decision making.

Probably the most compelling set of reasons given for President Nixon's bitter opposition to the release of the Pentagon Papers is that provided by Melvin Gurtov (1971), one of the authors of the secret Pentagon study and an outstanding political scientist specializing in Asian affairs. He spoke of three deceits in the current U.S. Vietnamese policy: "The first and most basic deceit is the Administration's contention that we're winding down and getting out of the war." In fact, he saw Vietnamization as a "domestic political ploy that really involves the substitution of air power for ground power." The second deceit was that "we're truly interested in seeing the prisoners of war released." Gurtov noted that "as far as this administration is concerned the prisoners of war are a political device, a device for rationalizing escalation, by saying these are acts that are necessary to show our concern for the prisoners." The third deceit was "that under the Nixon Doctrine the United States is not interested in making new commitments in Asia." In fact, the administration used the Cambodia coup "as an opportunity for creating for itself a new commitment in Southeast Asia, namely the survival of a non-Communist regime in Pnom penh." The outspokenness of his position indicates that the defense of the power elite of the past by President Nixon could just as well have been construed as a self-defense of the power elite in the present.

The Pentagon Papers provide much new light on theories of power elite and power diffusion and also provide an equal measure of information on conspiracy theory. While it is still true that conspiracy theory is bad theory, it is false to assert that no conspiracies exist or that none are perpetrated by the government. It might indeed be the case that all governments, insofar as they are formal organizations, have secrets, and we could call these secrets "conspiracies." From this point of view the interesting question is how so few leaks resulted from an effort of such magnitude and involving so many people as setting policy in the Vietnam War. Rather than be surprised that these papers reached the public domain four to six years after the fact, one should wonder how the government was able to maintain silence on matters of such far-ranging and far-reaching consequence.

Cyrus Eaton, American industrialist and confidant of many communist leaders, indicates that the Vietnamese were almost instantaneously made aware of U.S. policy decisions. There is serious doubt that they actually had copies of documents. Rather, like the American public, they were informed about the decisions but not the cogitations and agitations that went into the final decision. Perhaps all governments operate as the U.S. government did, as revealed in the Pentagon Papers; nonetheless, it is fascinating—at least this once—to be privy to the process and not simply the outcome and to see the foibles of powerful men and not just the fables manufactured after the fact for these men.

These papers tend to underwrite the common-sense point of view that governments are not to be trusted and to undermine the more sophisticated interpretation that governments are dedicated to the task of maintaining democracy at home and peace abroad. As bitter as it may seem, common-sense cynicism has more to recommend it than the sophisticated, well-elaborated viewpoint that takes literally the formal structure of government and so readily tends to dismiss the informal response to power and pressure from men at the top. The constant wavering of Johnson, his bellicose defiance of all evidence and information that the bombings were not having the intended effect, followed by his shock when his lieutenants, such as Robert McNamara, changed their position at midstream (almost constituting a betrayal in the eyes of the president), and shock in turn followed by a more relaxed posture and a final decision not to seek the presidency—all of this forms a human drama that makes the political process at once fascinating and frightful: fascinating because we can see the psychology of politics in action, and frightful because the presumed rationality is by no means uniformly present (cf. Horowitz 1971:37-46).

The publication of the Pentagon Papers, while a considerable victory for the rights of a free press and of special significance to all scientists who still uphold the principle of full disclosure as the norm of all political as well as scientific endeavor, is not yet a total victory for a democratic society—that can only happen when the concept of secrecy is itself probed and penetrated and when the concept of undeclared warfare is finally and fully repudiated by the public and its representatives. The behavior of the government in its effort to suppress publication of the Pentagon Papers cannot simply be viewed as idiosyncratic but rather as a part of the structure of the American political processes in which the expert displaces the politician, and the politicians themselves become so beholden to the class of experts for information that they dare not turn for guidance to the people they serve. For years, critics of the Vietnam War have been silenced and intimidated by the policy maker's insistence that when all the facts were known the hawk position would be vindicated. Many of the facts are now revealed—and the bankruptcy of the advocates of continued escalation is plain for all to see. Hopefully, this will firm up the critical capacities of those who, as an automatic reflex, assume the correctness of the government's position on military affairs.

REFERENCES

Abel, Elie
    1966   *The Missile Crisis.* New York: Bantam Books.
Commager, Henry Steele
    1968   "Can We Limit Presidential Power?" *New Republic,* 158 (February).
de Sola Pool, Ithiel
    1967   "The Necessity for Social Scientists Doing Research for Government," in I. L. Horowitz, editor, *The Rise and Fall of Project Camelot.* Cambridge, Massachusetts: M.I.T. Press.
DeWeerd, H. A.
    1961   *Concepts of Limited War: An Historical Approach.* Santa Monica: RAND Corporation, p. 2352 (November).
Gelb, Leslie, H.
    1971   *A History of U.S. Decision-Making Progress on Vietnam Policy* (The Pentagon Papers) New York: Bantam Books.
Graham, I. E. C. and E. Brease
    1967   *Publications of the Social Science Department of the RAND Corporation.* Santa Monica: RM-3600-4 (May).
Green, Philip
    1966   *Deadly Logic: The Theory of Nuclear Deterrence.* Columbus, Ohio: Ohio State University Press.
Gurtov, Melvin
    1971   "Reflections on The Pentagon Papers and the Vietnam War". *Life* (September 16).
Hoag, M. W.
    1957   *NATO Deterrent vs. Shield.* Santa Monica: RAND Corporation, RM-1926-RC (June).

1961   *On Local War Doctrine.* Santa Monica: RAND Corporation, RM-p. 2433 (August).
Horowitz, Irving Louis
1963   *The War Game: Studies of the New Civilian Militarists.* New York: Ballantine-Pocket Books.
1967   *The Rise and Fall of Project Camelot: Studies in the Relationship between Social Science and Practical Politics.* Cambridge, Massachusetts: M.I.T. Press.
1971   "The Pentagon Papers and Social Sciences" *Trans*action/*SOCIETY.* Vol. 8, No. 11 (September).
LeMay, Curtis
1963   Hearings Before the Committee on Armed Services, U.S. Senate. Washington, D.C.: Government Printing Office.
Liston, Robert A.
1966   *Tides of Justice.* New York: Delacorte.
McNamara, Robert S.
1963   Hearings on Military Posture, Committee on Armed Services, 88th Congress, 1st sess. Washington, D.C.: U.S. Government Printing Office.
New York *Times*
1962   *Cuban Crisis: A Step-by-Step Review* (November 13, 1962).
1971   Dean Rusk quoted in the New York *Times* (Saturday, July 3, 1971).
Pachter, Henry
1963   *Collision Course: The Cuban Missile Crisis and Coexistence.* New York: Praeger.
Posvar, W. W.
1964   "The Impact of Strategy Expertise on the National Security Policy of the United States" in J. Montgomery and A. Smithies, eds., *Public Policy* 13. Cambridge, Massachusetts: Harvard School of Public Administration.
Schlesinger, Arthur M. Jr.
1965   *A Thousand Days: John F. Kennedy in the White House.* Boston: Houghton Mifflin.
Smith, Bruce
1966   *The RAND Corporation: Case Study of a Non-Profit Advisory Corporation.* Cambridge, Massachusetts: Harvard University Press.
Sorenson, Theodore C.
1965   *Kennedy.* New York: Harper & Row.
Sparkman, John
1962   *Situation in Cuba:* Hearings Before the Committee on Foreign Relations and the Committee on Armed Services, U.S. Senate. Washington, D.C.: Government Printing Office.
Special Operations Research Office (SORO)
1964   "Working Paper Prepared For Office of the Chief of Research and Development, Department of the Army", in *The Rise and Fall of*

Project Camelot, edited by Irving Louis Horowitz. Cambridge, Massachusetts: 1974 (revised edition).

Speier, Hans and H. Goldhammer
    1959   *Some Observations on Political Gaming*. Santa Monica: RAND Corporation, RM-1679-RC (June).

United States Department of Defense
    1971   *History of the U.S. Decision-Making Process on Vietnam Policy* (The Pentagon Papers). New York: The New York *Times* and Bantam Books (July 1971).

Wheeler, Earle
    1963   Hearings Before the Committee on Armed Services, U.S. Senate. Washington, D.C.: Government Printing Office.

Wohlstetter, Albert
    1965   "Cuba and Pearl Harbor: Hindsight and Foresight," RAND Corporation, RU-4320-ISA (April).

CHAPTER
7

SOCIAL SCIENCE
PARTICIPATION IN U.S.
DOMESTIC POLICY

In a broad survey it is not possible to measure statistically the rate of failure and success in key policy operations involving an emphatic social science input. But what is clear from the cases of foreign policy involvement cited is that social science does not, in and of itself, help create policy cohesion. Beyond that, social science participation can not undo the wrongs committed by bureaucrats, politicians, and other elite groups. As if to deepen an appreciation of the ancillary, if important, role of social science, we see the same phenomenon operating in reverse within the United States proper. On domestic policy decisions, where a much higher consensus concerning U.S. national goals exists, one finds a much broader acceptance of social scientists by policy agencies and, in addition, a higher professional approbation for doing such consulting, advisory, and evaluating work.

If this line of analysis is correct, the assumption that social scientists behave as Platonic holders of power—or as Machiavellian advisors to power—is in need of drastic modification. For it is more nearly the case that social scientists, sharing as they do the liberal sentiments of that portion of the social stratification system from which they emanate, seek to implement such sentiments with the professional skills and know-how they possess. As a result, a reciprocity often exists between innovative domestic programs and avant-garde thinking in the social sciences (cf. Glazer 1972:149-81). But such inputs are more nearly indicative of a subordinate rather than a superordinate character. More bluntly still, social scientists perform essential janitorial "mopping up" duties as well as the mandarin services of rationalizing policy claims. They do not sit as Olympian deities over the conduct of U.S. affairs. A survey of major domestic policy programs and the social science participation in them, should help make this point more evident.

PROJECT CLEAR

The decision to desegregate the armed forces, which, in retrospect seems to have both an obvious and modest consequence of a World War fought on behalf of democratic principles, did not have quite so obvious a flavor a quarter century ago. Indeed, the executive, presidential attempts in this direction were frustrated by a military high command that did not wish to see the armed forces turned into an experimental camping grounds. In the words of General Omar Bradley, then Chief of Staff: "The Army is not out to make any social reforms. The Army will put men of different races in different companies. It will change that policy when the nation as a whole changes it" (cf. Baldwin 1948:51).

Given such a genuine and deep split between an executive branch of government that wanted to move quickly toward a more democratic army and a victorious military army equally unwilling to see traditional privilege and prestige tampered with, the use of the social sciences to bring off a new social policy must be seen as innovative as well as interesting: a precedent-setting achievement of even greater consequence than that imagined by any of the original participants.

In July 1948 President Truman issued Executive Order 9981, which stated that "there shall be equality of treatment and opportunity for all persons in the armed services without regard to race, color, religion or national origin." This order had an even greater impact on the outlook and aspirations of blacks than President's Roosevelt's earlier Order 8802 forbidding discrimination among war contractors, issued in June 1941 (cf. Broom and Glenn 1965:60). However, neither the executive order nor the military resistance perceived the actual modesty of the proposed reform. What was promised and delivered was equality of opportunity, not integration of the armed forces, and certainly not any program of "affirmative action" to advance blacks to officer ranks as rapidly as possible (Stillman 1968:43).

The urgings for racial reform in the armed forces were brought about by a combination of factors, the chief of which were a) the hard-headed recognition that black political strength in northern urban regions had to be taken into account, b) the relatively poor performance of racially segregated combat units both in World War II and in the early stages of the Korean conflict, and c) the military awareness that segregation required extra-strength units at a time of a shrinking overall manpower situation in the military (cf. Dalfiume 1969:204; Bogart 1969:10).

The question of desegration of the armed forces was hardly a matter confined to the military itself. It enlisted the cause of liberal congressional opinion as well as a solid phalanx of black political support against segregation; on the side of traditionalism and racial separation were the Dixiecrat Congressmen, professional career officers generally, and the usual bureaucratic inertia to avoid any controversy. Yet there was a shrewd realization that strong hierarchical structures such as the armed forces have been able to bring about desegregation more efficiently than institutions that depend upon voluntary action (cf. Bogart 1969:39). Under such circumstances, the role of the social sciences, clearly thrown in on the side of reform and racial equity, represented a considerable realization that simple legal mandate or executive order could not by themselves achieve the necessary public base of support that would convert an edict into a practice. There were many factors in the desegregation rulings that were crystalized in the military regulations published by the army in January 1950, establishing a policy of equality of treatment and opportunity for all persons in the army without regard to race, color, religion, or national origin. But above all, this process of conflict resolution took place largely without benefit of social science advisors.

An outstanding team of social scientists became involved with the Operations Research Office (ORO) in 1950, their charge "to initiate a project to determine how best to utilize Negro personnel within the army." The work done under the label "Project Clear" was characterized thusly by one high ORO official: "The Army wants to know what to do with all their niggers." The "research staff," then, was called into existence after and not before desegregation became the undeclared policy of the United States Army.

The social sciences were once again called upon as a legitimizing agency. Social scientists were to provide operational data on the use of manpower resources rather than on the desirability or feasibility of segregation or integration; the necessity for integration had already been widely acknowledged by high military officials. In his summation of social science and public policy on this matter Bogart (1969, p. 41) pointed out that:

The Army's desegregation was willed by historical necessity, not by research. It would have come about without *Project Clear*, and perhaps not very differently or very much later. Social research was conducted on a large scale and at a substantial expense in the process of arriving at the decision and in working out the procedure for implementing and enforcing it. This means that both the major decision and all the subsidiary decisions cannot really be divorced from the influence of the studies.

Project Clear reported four main findings on the "integration experience": a) strong hierarchical structures such as the army have been able to desegregate more efficiently than institutions depending upon voluntary action; b) black Americans in and out of the army resent enforced segregation; c) many black officers and noncoms hold positions of rank and privilege to which they could not return if the armed forces desegregation were to cease immediately; and d) there is de facto segregation in the army despite the de jure bans against segregation.

Project Clear enabled the armed forces to claim a pioneering role in the successful integration of black and white troops in a formerly segregated institution. It was also the precedent that provided a model for the civilian Job Corps two decades later and for the overall desegregation of government institutions. However, it must also be pointed out that such domestic good works also helped to point up the limitations of social science in policy roles. For at no point in the research did the scientists deal with the overall weakness in military structure or military system. The social sciences, like the federal agencies being served, were concerned with creating mechanisms to reform an institution, not to reveal how the very existence of such an institution itself might provide a limitation upon democratic premises and principles (cf. Coleman 1969).

BROWN VS. BOARD OF EDUCATION

This Supreme Court decision marks the most significant utilization of social science inputs into the direct transformation of domestic policy. On May 17, 1954, the Supreme Court of the United States handed down a ruling that announced the beginning of full citizenship for the country's largest minority. On that day the Court ruled that segregation in the nation's schools was unconstitutional. Twenty-one states that either permitted or required separate school systems for blacks and whites were told that "separate but equal" was no longer the law of the land. "Separate educational facilities are inherently unequal," declared Chief Justice Earl Warren for the unanimous court.

The school decision was bound to be controversial, for in spite of a score of rulings against higher-education segregation in the nation's highest courts, the principle of "separate but equal" as enunciated in *Plessey* v. *Ferguson* had never been challenged. It is probable that those Southerners who were watching the pattern of decision making in the courts expected that, sooner or later, segregation would have to come to an end. But it is likely that they expected an incremental step; the sweeping nature of the prounouncement—which, after all, was made by a court comprised of three Southerners and a brand-new chief justice with very little judicial background—fueled the outrage with which it was greeted in the South.

It was a surprising decision, not especially because it ruled for the black appellants but because of the apparent basis of the decision. The court made virtually no effort to argue from legal precedent. The basis of the decision was, in effect, that times had changed: modern sociological and psychological evidence showed separate educational facilities to be damaging to blacks. The courts quoted with favor the finding of the Kansas case court:

> Segregation of white and colored children in public schools has a detrimental effect upon the colored children. The impact is greater when it has the sanction of the law; for the policy of separating the races is usually interpreted as denoting the inferiority of the negro group. A sense of inferiority affects the motivation of a child to learn. Segregation with the sanction of law, therefore, has a tendency to retard the educational and mental development of negro children and to deprive them of some of the benefits they would receive in a racially integrated school system [cf. Clark and Kamisar 1969, p. 330].

The social science evidence presented and discovered through its own research, the Court stated, led the Court to conclude that the plaintiffs were, by reason of segregation, "deprived of the equal protection of the law guaranteed by the Fourteenth Amendment." The decision to a significant degree represented and, more importantly, was perceived as a shift from judicial decision based primarily (if not exclusively) on legal precedent to one based on presumed facts of social change. That perception had no disastrous consequences for the Court or the decision but it ushered in a period of intense criticism from conservative sectors that argued that the court was acting as a policy-making body by using nonlegal evidence to reach its decision, that social science was an improper form of evidence, and that if the evidence used was invalid the decision must also be invalid (cf. Garfinkle 1959; LaFarge 1953).

Social scientists themselves were not entirely confident of the worth of the evidence submitted in the school segregation cases. The argument went that since the Court itself has criticized the introduction of nonlegal evidence on numerous occasions, and of social science evidence in particular, a decision based on such evidence was clearly erroneous. There was also some effort to impugn the integrity of the experts called upon to testify: Kenneth Clark was said to be biased since he was employed by the NAACP; Gunnar Myrdal was called a Socialist who had been unforgivably critical of the United States in the work cited (*An American Dilemma*). The attempt overall was clearly to attack both the use of social science in general and the quality of the social science cited. A third tactic is suggested by a speech by Strom Thurmond after the implementation decision. "We might do well," he said, "to adopt the tactics of our opponents. If propaganda and psychological evidence are effective for our opponents they can be effective for us. Our worthy objective of preserving the Constitution justifies the method" (Thurmond 1956, p. 22-32).

In other words, if one cannot prove that social science is not a legitimate form of evidence in the courts and that the social science used was poor social science, one should present one's own social science evidence to the contrary. A concerted effort was mounted in the period after 1955 to persuade the Court to reverse itself and to gain support among the public for the idea that blacks are inherently inferior. After the school desegregation decisions, an attempt was made to formulate a scientific defense for segregated education. The evidence for segregation usually took the form of investigations of comparative racial intelligence, psychological test results, and the relative intellectual capacity of whites and blacks. Research also began to appear on the psychic traits and personality characteristics of the races and the extent to which they are transmitted by heredity or dictated by environment. The debate has persisted to this day, despite the legislative success of the advocates of civil rights, and many of those who argue the case for innate racial differences have been taken quite seriously. Arthur Jensen and Robert Herrnstein are the most recent examples.

The attempt to set up a countervailing body of popular opinion, buttressed by the expert opinion described above, was reinforced by supporters who, whether or not they agreed with the decision, were concerned about some of its implications. Advocates of states' rights felt that the decision granted too much power to the federal government and that it represented a fundamental interference with the right of a state to educate its children in accordance with the majority of its citizens' wishes. Strict constitutionalists felt that it signified an imbalance of power in the judiciary, and judicial conservatives worried about the implications of the use of something so temporal as social science. Unlike legal evidence, it was argued, social science evidence may change with the frame of mind of the researcher. It is very close to opinion and is certainly not a "science" such as physics, for example. This attitude, which was far from uncommon, suggests a fundamental misunderstanding about the nature of social science. Because social scientists could not point to a body of social science "law," some laymen concluded that it could not be taken seriously. Some social scientists were not certain that they liked social science being used as advocacy. The 1950s were, after all, the heyday of functionalism, which advocated that social scientists strive toward a value-free orientation. Social science research, according to this school of thought, should not be contaminated by anything so demeaning as politics. Even some liberals were nervous about the implications of the political use of social science research (Berger 1957:471-77). The Court had used the social science evidence presented by the plaintiffs to show that they had suffered damage to their personalities as a result of segregation. What if, some social scientists wondered aloud, this became legal precedent, and one had to prove damage to ensure equality under the law? The right to equality should be protected, it was argued, even if it made no difference to an individual or even if it were not harmful to another party. Some lawyers who supported the decision fretted about the poor quality of logic exhibited in the decision and regretted that the decision was not more firmly based on legal precedent (cf. Cahn 1955:150-59).

Once the school desegregation decision was made, other political factors came into play. The administration's low-key reaction to southern indignation in the wake of the decision was, perhaps, designed to avoid fanning the flames by involving President Eisenhower in the controversy; the civil rights actions taken on behalf of blacks through administrative directive were accomplished quietly— and slowly. At worst, the Eisenhower administration's inaction resulted from the president's own tepid feelings about civil rights. But whatever the motivation, the result of the lack of administration support was that the Supreme Court's decision became vulnerable to attack; lacking any legitimacy ascribed to it by the executive branch, it had to stand or fall on the prestige of the Court.

The decision was scrutinized for flaws. Many of the arguments made by the appellees in the argument before the Court began to appear in the popular media and found their way into speeches by southern congressmen and southern sympathizers. Critics fastened on the social science aspect because that was the most novel element of the decision. Both the decision's critics and its supporters perceived that the use of social science in this new and, to some, radical way made the decision vulnerable. Yet, as the arguments presented by the critics shifted from "all social science is inexact and therefore inadmissible evidence" to "this particular social science research is wrong, and here is the evidence to the contrary," in short, as the critics began to use social science to *refute* the social science presented in the Brown case, they gave up the battle. For in so doing, prosegregationists were accepting the legitimacy of social science as evidence; in adopting the genre of evidence used by opponents of segregation, they were conceding the validity of social science advocacy. Today, no one questions whether or not social science may legitimately be used by any court to reverse a legal precedent; in a recent discussion of a forthcoming Supreme Court ruling on busing, Christopher Jencks listed three possible bases upon which the Court could reverse busing precedents, and one of them was social science evidence (Jencks 1972:41).

The quality of the social science evidence presented in the school segregation decision remains to be discussed. In all frankness, it was not very high. The most superior evidence was presented by Kenneth Clark, and, as the counsel for South Carolina was quick to point out, there were serious problems in the formulation of Clark's conclusions. He could not, for example, convincingly account for the higher incidence of "negative self-identification" on the part of northern blacks. One-third of the social scientists sampled by Isidore Chein, who said they felt that segregation was harmful to both black and white children, also said that they based that decision upon their own research, and two-thirds gave others' research as the primary influence. Yet since very little research on the effects of segregation had been published in the academic journals, and, in any case, since the Court could not evaluate the research to which it referred, its response constituted opinion, nothing more. In fact, research on black/white differences did not really begin in earnest until after the Supreme Court decision, which itself stimulated great interest in and emphasis upon research on blacks. After 1955 a number of journals and newsletters began to appear that published the regular reports on such research and where it was being conducted. Prior to the decision virtually the only major research done had been commissioned by the NAACP or appeared in special-interest publications, such as the *Journal of Negro Education*. Funding for such work was simply not easily available. Aside from civil rights organizations, Jewish organizations, and some foundation sponsorship there was little money around for such research; certainly no government funding was available.

The criticism of the social science evidence presented before the Supreme Court by the proponents of segregation had a great deal of validity. The empirical evidence for integration was hardly conclusive. Moreover, the works cited by the Court appear to have been almost arbitrarily selected, as critics have charged. The Court did not make an extensive or systematic effort to find out on its own what social science had to say about the subject. On the contrary, there is a random quality to its citations of social science evidence; less important authors and less relevant works of important authors are cited, and fundamental works and authors are omitted. The social science research that had been done prior to the *Brown* decision by no means *proved* that segregation caused the educational and mental retardation of black children; that variable has simply not been isolated. Furthermore, except for Clark's tests, very little evidence had been presented to show conclusively that damage had actually been done to the educational and mental development of black children.* (cf. Pasamanick and Knoblock 1958).

---

*In fact, recent research on desegregation and its effects has indicated that the questions and answers are considerably more complex than would be supposed from the 1954 decision (cf. Jencks 1972:120).

This is not to argue that the decision should not or could not have been made. The point is, instead, that the Court made its decision on the basis of its sense of the effect of segregation and the requirements of the Fourteenth Amendment. Members of the Court may have been swayed by the testimony presented by the social scientists; Clark's tests were said to have been particularly convincing. Two NAACP staff members, Herbert Hill and Jack Greenberg, assessed the effect of oral testimony very highly: "The experts were cross-examined, and their testimony was subject to rebuttal; this gave the defendants (arguing for the legality of segregation) a certain opportunity but it enhanced the persuasiveness of the testimony if it could not be shaken" (Greenberg and Hill 1957:474).

But social science was not the *foundation* of the decision; it was used to lend weight to what the justices clearly were persuaded was true: that segregated education is unequal education. The problem that the proponents of segregation faced was not that social science led the Court down an erroneous path; rather it was that the time had come in the judgment of the Court—and, judging from the initial media response, in the opinion of many opinion makers—for the black to take his place as a full-fledged U.S. citizen. Given the widespread faith in education as a panacea for all social ills, the hope was that equal opportunity in education would be enough (cf. Sutherland 1954). Certainly, no one foresaw the massive social revolution that was loosed by the *Brown* victory. The segregationists held a bad deck; but the Court had to find a way to reverse *Plessey* without seeming to do so. The solution was the argument that the situation in 1954 was no longer what it was in 1896, that times have changed: "In approaching this problem, we cannot turn the clock back to 1868 when the Fourteenth Amendment was adopted or even to 1896 when *Plessey* v. *Ferguson* was written. We must consider public education in the light of its full development and its present place in American life throughout the Nation" (cf. Clark and Kamisar 1969:329; see also Clark 1955).

The Supreme Court is, then, a policy-making body, and like any such body it recognizes that there is no truth or untruth, no right or wrong, that there are only degrees of each. Perhaps the Court is less swayed by political winds than are other branches of the government (the justices are, after all, appointed for life, or until retirement), but though it has no constitutency, it does respond, as is clear in the *Brown* case, to its sense of the needs of the body politic, as well as to its awareness of its own limitations. It is also clear that the Court is not above internal politics; recent studies (by social scientists) of voting behavior on the Court have subjected it to the same scrutiny given any other branch of the government (cf. Schmidhauser and Berg 1972). It is now recognized—if it was not before—that the appointment of a Supreme Court justice is a political act; that justices vote alone distinguishable lines of judicial conservatism or liberalism, strict constructionism or activism (cf. Glick 1971).

Social science can play an important role in the process of judicial policy making, just as it has contributed to the formulation of policy by other branches of government. The important point is that social science has little discernible influence unless it is taken up and exploited for political reasons. We have only to look at the lack of positive reaction by political figures when social science research does not come up with the expected or desired answers: hence, the sad fate of the presidential commission on drugs, the rejection of the president's commission on obscenity and pornography, and the dismissal of the Population Council's recommendations for liberalized abortion laws and wider dissemination of birth-control devices. Despite the claims of critics of and participants in the decision alike, the role of social science in the school desegregation cases was not decisive. By the 1953 argument the Court asked its "five questions," because it had not found the information presented in the 1952 brief conclusive and was searching for another basis for decision. When neither side was able to present an air-tight historical or constitutional case, the Court was forced to turn back to the social science argument. But even then the strongest statement for social science in the decision originated in the Kansas case and was merely quoted by the Supreme Court. Moreover, the Court was not consistent in its reliance on social science evidence; otherwise, it would have been more sanguine about the possibilities for peaceful integration, even in the South, and would have given a more vigorous order to integrate.

Though, in fact, the role of social science in the school segregation cases may be more modest than has been claimed, the cases represented a significant advancement for the social sciences. For the first time social science played a role in judicial advocacy that resulted in a significant policy decision and initiated what Bayard Rustin has characterized as the decade in which "the legal foundations of racism in America were destroyed" (cf. Rainwater and Yancey 1967:9). Brandeis had used social science to prevent a conservative judiciary from holding back progress; now the Court was taking an active role in molding a social consensus. In the process the social sciences acquired new legitimacy, even though under severe attack, and within and outside the social science profession their power and potential influence began to be taken seriously (cf. Curtis 1973).

THE WAR ON POVERTY

The war on poverty, rather like the war in Vietnam, was preeminently the conception of the liberal, policy-oriented intellectuals, especially those who gathered in Washington and in a significant sense came to power in the early 1960s under the presidency of John F. Kennedy. Kennedy's presidential campaign had propounded a fairly radical critique of American society. The Eisenhower era had not been barren of government initiatives, but even when these were of massive dimensions, as in the case of the Interstate Defense and Highway Program, they had tended to be directed toward the needs and interests of the middle classes of American society. A major architect in the war-on-poverty program, Wilbur J. Cohen (1970:4) provides an excellent description of the legislative background to antipoverty efforts in the post-World War II age of prosperity:

During the 1940s and 1950s relatively little attention was focused on the poor. Although some improvements were made in the social security, unemployment insurance and public assistance programs, it was not until the 1960s that the conscience of the American people, under the leadership of Presidents Kennedy and Johnson, was awakened to the needs of the disadvantaged. The paradox of poverty amidst a nation of plenty became a major social and political issue.

While the vast majority of Americans was sharing in the gains of a prospering economy, about 22 percent of the population was poor in 1959. President Kennedy took up the cause of the forgotten poor and planned an intensified attack on poverty that President Johnson put into effect. Congress expressed the nation's commitment in 1964: "It is the policy of the United States to eliminate the paradox of poverty in the midst of plenty in this nation" (House Committee on Education and Labor 1964). To carry out this commitment, far-reaching, wide-ranging social legislation was enacted over the next four years. The Economic Opportunity Act, the Elementary and Secondary Education Act, Medicare and Medicaid, Social Security amendments, the Civil Rights Act, and the Rent Supplement Program are a few of the many laws that were enacted to attack poverty on many fronts. Federal funds assisting the poor increased from $9.9 billion in 1960 to $24.6 billion in 1968. The combination of innovative and imaginative programs backed by federal resources and enlightened economic, fiscal, and monetary policies that stimulated economic growth, providing record levels of employment, reduced the number of persons living in poverty from 39 million in 1959 to 24 million in 1969. As a result of substantial social security benefit increases in 1965 and 1967, the incomes of about one and a half million persons were raised above the poverty line. Job training, rehabilitation, and health and educational programs made it possible for millions of others to participate in a sustained, prospering economy.

The level and volatility of criticism against the war on poverty in the 1970s has become so extensive that it is hard to recollect that the start of the 1960s was a period of deep concern about poverty, especially the impoverishment of black people (cf. Moynihan 1968). The profusion of programs that came forth during this period may not have led to the eradication of poverty, but it did make possible the rise of black economic possibilities that permitted that huge section of the American population to take a leading part in the economic expansion that was so notable a feature of the country during the decade (cf. Silberman 1964; Sundquist 1969). As Moynihan wryly observes: "Whatever else is said about us, it makes social statistics look good." He goes on to add:

Between 1960 and 1969 the number of nonwhite craftsmen and operatives, the basic blue-collar occupations which make up about one third of the work force, increased 40 percent, whereas the number of whites in such jobs rose only 7 percent. The real earnings of nonwhite men averaged a 55 percent gain during this period, double the increase for whites. In 1968 an event of significance occurred. The median income of young husband-wife black families outside of the South reached parity with those of white families. In 1969 even more impressive gains occurred. Outside the South, the median earnings of husband-wife Negro families headed by a male twenty-five to thirty-four years of age were 91 percent of the pay of their white counterparts, while for similar families with a head age fourteen to twenty-four years, the midpoint of black income reached 107 percent that of whites. This was surely the first time in the history of the United States that a broadly defined category of blacks had higher incomes than did their white equivalents [Moynihan 1969].

As the decade wore on, the economic boom wore out. Only a portion of the black community was able to participate in the national growth. Following these changes, the ghettos became ablaze and the cities further impoverished; the university campuses were disrupted by a cycle of administrative blunders, faculty indifference, and student opposition. Under such circumstances, President Johnson decided against seeking another term in office. When the Democratic party held its 1968 convention in Chicago, protestors were attacked by trained riot police. The war on poverty was attenuated by the drain of other priorities: the war in Vietnam, growing military expenditures, and a general unwillingness to redistribute and reorient economic resources. Yet even more central to the mortification of the war on poverty was the breakdown of a national consensus to do away with poverty in the United States. The war on poverty embodied more than a collection of congressional actions. In the war on poverty were people in community action, action-oriented towards helping the disadvantaged and nourished by hope and optimism (Pilisuk and Pilisuk 1973:7-8).

Federal antipoverty programs were originally conceived of to deal with issues of adequate housing, training for meaningful jobs, maintaining an adequate income, and supplying food to the needy. When efforts to meet these needs began to conflict with entrenched urban political interests, support for antipoverty efforts began eroding. An apolitical view of the situation of the poverty-stricken meant that the structural causes could not be attacked. When a localized group began attaining power it would surely collide with an entrenched power determined to achieve obstruction or co-optation of the local group. Minority group members can be trained to occupy skilled labor occupations. Yet unless other new job opportunities are created for white workers there will only have been replacement, not upward mobility. The white worker will then become the opponent of the newly-trained minority-group member. This fact will further ameliorate labor consensus on poverty issues. Minority communities, appreciating this reality, resist broad programs presented to them as *fait accompli* by well-intentioned reformers. Thus, poverty-stricken groups must decide either to actively participate in the formulation and modification of programs affecting their lives, or to become the victims of misdirected albeit well-meaning reformers (cf. James 1972).

The structure of power was threatened by far more than community-action programs and organized groups of poor people. Social science professions and associated paraprofessionals were also considered threats. These social scientists performed as intermediaries between the powerful and the powerless. In this role of delivering services to the poor, the social scientists could not present themselves as neutral observers calling on the economic and power resources of the American power structure. Thus, the participation of social scientists in the community life of the poor meant that their actions were interpreted as a threat by the government sponsors and the larger public (Pilisuk and Pilisuk 1973:10-12).

Another aspect of community participation is the demand that the poor participate in focusing their own programs. This demand demonstrated that the program was readily subject to the influence of established sources of power. When community action became widespread, it provoked local interests wherever action programs operated. The war on poverty tapped public funds and used public institutions to devote significant attention to local problems. The local interests, therefore, had to be heeded (or at least not disregarded), and in this case the local interests were represented by city mayors. The local city officials discovered that they had powerful allies in the federal government to whom they could turn. This alliance focused pressure on the heart of the war on poverty: the Office of Economic Opportunity. For example, after a mayor's conference the instrument of pressure on the OEO was the Bureau of the Budget: "The Budget Bureau, the fiscal arm of the White House, has told the Office of Economic Opportunity that it would prefer less emphasis on policy-making by the poor in planning community projects" (cf. Rainwater and Yancey 1967).

The federal government and most local governments would permit some flexibility in programs in terms of cash-transfer programs and power given to the poor—so long as these programs remained localized in such areas as the deep South. However, these programs soon spread to the urbanized North. When this suffusion took place, to the presumed detriment of whites and their elected officials, consensus evaporated. When such grass-roots agreement disappeared, the utility of the social science to these programs was eliminated (Marris and Rein 1973:218-19). OEO's goal was the construction of an interest group consisting of poor people and the supporters of the poor. This constituency would become strong enough to make the antipoverty programs politically self-sustaining. If the community-action programs were successfully co-opted by local power structures, contemporary institutions would be the pathway of funds to the poor. This essentially meant that the war on poverty would become devoted to the sustenance of these local governments and institutions. The militancy of many of the poor in urban ghettos was running high enough to avoid such a fate. However, if only the poor supported a program, they would not be able to constitute a politically viable force. Faced with this dilemma, OEO attempted to insist that the poor have very significant representation in community-action programs. At the same time that OEO applied pressure on the local city governments to share their power with these community-action programs. OEO sometimes incorrectly estimated this compromise on such occasions as when one of its funded projects conflicted with a government operation in the same area. These situations could not be avoided and conflict was necessary to clarify OEO-city hall jurisdictional boundaries. The development of the Model Cities program verifies that the question of community participation could not be side-stepped through the alteration of guidelines, laws, and administrative directives. The programs hinged on a compromise that would balance community participation with local city government (Marris and Rein 1973:271).

Lack of a constituency was not the central problem facing advocates of community-action programs. Instead, the barrier was that too many disparate groups with contravening goals competed for limited available resources. This stand-off between competing factions led to frustration that eroded community-action consensus. Despite these shortcomings, some lasting accomplishments were attained by the war on poverty. Articulate pressure groups formed in isolated instances. Legal programs have proved to be remarkably successful in servicing the needs of the poor. Principles of social evaluation and planning are now commonly-accepted traits of governmental social-program construction. Yet, lacking any broad-based constituency or any ties to a wider consensus, the antipoverty program was unable to produce a constituency that could generate its own political defense and support.

The war on poverty was denied adequate resources for its mission because there was fear of overcommitting the president on a politically uncertain issue. By not clearly defining community participation, the programs' supporters became alienated, confirming initial suspicions about the effectiveness of the program. Yet the concept of community action tapped dimensions that transcended the search for diluted idealism in combination with political expedience. The war on poverty directly addressed the problems of making democracy work in American society. By attempting to modify, or at most, reform structural shortcomings of representative government, the community-action program sought to alleviate the deprivation of millions of Americans. Thus the war on poverty faced "an issue more profound even than poverty—the viability of democracy itself" (Marris and Rein 1973, pp. 271-72).

Few social scientists involved in the war on poverty were properly able to assess the extent to which they were not so much innovating programs as responding to a national crisis in race relations that had to be met more candidly than it had been during the Eisenhower administration in the 1950s. Indeed, one early critic, Saul Alinsky, saw the entire war on poverty as an effort employed "to suffocate militant independent leadership and action organizations which have been arising to arm the poor with their share of power" (Alinsky 1968:173). If such a judgment is tinged with more than a fair share of hyperbole, it is a fact that even more careful and less partisan observers have noted that the war on poverty programs became vulnerable precisely when they stretched beyond the limits of established political lines of authority. Ultimately, protest depended on government tolerance, not to mention federal funding (Marris and Rein 1973:292-93). Under such circumstances, the war on poverty had severely circumscribed limits that the social scientists could barely explain, much less move beyond.

In retrospect, it becomes apparent that the war on poverty was specifically an attempt by the Democratic party to maintain and increase its black urban voting base. This further implies that community-action programs were to be designed to keep both money and power out of the hands of state legislatures controlled by the Republican party, placing money and power rather into the hands of urban ethnic white and black groups. The additional element was the circumventing of those city governments that could not be trusted to make sure that benefits actually reached ghetto voters. Thus, the war on poverty was a delicate balancing act for maintaining traditional constituencies, but it was also certain to pick up new constituencies (Piven and Cloward 1971:262-63). Thus, the circumstances that compelled the Democratic party's national leadership to emphasize the needs of the black community coincided precisely with the researches being conducted by the social scientists on black communities indicating that in the past blacks had been denied both economic and political equity.

The social science critics of the war on poverty, at this writing, probably outnumber its adherents. In part, this is a consequence of an intense polarization over the role of community-action programs. Those on the Left, such as Clark and Hopkins (1970:245-46), viewed such programming as serving to quell any sense of civil outrage among the poor, while those on the Right, such as Banfield (1970:128-31), saw any such federally-sponsored programs as a dangerous continuance to exacerbate civil strife among social classes. The most recent point of view, and perhaps the most sophisticated in retrospect, is that of Greenstone and Peterson (1973:305-15), who view the war on poverty as basically a structure that exploited pluralistic bargaining norms on behalf of black interests. They hold this view to be thoroughly consistent with the primacy of the racial, rather than the class, problem in the United States, and no less consistent with the American approach to cultural diversity:

> For blacks, this policy has the advantage, unlike demands for social integration, that it does not directly attack the validity of other minority cultures or even, except indirectly, the dominant largely white Protestant culture of the whole society. Moreover, this policy would have the blacks rely more on their own gradually increasing resources rather than on the wisdom, generosity and benevolence of white American cities. Although racial oppression and inequality often seem virtually intractable, the policy most likely to eradicate it must follow the path of collective self-development that other ethnic groups utilized to establish themselves in a society that was at once white Protestant in its dominant cultural orientation, capitalist in its economic values, and only partially egalitarian in its political aspirations. Community control, for all its faults, can facilitate the forward thrust of black power in the American regime.

By the late 1960s, when the national consensus on the war on poverty had badly deteriorated and reached a near-breakdown level, the social scientists themselves lost their unified response to what the war on poverty could do for the poor and the minorities. While those most closely associated with the federal programs remained dedicated to its continuation in one form or another, voices of opposition began to multiply within the social sciences. Silberman (1968:95-96) pointed out that OEO, through its insistence that community-action agencies be broadly based, had the actual result of reducing either local initiatives or innovation. Alinsky (1968:177) viewed the war on poverty as the latest phase of a welfare industry, aiding profit-making firms rather than the poor. He felt, and not without considerable support from black activists, that the war on poverty had swollen bureaucracies, increased the number of professional consultants and coordinators, and generally drained off the lion's share of funds targeted for the poor and the minorities: "Their voracious appetite insures that only discarded droppings will drip down to the poor. . . . Poverty is a blue chip investment." That is, it may have been the displacement of the Johnson-Democratic era with the Nixon-Republican era that brought to an abrupt halt the war on poverty. First through agency reorganization, next through staff reductions, and finally through fiscal cutbacks, the war on poverty was wound down, almost as rapidly as it had been initially mounted.

It is a curious fact that the social scientists were able to lend their support to the war on poverty at the appropriate time and to lend the weight of criticism when that seemed called for (cf. Rossi 1973). This illustrates a central fact for all social science in relation to public policy in the United States: when a genuine, broad-based consensus exists, the social scientists perform major legitimizing and rationalizing services, but when a dissensus is present, the social scientists can only serve to reflect that situation in the very polarities of their own professional writings and researches.

THE NEGATIVE INCOME TAX

Discussions of negative income taxation have been an ongoing feature in the economic community for some time. The subject was informally discussed as early as the 1940s by economists Walter Heller and William Vickery, the latter of whom was at the time a member of the Treasury Department's Division of Tax Research. The idea of negative income was first touched upon in a 1946 article in the *American Economic Review* (Stigler 1946:365). But it was then an idea whose time had not yet come. Chicago economist Milton Friedman originated a negative income tax plan in a series of lectures at Wabash College in 1956. His plan was formally introduced in his book *Capitalism and Freedom* (1962). Friedman viewed the negative income tax proposal as an alternative to ongoing welfare programs. The benefits of the plan, according to Friedman, would include that a) it would make the cost to society explicit; b) it would operate outside the market; and c) although reducing individual incentive, it would not eliminate incentive entirely (Friedman 1962:192).

Robert J. Lampman, an economist at the University of Wisconsin and a member of the staff of its Institute for Research on Poverty, developed an alternative negative income tax approach. Lampman saw his negative tax plan as a supplement rather than a substitute for existing welfare programs. He recommended the use of an income-gap measurement as a base for the negative tax. This was in opposition to the Friedman plan, which advocated basing a system on unused exemptions and other deductions. Other variations of the negative income tax (NIT) have been advanced by Tobin (1965) and Marmor (1971), among other social scientists (cf. Green 1967; Meyer 1970; and Zeckhauser 1971).

A guaranteed annual income, revolving around some form of NIT, was a central feature in a set of recommendations formulated by the President's Commission on Income Maintenance Programs (Heineman Commission). This commission was formed in Johnson's administration but concluded its work during the first year of the Nixon administration (President's Commission 1969:197). At that time, under a grant from OEO, the Institute for Research on Poverty (IRP) at the University of Wisconsin at Madison began a study on the NIT. Commencing in 1968 the Graduated Work Incentive Experiment (GWIN) aimed at determining the labor-supply response to a range of alternative simple income plans. By the winter of 1969 HEW enlisted IRP's assistance in undertaking a large-scale program of experimentation in income maintenance, an area in which the Institute already had centered its resources (cf. McNown 1973; Etzioni 1969).

In association with Mathematica of Princeton, New Jersey, the IRP developed a research agenda. The research, under the direction of Harold Watts, took a multidisciplinary thrust, experimenting with 1,200 families in Trenton, Paterson, Passaic, and Jersey City, New Jersey, and in Scranton, Pennsylvania. The program, also supported by OEO, investigated graduated work incentives on the lives of the welfare families under study (cf. Orr et al. 1971).

With lead-in money provided by the Ford Foundation, the IRP generated comparative data with a rural contrast to the New Jersey studies. This project was absorbed by OEO and established larger programs in 1969, studying 825 families in Iowa and North Carolina over a three-year period. Besides permitting a rural-urban contrast, this study also allowed a Northern-Southern comparison. Taking an interdisciplinary approach, the study broached the fields of economics, agricultural economics, sociology, political science, law, and social work. It examined and measured the effect of work on incentives, changes in expenditure patterns, alternations in family structure, adult education, health, attitudes, and social and political activities (Bawden 1970).

To complement these two studies the OEO added two more experimental programs to evaluate NIT and GWIN proposals. One area selected was Gary, Indiana, which added black, female-headed families. Day-care treatments were also added to the experimental design (Kelley and Singer 1971). The other study viewed the contrast of the earlier studies with the Western United States by studying Seattle, Washington. The Gary study made use of the resources of the Urban Institute and Indiana University. The Seattle study worked through Stanford University and Stanford Research Institute (Kurz and Spiegelman 1971).

Social scientists and economists have done a considerable amount of background, supportive, and evaluative work of NIT and GWIN. For example, Orcutt and Orcutt (1969) made an in-depth evaluation of the problems of social experimentation in the area of income maintenance. Cavala and Wiladavsky (1970) studied the political feasibility of income maintenance, focusing on congressional resistance and means of overcoming such resistance (1970). Social scientists have also played a major role in the establishing of the family assistance plan (FAP), and sociologist Daniel Moynihan is given major credit for selling FAP to the Nixon administration (cf. Moynihan 1972). Social scientists gave testimony on FAP and even earlier ground-laying inquiries (see U.S. Congress, Joint Economic Committee, 1968, 1973; U.S. Senate Committee on Finance, 1972).

The studies discussed above, although not nearly completed or analyzed, played a significant part in the discussions on family assistance and maintenance. For example, the early results of the New Jersey study were "displayed prominently as part of the early presentation of the family assistance plan to Congress" (Watts 1969:71). Harold Watts, the director of the New Jersey program commented that the premature exposure of GWIN and NIT programs may have been inimical to the implementation of the plan: "It is at least questionable whether preliminary results at such an early stage of the experiment should have been drawn off and used as a part of a major policy debate. One cannot expect the process of public policy formation to wait upon the completion of scientific studies" (Watts 1969:71).

The idea of income redistribution remains firm on the social science agenda, despite the severe loss of George McGovern in the 1972 presidential elections. Herbert Gans (1974, p. 62) claims that despite the setbacks "it will reappear in future presidential campaigns and may some day become the law of the land." Increasingly, sociologists have joined economists in proposing some variant of the negative income tax on the supposition that the social effects of income redistribution, in providing a cushion against total immersion, would be greater than its economic effects, since redistribution would still leave the overall ratios of affluent to poor and of male to female household heads very much intact (cf. Greenberg and Kosters 1970; DaVanzo 1972; Elesh 1973; Katz 1973).

Gans summary indicates that middle-income group support for income redistribution will grow once middle-income groups realize that it will mean additional money in their pockets. Nevertheless, the traditional hostility to welfare and the equal emphasis on work as a fundamental answer to poverty make the negative tax at best a marginal factor in new policies aimed at alleviating poverty:

As long as most Americans believe that income should be derived from work and as long as they favor policies which put people to work rather than on the dole, the poor are most likely to obtain higher incomes through programs for full employment and deliberate job creation. Such programs must therefore be part of the legislative package when the time comes for America to adopt income redistribution. From a longer perspective that legislative package is still only a first step, for eventually America must also consider the redistribution of wealth. Unequal income rests on a foundation of unequal wealth, and someday that foundation must be dismantled by such policies as the breakup of old fortunes, the levying of stricter inheritance taxes, the sharing of unredistributed corporate wealth and the dispersion of stock ownership. If income redistribution ever becomes politically feasible, the need for greater sharing of the wealth will soon be apparent, and if Americans feel that wealth which is not derived from work does not deserve the same protection as income which is derived from work, policies for redistributing wealth may gain a more widespread political acceptance than policies for redistributing income [Gans 1974, p. 69).

Thus far, liberal social scientists have convinced only liberal politicians. The task of reshaping the attitudes of the conservative politicians and the middle classes remains a future step in the pursuit of social equity by social scientists. And beyond that, the goal of positively effecting the conditions of the working classes and the welfare masses remains an elusive, unfulfilled goal.

REFERENCES

Alinsky, Saul D.
1968   "The War on Poverty—Political Pornography" pp. 171-80 in C. Waxman (ed.) Poverty: *Power and Politics*. New York: Grossett and Dunlap.
Baldwin, Hanson
1948   "Segregation in the Army: General Bradley's View is Held to Put Morale Above Compulsory Change" New York *Times* (August 8, 1951).
Banfield, Edward C.
1970   *The Unheavenly City*. Boston: Little, Brown.
Bawden, Lee
1970   "Income maintenance and the rural poor: An experimental approach." *American Journal of Agricultural Economics* 52:438-41.
Berger, Monroe
1957   "Desegregation, Law and Social Science" *Commentary* (May).
Beyer, Gregg
1974   "Revenue Sharing and the New Federalism" *Society* 11 (2):58-61.
Bogart, Leo (ed.)
1969   *Social Research and the Desegregation of the U.S. Army* (including two original 1951 field reports). Chicago: Markham.
Broom, Leonard and Norval Glenn
1965   *Transformation of the Negro American*. New York: Harper & Row.
Cahn, Edmond
1955   "Jurisprudence" *New York University Law Review*. 30.
Cavala, William and Aaron Wildavsky
1970   "The political feasibility of income by right." *Public Policy* 18:321-54.
Clark, Kenneth B.
1955   *Prejudice and Your Child*. Boston: Beacon Press.
Clark, Kenneth and Yale Kamisar
1969   *Argument: The Oral Argument Before the Supreme Court in Brown v. Board of Education of Topeka 1952-1955*. New York: Chelsea House Publishers.
Clark, Kenneth and Jeannette Hopkins
1970   *A Relevant War Against Poverty*. New York: Harper & Row.

Cohen, Wilbur J.
1970   "Government Policy and the Poor: Past, Present and Future."
        Journal of Social Issues, (March 26:1-10).
Coleman, James S.
1969   "Race Relations and Social Change"—Pp. 274-341 in Irwin Katz
        and Patricia Gurin (eds.). *Race Relations and the Social Sciences*,
        New York: Basic Books.
Curtis, Mary Ellen
1973   "Social Science and the Law: An Analysis of the School
        Segregation Decisions of The Supreme Court"—unpublished
        manuscript, Department of History. Rutgers University.
Delfiume, Richard M.
1969   *Desegregation of the U.S. Armed Forces; Fighting on Two Fronts,
        1939-1953.* Columbia: University of Missouri Press.
Da Vanzo, Julie
1972   *An analytical framework for studying the potential effects of an
        income maintenance program on U.S. interregional migration.* (R-
        1081-EDA). Santa Monica: Rand Corporation.
Elesh, David
1973   "Poverty theories and income maintenance: Validity and policy
        relevance." *Social Science Quarterly* 54:359-73.
Etzioni, Amitai
1969   "Insuring the poor." *New Leader* 52 (March 3:10-11).
Freidman, Milton
1962   *Capitalism and Freedom.* Chicago: University of Chicago Press.
Gans, Herbert
1974   "More equality: Income and taxes." *Society* 11 (2):62-69.
Garfinkel, Herbert
1959   "Social Science Evidence and the School Segregation Cases."
        Journal of Politics 21, No. 1.
Glazer, Myron
1972   *The Research Adventure: Promise and Problems of Field Work.*
        New York: Random House.
Glick, Henry Robert
1971   *Supreme Courts in State Politics: An Investigation of the Judicial
        Role.* New York: Basic Books.
Green, Christopher
1967   *Negative Taxes and the Poverty Problem.* Washington: Brookings
        Institution.
Greenberg, David and Marvin Kosters
1970   *Income guarantees and the working poor: The effect of income
        maintenance programs on the hours of work of male family heads*
        (R-579-OEO). Santa Monica: Rand Corporation.
Greenberg, Jack and Herbert Hill
1957   A Citizen's Guide to Desegregation. Cited in Monroe Berger,
        "Desegregation, Law and Social Science." *Commentary* (May).

Greenstone, J. David and Paul Peterson
  1973   *Race and Authority in Urban Politics: Community Participation and the War on Poverty.* New York: Russell Sage Foundation.
James, Dorothy D.
  1972   *Poverty, Politics and Change.* Englewood Cliffs: Prentice-Hall.
Jencks, Christopher
  1972   "Busing—The Supreme Court Goes North." The New York *Times Magazine* (November 19, 1972).
Katz, Arnold
  1973   "Income maintenance experiments: Progress toward a new American national policy." *Social and Economic Administration*, 7:126-35.
Kelley, Terrence and Leslie Singer
  1971   "The Seattle experiment: The Combined effect of income maintenance and manpower investments." *American Economic Review* 61:22-29.
Kurz, Mordecai and R. G. Speigelman
  1971   "The Seattle experiment: The Combined effect of income maintenance and manpower investments." *American Economic Review* 61:22-29.
LaFarge, John
  1953   "Judgment on Racial Segregation." *America.* 90 (December 12, 1953).
Marris, Peter and Martin Rein
  1973   *Dilemmas of Social Reform.* Chicago: Aldine.
Marmor, Theodore (ed.)
  1971   *Poverty Policy: A Compendium of Cash Transfer Proposals.* Chicago: Aldine.
Mc Nown, Robert
  1973   "The story of the Family Assistance Plan." *Current History* 65 (August):57ff.
Meyer, Charles
  1970   "A base for the negative income tax." *Social Science Quarterly* 51:263-74.
Moynihan, Daniel P. (ed.)
  1968   *On Understanding Poverty.* New York: Basic Books.
Moynihan, Daniel P.
  1969   *Maximum Feasible Misunderstanding.* New York: Macmillan.
Moynihan, Daniel P.
  1972   *The Politics of a Guaranteed Income.* New York: Random House.
Orcutt, Guy and Alice Orcutt
  1969   "Incentive and disincentive experimentation for income maintenance and policy purposes." *American Economic Review* 58:754-72.
Orr, Larr et al. (eds.)
  1971   *Income Maintenance: Interdisciplinary Approaches to Research.* Chicago: Markham.

Pasamanick, Benjamin and Hilda Knobloch
    1958   "The Contribution of Some Organic Factors to School
            Retardation in Negro Children." *Journal of Negro Education* 27
            (1):4-9.
Pilisuk, Marc and Phyllis Pilisuk (eds.)
    1973   *How We Lost the War on Poverty.* New Brunswick: Transaction.
Piven, Frances Fox and Richard Cloward
    1971   *Regulating the Poor; The Functions of Public Welfare.* New York:
            Pantheon.
President's Commission on
  Income Maintenance
    1969   *Poverty Amid Plenty: The American Paradox.* Washington.
Rainwater, Lee and William L. Yancey
    1967   *The Moynihan Report and the Politics of Controversy.*
            Cambridge, Massachusetts: M.I.T. Press.
Rossi, Peter (ed.)
    1973   *Evaluating Social Programs.* New York: Seminar Press.
Ribicoff, Abraham
    1973   "He left at half time." *New Republic* 168 (February 17):22-26.
Schmidhauser, John R. and Larry L. Berg
    1972   *The Supreme Court and Congress: Conflict and Interaction 1945-
            1968.* New York: The Free Press/Macmillan.
Senate, Committee on Finance
    1972   *Income maintenance experiments* Submitted by the Department
            of Health, Education and Welfare (Committee Print).
Silberman, Charles E.
    1964   *Crisis in Black and White.* New York: Random House.
    1968   "The Mixed-up War on Poverty." Pp. 81-100 in Chaim Waxman
            (ed.) *Poverty: Power and Politics.* New York: Grossett and
            Dunlap.
Stigler, George
    1946   "The economics of minimum wage legislation." *American
            Economic Review* 36:287-91.
Stillman, Richard J. II
    1968   *Integration of the Negro in the U.S. Armed Forces.* New York:
            Praeger.
Sundquist, James (ed.)
    1969   *On Fighting Poverty.* New York: Basic Books.
Sutherland, Arthur E.
    1954   "The Supreme Court and the Public School." *Harvard
            Educational Review* 24:71-85.
Thurmond, Strom
    1956   "The Constitution and the Supreme Court" Vital Speeches. 22
            (January 15, 1956).
Tobin, James
    1965   "Improving the economic status of the Negro." *Daedalus* 94:889-
            95.

U.S. Congress, House Committee
  on Education and Labor
    1964   *Hearings on the Economic Opportunity Act 1964, 88th Congress,*
              2nd Session: 207-12, 301-39.
United States Congress,
  Joint Economic Committee
    1968   Subcommittee on Fiscal Policy "Hearings on income maintenance
              programs" June 11-27.
    1973   "Studies in public welfare". *Issues in welfare administration;
              implications of the income maintenance experiments.*
Watts, Harold
    1969   "Graduated work incentives: An experiment in negative taxation."
              American Economic Review 58:463-72.
Zeckhauser, Richard
    1971   "Optimal mechanisms for income transfer." *American Economic
              Review* 61:324-34.

CHAPTER

8

CONFLICT AND
CONSENSUS BETWEEN
SOCIAL SCIENTISTS
AND POLICY MAKERS

The last area of our discussion on social science and public policy in the United States is itself involved in the sociology of political mobilization—that is, in the ways that politicians, in turn, evaluate and assess social scientists, especially the academic community most intimately involved in the affairs of the political domain. The problem is to locate either the mutuality or the incompatability of interests that are involved between the two sectors.

PROBLEMS AND PROSPECTS IN THE INTERACTION BETWEEN SOCIAL SCIENTISTS AND FEDERAL ADMINISTRATORS

To construct a satisfactory framework we should focus on problem areas that are decisive for both groups. We will first discuss the social scientists' perception of the interaction and then present the problem areas perceived by political men. Apart from the interaction itself, a shadowy area of consequences on the network of proposals and responses follows from the relationship between the two contracting parties. For social scientists and politicians not only interact with one another, but the professional ideologies they arrive at and the norms they establish also guide present and future interactions as well.

One of the most crucial, and at the same time one of the most difficult, aspects of the relationship of social scientists to politicians to be discussed is concerned with determining at what point normative behavior leaves off and conflictual behavior starts. Only with the latter sort of interaction does a true problem-solving situation exist. For example, the norm of secrecy that guides bureaucratic behavior contrasts markedly with the norm of publicity governing most forms of academic behavior. There is little question that this normative

147

distinction leads to a considerable amount of exacerbated sentiment. Yet the differences at this level between the two groups seem intrinsic to the nature of sovereignty and to the nature of science. Such differences can hardly be "ironed out" or "smoothed over" simply because we would have a nicer world if they were. Thus, at best, an explication of the issues can admit an intellectual and ideological climate in which differences can be appreciated—and in this way can come to be lived with. This must be stated explicitly: those who expect a set of recommendations for the governance of relations between social scientists and politicians should be dissuaded from the advisability of such an approach, lest they find themselves manufacturing perfect doctrinal formulas and juridical restraints that prove far worse than the initial problem being considered.

PROBLEM AREAS PERCEIVED
BY SOCIAL SCIENTISTS

The first and perhaps most immediate experience that social scientists have with politicians or their counterparts on various federal granting agencies relates to the financial structure of contracts and grants. At this point, the difference between contracts and grants should be explained. For operational definitions, we can speak of contracts as those agreements made with social scientists that originate in a federal bureaucracy (most research on Thailand and Southeast Asia or on Pax Americana is contract work); we can speak of grants as those projects that are initiated by the social scientists. Nonetheless, the distinction between contracts and grants should not be drawn too sharply, since, in fact, if not in law, many contracts do originate with social scientists. Such agreements may be structured broadly to give the researcher a vast range of freedom, or they may be narrowly conceived to get a project tailored to an agency's "needs." The entrepreneurial spirit of social scientists, particularly those working in nonacademic research centers, makes them ingeniously adept at discovering what a government administrator is ready to pay for. Thus, while a de jure distinction between contracts and grants is useful, it is limited on de facto grounds by the inability to track down the originator of a proposal, as well as the party that really shapes the final project.

Perhaps more important than the formal distinction between contracts and grants are the disproportionate funds made available by various federal agencies for social scientific purposes. In fiscal year 1967 DOD budgeted 21.7 percent of its research funds for the social sciences. DOS budgeted only 1.6 percent of its funds for the social sciences—and most of this was in the separately administered AID. This disparity indicates that the "modern" DOD is far readier to make use of social science results than is the "traditional" DOS. A related complaint is that most contracts issued, in contrast to grants awarded, by agencies, such as the HEW or NIH, allocate little money for free-floating research. Funds are targeted so directly and budgeted so carefully that, with the exception of the overhead portion, which is controlled by administrators rather than by scholars, little elasticity is permitted for work that may be allied to but not directly connected with the specific purpose of the contract itself. This contrasts markedly with contracts made with many physical scientists and even with researchers in the field of mental health, who are often able to set aside a portion of their funds for innovative purposes. Even so-called "kept" organizations, such as IDA (Institute of Defense Analyses), SDC (System Development Corporation), or RAND, enjoy more latitude in developing their work programs than the usual "f- university researchers.

Related to this matter of financial reward for "hardware" and "high- research is the funding available for social science research as a whole. Social scientists often claim that the funding structure is irrational. Government funds are available in large sums for big-team research, but little spillover is available for individual scholarly efforts. The government reinforces big-team research by encouraging large-scale grants administered by agencies and institutes and by its stubborn unwillingness to contribute to individual scholarly enterprise. The assumption is made that large-scale ideas can be executed only by large-scale spending—a fallacy in logic, if not in plain fact. Large-scale grants are also made because they minimize bureaucratic opposition within the government and eliminate specific responsibility for research failures. But at the same time, this approach contributes to the dilemma of the scholar who is concerned with research at modest "retail" levels that may be far more limited than the grant proposal itself indicates. The present contract structure encourages a degree of entrepreneurial hypocrisy that is often alien to the spirit of the individual researcher and costly to the purchaser of ideas and plans. And while efforts by individual agencies—notably, by the NSF—have moved counter to this bureaucratic trend, the bulk of funds continues to be made available without much regard for the persons actually engaged in the researches.

A question arising with greater frequency now that many social scientists are doing federally-sponsored research concerns the relationship between heuristic and valuative aspects of work. Put plainly, should the social scientist not only supply an operational framework of information but also assist in the creation of a viable ideological framework? Does he have the right to discuss, examine, and prescribe the goals of social research for social science? Whether social scientists in government service ever raise such issues is less important than the fact that some might refuse any connection with the federal bureaucracy for this reason. Many social scientists, especially those working on foreign area research, bitterly complain that government policy makers envision social science to be limited to heuristics, to supplying operational code books and facts about our own and other societies, and that the social scientist is supposed to perform maintenance services for military missions. Social scientists, however, also consider their work in terms of its normative function, in terms of the principles and goals of foreign and domestic policy. Given their small tolerance for error, policy makers cannot absorb mistaken evaluations. This inhibits the social scientist's long-range evaluations and renders empiricism the common denominator of investigation. Factual presentations become not only "value free" but "trouble free."

This is not so much indicative of a choice between pure and applied social science research as a consequence of differing perspectives on the character of application. Social scientists working for the political establishment realize that applied research is clearly here to stay. They are the first to announce that it is probably the most novel element in American—in contrast to European—social science. But federal bureaucrats operate with a concept of application that often removes theoretical considerations from research. Designing the future out of present-day hard facts, rather than analyzing types of action and interests and their relations in the present, comes to stand for a limited administrative utopianism and creates the illusion that demands for theory and candid ideological commitment have been met.

The social world is constructed like a behavioral field, the dynamics and manipulation of which are reserved for policy makers, upon which they design futures. But social scientists are aware that "interests" and their representative values are contending for influence on that field and that social planning is often a matter of choosing among these values for the sake of political goals. Thus, tension arises between social scientists, who consider their work set in highly political terms, and federal bureaucrats, who prefer to consider the work of the social scientists in nonpolitical terms. Indeed, federal administrators particularly go out of their way to depoliticize the results of potentially volatile social research so as to render it a better legitimizing device for their own bureaucratic activities. Social scientists come to suspect that their work is weighed for efficiency and applicability to an immediate and limited situation. The ability of the social system to confront large-scale and long-standing problems is left out of reckoning.

Federal bureaucrats measure the rewards of social science involvement in the government in terms of payoffs generated. These are conceived to be the result of "big-team" research involving heavy funding (like the Model Cities Program). Moreover, the high status of individuals is appreciated when they are at the center rather than the periphery of policy performance, having an opportunity to influence policy at high levels, secure valuable information, and give prestige to projects in which they participate. (And, it might be added, many social scientists who contract research from the government seek just such power rewards.)

Even those social scientists most deeply involved with the government—as employees rather than as marginal consultants—express profound reservations about the reward system. First, as we have noted, social scientists operate under various degrees of secrecy that stifle their urge toward publicity for the work they do. Recognition goes instead to those for whom they work. Second, social scientists must share responsibility for policy mistakes. Thus, they may be targeted for public criticism under difficult conditions more frequently than praised when they perform their duties well. Finally, those social scientists closest to policy agencies are most subject to congressional inquiry and to forms of harassment and investigation unlike anything that may befall strictly academic men.

The government-employed social scientist runs risks to which his colleagues at universities are not subject. He often contends that these risks are not properly understood by academics or rewarded by policy makers (salary scales, for example, are adequate in federal work but not noticeably higher than academic salaries). Marginal financial payoffs resulting from publication are often denied the federally-sponsored social scientists. And publication is a sensitive area for other reasons, as discussed above. Social scientists' fears concerning their removal from channels of professional respectability and visibility seem to increase proportionately to their distance from the academy. Few of those in federal work receive recognition from their own professional societies, and few gain influential positions within those professional establishments. Because of the marginality produced by federal work, scholars willing to be funded through government agencies or even to accept consultantships will reject primary association with a federal administration. For this reason the list of high-quality social scientists who choose to remain in the government as professional civil-servants remains low.

While outsiders may accuse federally-sponsored social scientists of "selling out," the latter defend themselves by pointing out that they make sacrifices for the sake of positively influencing social change. This self-defense, however, is often received skeptically by their colleagues in the academic arena (as well as by their would-be supporters in the federal bureaucracy), who regard such hypersensitive moralism with suspicion. The upshot of this matter of "rewards" is, then, that status derived from proximity to sources of power is offset by isolation from the actual wielders of power—academic no less than political.

PROBLEM AREAS PERCEIVED
BY POLITICIANS

Social scientists' complaints about their difficulties with government-sponsored research have received more attention than administrative complaints against social scientists simply because social scientists tend to be more articulate in examining their feelings and in registering their complaints about the work they do. Also, the relationship of the social scientist to the bureaucrat has a greater import for the social scientist than for the bureaucrat. It is small wonder that government complaints about social scientists have been poorly understood.

Federal agencies and their bureaucratic leaderships remain skeptical about the necessity for employing basic social science data in their own formulations. Among traditionally-appointed officials the local lawyer or party worker is the key means for transmitting information upwards. For many sectors of the military, expertise comes mainly from military personnel performing military functions and does not require outside social science validation. As we witnessed in the military response to the Department of Defense "Whiz Kids," outside efforts may be considered intrusions. High military brass (as well as a number of politicians) "sounded off" hotly against DOD and echoed in their critiques a traditional posture that pits military intuition and empirical proximity to the real world against mathematical techniques and "ivory tower" orientations.

When social scientists attempt to combat these doubts and suspicions by preparing memoranda and documents that prove the efficacy of social science for direct political and military use, they may do more to reinforce negative sentiments than to overcome them. When the academy responds that way to the polity (as it did in its recommendations to the Defense Science Board), it underwrites its own lack of autonomy, if not its own ineptitude. It cannot prove its worth by moral declarations and public offerings to bureaucratic agencies. The total service orientation of social research, in contrast to the independent "feudal" academic orientation, is one that breeds contempt for the performer of such services and a lack of faith in his results. This helps to explain the resentment for social science research extending from the Joint Chiefs of Staff to the Senate Foreign Relations Committee. Suppliers of intellectual labor are well paid if they have a powerful union or guild (as many social sciences have), but they hardly command high status in a political atmosphere that strains toward quick and inexpensive solutions.

The first and perhaps most significant criticism made by administrators against the academy is that social scientists make excessive demands for funds and special treatment while working on projects that frequently have little tactical value. This is translated into a charge of impracticality. Typical is the critique made by the General Accounting Office against the Hudson Institute, headed by defense strategist Herman Kahn. Underlining charges made by the Office of Civil Defense, it scored the work of the Hudson Institute in the area of the behavioral sciences for being "less useful than had been expected," and cited the work as unacceptable without "major revision." Various social science reports, particularly those prepared by semiprivate agencies, have been criticized for their superficiality, for their "tired" thinking, for their sensationalism, and, above all, for their lack of immediate relevance. In response, social researchers claim that the purpose of a good report is imaginative effort rather than practical settlement of all outstanding issues. Government agencies should not expect a high rate of success on every research attempt, they argue. One reason for the persistence of this line of criticism is that demands for high-payoff utilitarian research are seldom contested. The questionable practicality of much social science research remains a sore point in the relationship and cannot be resolved until and unless social scientists themselves work out a comfortable formula governing the worth of relevance in contrast to the demand for relevance.

Another criticism leveled at academics by federal sponsors issued from the first: namely, that there are no systems for ensuring that results obtained in research are usable. A gap exists between the proposal and fulfillment stages of a research undertaking and there is an equally wide gap between the results obtained and the processes involved in grappling with problems. Proposals that are handsomely drawn up and attractively packaged often have disappointing results. And while many sophisticated agencies, such as NIH, NSF, or OEO, are aware of the need for permissiveness in research design those agencies more firmly rooted in hard science and engineering traditions are not so tolerant of such experimentation. Moreover, it is charged that academics engaged in government research "overconservatize" their responses to placate a federal bureaucracy. This "overconservatizing" may come, however, at the very point when the administrator is trying to establish some liberal policy departures. The chore of the federal agency becomes much more difficult, since it must cope not only with bureaucratic sloth and the conservative bias of top officials but with reinforcements for that bias in research reports by the social scientists from whom more liberal formulations might have been expected. Thus, not only is there a gap between proposal and fulfillment stages in the research enterprise, but also some reports may structure conservative biases into the programs assigned to the federal bureaucracy by congressional committees or by executive-branch leadership.

The charge of inutility is often related to a differential intellectual style or culture. The government-versus-academy cleavage is largely a consequence of intellectual specialization of a kind that makes it difficult for the typical bureaucrat to talk meaningfully with the typical "modern" behavioral scientists. Most government officers in DOS, for example, are trained either in history or in a political science of a normative sort. International relations taught in the descriptive traditions of the 1920s or, at the latest, in the style of a Morgenthau or a Schuman continue to prevail. Whatever difficulties may exist between the academy and the polity at the level of role performance can at least be overcome by those who share a common intellectual formation. But often communication cannot be achieved with those behaviorists whose vocabulary, methods, and even concepts seem esoteric, irrelevant, occasionally trivial, and not rarely fraudulent. Thus, at the root of the charge of inutility is a conflict of intellectual cultures that negatively affects the relations between the academics and the politicians.

Federal administrators point out that academic men often demand deferential treatment, contrary to the norms that govern other federal employees. They charge that social science personnel do not really accept their role as government employees but rather see themselves as transiently or marginally connected to the government. Particularly in areas of foreign affairs, the academic appears to want the advantages of being privy to all kinds of quasi-secret information and of being involved in decision making, yet avoiding normal responsibilities that are accepted by other government employees.

Such attitudes smack of elitism to federal officials—an elitism built into the structure of social scientific thinking. Trained to analyze problems rather than to convince constituencies, social scientists become impatient with the vagaries of politics, preferring to challenge policy. One reason adduced by elected officials for preferring legal rather than scientific advisors is that the former have a far keener appreciation of mechanisms for governing people and being governed by them. The legal culture breeds a respect for the "popular will" rarely found among social scientists attached to government agencies. Indeed, the resentment expressed by many House and Senate committees against DOD and DOS social scientists is a direct response to the elitist streak that seems to characterize social scientists in government.

This is the reverse side of the involvement-autonomy debate, in which the government pushes for total involvement and participation, while the social scientist presses for autonomy and limited responsibility in decisions directly affecting policy. Elitism rationalizes the performance of important service while enabling the social scientist to maintain the appearance of detachment. Although social scientists view their own federal involvement as marginal, at the same time they demand access to top elites so that they may be assured that their recommendations will be implemented or at least seriously considered. But access at this level entails bypassing the standard bureaucratic channels through which other federal employees must go.

The social scientist's demand for elite accessibility, though said to be inspired by noble purpose, tends to set the social scientist apart from other employees of the federal government. He sees himself as an advising expert instead of as an employee. The social scientist takes himself seriously as an appointed official playing a political role in a way that most other federal workers do not. The federal bureaucracy finding that the social scientist has come to Washington to "set the world on fire," thinks that a presumptuous intention, unmindful of the flame that also burns in the heart of staff administrator.

The question of ready access to leadership rests on notions of the superior wisdom of the social scientist; however, it is precisely this claim that is most sharply contested by federal administrators. Reflecting popular biases, administrators claim that the easy admission of social scientists to the halls of power presumes a correctness in their policy judgments not supported by historical events and not warranted by mass support from popular sectors. The separation of science and citizen roles often justifies lack of citizen participation. The scientific ethos thus comes to serve as a basis for admission into a system of power by circumventing the civic culture. This precisely is why federal bureaucrats feel that they are defending their political constituencies (and not, incidentally, their own bailiwicks) by limiting social science participation in the decision-making process.

If social scientists chafe at being outside the mainstream of academic life during their period of involvement with the political system, federal bureaucrats are themselves highly piqued at the degree of supplemental employment enjoyed and desired by social scientists. Also, in clear contrast with other federal governmental personnel, social scientists are able to locate supplemental positions in the Washington, D.C., area. They work as teachers and professors; they do writing on the side for newspapers and magazines; they edit books and monographs; they offer themselves as specialist consultants, capitalizing on their government involvement. They become active in self-promotion to a degree far beyond the reasons for their being hired.

In the more loosely structured world of the academy, such self-promotion not only goes uncriticized but is rewarded. Royalty payments for textbook writing, involvement with publishing firms in editorial capacities, honoraria connected with membership in granting agencies, and payments for lectures on campuses are all highly respected forms of supplemental "employment." But federal government employment is a 12-month yearly, 24-hour daily involvement. This condition and its demands are far different from the nine-month yearly commitment and fluid scheduling endemic to most social scientist relations with academic institutions. Federal agencies disdain the marginal aspects of the academics' involvement in political life, and their awareness that men involved in government effort are often enough not representative of the most outstanding talent available in the social sciences also disturbs them, particularly because they traffic in the status spinoff of both the academy and the polity. The anomaly exists that men who may not have been especially successful in academic life make demands upon the federal bureaucracy as if in fact they were the most outstanding representatives of their fields. The same problems might well arise in connection with outstanding representatives from the social sciences, but the situation becomes exacerbated precisely because the federal bureaucrats know that they are dealing with—at least in many instances—second- or even third-echelon federally employed social scientists.

IMPROVING INTERACTION

In this profile the academics and federal administrators alike have been presented as more uniform in their responses to each other than is actually the case. It should not be imagined that the two groups spend all their time in bickering criticism of each other, for then certainly no stable relationship worth speaking of could exist. Still, the roles acted out by both parties make it clear that the present is a period of extensive redefinition. The criticisms that academics and politicos have of each other often have a mirror-image effect, each side sharply focusing on the least commendable features of the other. Significantly, the political context and content of this issue has in the main been unconsciously suppressed by both sides. The academics have preferred to emphasize their scientific activities in objective and neutral terminology, while the politicos express their interests in organizational and bureaucratic terms. The strangest aspect of this interaction, then, is that in the world of politics it seems that nothing is more embarrassing than political analysis and synthesis. As if by common consent, social scientists and policy makers have agreed to conduct their relations by a code of genteel disdain rather than in open confrontation. The gulf between the two groups requires political distance as an operational equivalent to the social distance between competing tribal villagers.

There may be cause for concern that federal government sponsorship corrupts the character of social science output because it emphasizes big money, an overly practical orientation, and limited dissemination of information, and because it fails to accept the fact that any research may be potentially subversive. But, ironically, timid or opportunistic social science personnel are not recruited by the government. Most often, the social scientist seeks the federal sponsor and becomes overly ambitious in the process of pressing exaggerated claims for unique research designs and high-payoff promises. The chief danger for the academic who has come to depend on the federal bureaucracy for research funds and its variety of career satisfactions is not more financial dependence; rather, it is that he may begin to develop the loyalties and cautionary temperament of the opportunistic civil servant per se.

Many interlocking appointments between the academy and the polity have occurred at the organizational level without resolving persistent questions as to what constitutes legitimate interaction between social science and public policy. This indicates that the line between the academy and the polity is blurred enough to require precise determination of exactly who is stimulating what kind of research and under what conditions. As it becomes increasingly clear that social scientists are the stimulants and administrators the respondents in a majority of instances, it becomes obvious also that criticism must be leveled at social science participation, rather than at federal practice. To understand fully the sources of tension in the interaction between academics and administrators, it is necessary to illuminate the range of attitudes toward connection between the government and the academy, which extends from advocating complete integration between administrators and academics to calling for complete rupture between the two groups. A spectrum of positions is presented on this matter.

The quarter of a century from 1945 to 1970 represents a range of attitudes from complete integration to complete rupture. From World War II, and even prior to that during the era of the New Deal, optimism prevailed about an integrated relationship between academics and administrators. This was perhaps best expressed by the "policy-science" approach frequently associated with the work of Harold D. Lasswell (1951). In his view the relationship between social science and the political networks would be an internal affair, with political men involved in scientific affairs just as frequently and as fully as scientific men would be involved in political affairs. The policy-science approach was a noble effort to redefine familiar departmental divisions of labor. Sociology, political science, economics, and the other social sciences would be absorbed by a unified policy science that involved a common methodological core. The problem with his exchange network, as Lasswell himself well understood in later years, is that federal administrators speak with the presumed authority of the "garrison state," while academics (even those temporarily in government service) speak with the presumed impracticality of the "ivory tower."

The policy-science approach did in fact have direct policy consequences. The end of World War II and the 1950s saw the rise of new forms of institutional arrangements for housing social science. But more than organization was involved. A new emphasis cut across disciplinary boundaries. Area studies emerged in every major university. Communism was studied as part of the more general problem of the role of ideology in social change. This was followed by centers for urban studies and the study of industrial and labor relations. Despite the rise of institutionalized methods for uniting specialties, however, university department structures had a strange way of persisting, not just as lingering fossils but as expanding spheres of influence. It soon became apparent that in the struggle to influence the graduate-student world and to decide who will or will not be appointed and promoted in university positions the "department" held final authority. The separate departments of the social sciences enabled the disciplines to retain their vitality. At the same time that the policy-science approach was confronting departmentalism, disciplinary specialization was increasing. During the postwar period, anthropology insisted on departmental arrangements that distinguished it from sociology and theology, while other areas, such as political science and social work, became more sharply delineated than ever before. The policy-science approach was able to institutionalize all sorts of aggressive and at times even progressive reorderings of available information, but it failed to establish the existence of a policy-science organization. And this proved fatal to its claims for operational primacy.

The policy-science approach of the 1950s was supplanted by the "handmaiden" approach of the early 1960s, in which social science was to supply the necessary ingredients to make the political world function smoothly. The reasoning was that the social sciences were uniquely qualified to instill styles in federal decision making based on confirmed data. This was not, however, to entail complete integration of services and functions. The handmaiden approach was considered more suitable to the nature of both the sciences and the policy-making aspects of government and was materially assisted by a rising emphasis on applied social research. The new emphasis on application and on large-scale research provided the theoretical rationale for janitorial "mop-up" services. Applied research was to make the search for the big news, for the vital thrust; participation in this intimate consensual arrangement would deprive the social sciences of their freedom but would guarantee relevance. The "theoryless" service approach was thus wedded to an action orientation.

Advocates of the handmaiden approach, such as Ithiel de Sola Pool (1967) vigorously defended social scientists' obligation to do meaningful research for government. It was noted that an organization such as DOD has manifold needs for the tools of social science analysis as a means for better understanding its world. It was pointed out that the intelligence test had been an operational instrument in manpower management since World War I and that DOD and other federal agencies had become major users of social psychology in military and sensitive areas. As the world's largest training and educational institution, the U.S. government had to acquire exact knowledge for the selection and training of an enormous number of human subjects. Equally significant was the federal government's needs for exact foreign-area information. This thirst for knowledge of the particular cultural values and social and political structures of foreign countries increased as the world was carved up into potential enemies or potential allies of the United States.

The ironic aspect of this support for useful research is that although the handmaiden approach ostensibly left social science autonomy intact, it reduced that autonomy in fact by establishing criteria for federal rather than social science "payoff." High-yield research areas uniformly involved what the social sciences could do for the political structures and not necessarily the other way around. Thus, while the policy-science approach gave way to the service-industry orientation of the handmaiden approach, the latter, too, was not based on any real parity between the academy and the polity.

A new approach, considerably removed from both the policy-science and handmaiden approaches, has been finely articulated by David B. Truman (1968). As theory, it expresses a renewed sense of equity and parity between social scientists and administrators. Under Truman's arrangement there would be frequent but largely unplanned interchanges between federal bureaucratic positions and university positions. This exchange of roles would prove valuable and could eventually be explored and encouraged on a systematic basis. Meanwhile, the selective-participation approach advocates minimal formal structure in the system.

The most important aspect of the selective participation approach is that it is based upon a norm of reciprocity. A partial interchange of personnel could be accomplished primarily through regular seminars and conferences mutually attended by social scientists and government administrators, each cluster of men representing carefully-designed combinations. Another method might be alternating presentation of scientific development and policy problems at these meetings. Unlike the normal consultant relationship of the handmaiden style, this would guarantee some kind of equity between the academy and the polity. Selective participation would include securing grants and promoting federal research for multidisciplinary teams of academics working on political problems, instead of the usual outright political employment of individual social scientists or academic talent. This, it was hoped, would provide a flexible arrangement of specialties that would fill the gap between scientific knowledge and public purpose without detriment either to social scientists or political policy makers. Operationally, it meant a greater flow of funds from government agencies to research institutes housed on university campuses—a not inconsequential change over the policy-science approach, which projected a much more intimate ecological as well as ideological network.

The dilemma was that the selective-participation approach implicitly assumed an exchange network with a parity of strength between political decision makers and academics. The approach failed to demonstrate that the academic would be on a par with the administrator, for the latter had financial inputs while the former had the informational outputs. In point of fact the government agency still does the hiring, even in the selective-participation approach, and the academics participate in a policy-making role without much expectancy of a payoff for social science theory or methodology.

This situation has given rise to what might be called the principle of "nonparticipation," which is increasingly being adopted. Social scientists continue to write and publish in areas of foreign research or in sectors vital to the national political arena but do not do so under government contract or as a direct response to a federal agency. It was felt that if the autonomy of the social sciences means anything at all, uses and findings legitimately arrived at will be incorporated into federal policy making whether or not social scientists participate actively or critically. The principle of nonparticipation tended to be adopted by many conservative as well as radical social scientists who saw in the growth of federal social research a threat to the standard forms of status advancement in the professions and also a movement toward applied social planning that violated their own feeling for the generalizing nature of social science. On organizational and intellectual grounds, the principle of nonparticipation served as an effective response to the policy-science approach. The underlying assumption of the notion of nonparticipation is that the federal government has more to gain than does the social scientist by the interaction between them. Although interaction would be maintained, the order of priorities would be changed so that social scientists no longer would have the onerous task of providing high-payoff research for others, with low yields to themselves.

In many ways the principle of nonparticipation suggested that the university department remain the primary agency in the organization of social science instead of the federal research bureau. The nonparticipant in federal programs often found himself to be the critic of bureaucratic research in gereral and of bureaucratic agencies attached to universities in particular. He did not want to have his research controlled by federal decision making; more importantly, he did not want a federal agency to usurp what was properly a judgment in the domain of a university department. At the same time, the principle of nonparticipation spilled over into the principle of active opposition. This opposition was registered in the main by younger scholars in areas such as history and by graduate students in the social sciences—that is, among those often involved in student protest movements. From their point of view the matter could not be resolved on the essentially conservative grounds of the selective use of the best of social science by the government. A conscious attempt must be made to use scholarship for partisan or revolutionary goals that could under no circumstances be employed by the establishments linked to government agencies. As Hans Morgenthau indicated, this represented a movement away from the belief that the social scientist and the federal administrator inhabited mutually exclusive institutions to a belief in a more active opposition because they occupied mutually hostile positions with antithetical goals.

In one sense, the radical posture accepts the policy-science appraisal of a political world dominated by the "garrison state" but rejects its remedy of social science immersion to reorient government away from its predatory world missions. The policy-science view assumed the educability of military-minded rulers. The antiparticipation view assumes the reverse, namely, the ease with which social scientists become incorporated into the military and political goals of men of power.

Radical critics, such as John McDermott, assert that in practice the goals of the academy and the polity have become antithetical. Furthermore, they say that, theoretically, those goals ought to be antithetical. A transformation of the dream of action into the nightmare of federal participation, in which the academy became in effect an adjunct of the federal establishment, has been brought about. The academic social scientists' dream of position and prestige has in some sense been realized by their transformation into men of action: academic men have become high priests of social change. The desire for social change has, in effect, overwhelmed the goals toward which such change was directed.

The move toward active opposition is a critique of the way in which the university, no less than the government, is structured. Those who moved away from federal participation simultaneously turned their energies on the university system. They hold that the academy itself, as beneficiary of federal funds, has become the political party of the academic man. The rash of student attacks against the university must be considered as, in part at least, symbolic attacks against the notion of the integration of policy making and academic performance. The most well-guarded nonsecret of the present era of university relationships to the government, at least insofar as these ties bear upon the notion of active opposition, concerns the general political and ideological climate that now prevails. Surrogate politics has now become a rooted pattern in American academic affairs, partly because academics come to politics by way of moral concern, while politicians come to moral concerns by way of political participation. Surrogate politics is also a reflex action of the expanding articulate but impotent social sectors against what have become the dominant political trends of the United States at this time.

Surrogate politics has its place in national affairs. Indeed, the question of the relationship between the academy and the polity is precisely a question of surrogate politics. A common undercurrent of moral revulsion for professional hucksterism and amateur gamesmanship has forced the present review of the status between social scientists and policy makers. This same reexamination should have taken place a quarter of a century ago, despite the difficulties of the situation. But precisely because of the optimal consensus that existed in the past concerning the political climate, the issues now being discussed were considered improper topics for social scientists in pursuit of truth.

During the 1941-45 period, when the United States was engaged in a world conflict in which the overwhelming number of its citizens felt involved in the very survival of civilization itself, there were no pained expressions about government recruiting on campuses. There was no resentment toward the retooling of universities to satisfy military research needs and psychological warfare, propaganda research, or conventional bombing surveys. Nor were any scholarly panels held at professional meetings concerning the propriety of social scientists who accepted appointments under the Roosevelt administration in the Office of War Information or in the Office of Strategic Services, such as those panels that now discuss the propriety of relationships between social scientists and the Federal Bureau of Investigation or the Central Intelligence Agency.

Between 1946 and 1960, or from the end of World War II to the beginning of the Kennedy era, the United States was involved in a cold war, with the Soviet Union as its primary antagonist. We obviously are not concerned here either with the origins or sources of the cold war but with the fact of its existence. It was during this period that social science was perhaps most partisan in its commitment to the U.S. foreign-policy posture. This partisanship was manifested in many ways: the rise of think tanks with direct federal sponsorship for applied social science research; the emergence of specialized centers, such as Soviet centers, Southeast Asian centers, and Latin American research councils, that once more were harnessed to the tasks of U.S. foreign policy. Beyond that was the automatic assumption that social science did indeed have values: the values of the "American century." The fanciful illusion that this did not constitute an ideology was nothing more than a chimera behind which the values of social science meshed more perfectly, either before or since, with the tasks of U.S. foreign policy.

This same era was not so much one of transition from wartime to peacetime but rather a movement from an overt world struggle between democracy (then defined as both capitalist and socialist in character) and fascism to one between capitalism and communism. As a result, this specific era witnessed a growing resurgence in the West of private enterprise. But in the United States, at least, this resurgence was more ideological than organizational. The bulk of funding for research and development continued to flow in ever-increasing amounts from public government sources. As a result, the real gap between state capitalism and state communism was far narrower in practice than in theory. It has been noted that this was also the period in which the real gap between scientific disciplines diminished to a commensurate degree (cf. Price 1965:5, Salomon 1973:46-48). This ambiguous line between disciplines reflected itself specifically in the emergence of task-oriented social research. The rise of "team" efforts, oriented toward predetermined "projects," had the result of making policy central. The scientific background of key personnel mattered far less than the social (or, as it sometimes turned out, antisocial) goals of the research design.

Between 1960 (the beginnings of the thaw) and 1972 (the end of the Vietnamese conflict) controversy over the relationship between social science and political performance increased in both intensity and quantity. The breakdown of the consensus was evident within the social scientific communities by a series of surrogate discussions over the legitimacy of the war in Vietnam, Latin American self-determination, or civil strife in ghettos in the United States. Unable to address such issues directly and unprepared to design structures for future alleviation of such world and national pressures, social scientists exaggerate the politics of inner organizational life. Professional societies engage in mimetic reproduction of central social concerns on a low-risk and probably a low-yield basis.

During this period, inner-organizational struggles also received the encouragement and support of corresponding professional people and societies from the Third World and from minority groups. It is no accident that federal projects that had Latin American targets have come under particularly severe assault. The existence of a counter-social-science establishment in countries such as Mexico, Chile, Argentina, and Brazil provides vocal support for domestic United States academic opposition and for firming up such opposition by posing the threat of total isolation from foreign area research for a failure to heed the dangers of certain kinds of political research. Increasingly, black militants in this country have adopted a similar posture of nonparticipation in social science projects without clearly stating preconditions of protection of the "rights" of the subjects or sovereigns.

Since 1972 the fervor over heedless involvement in policy has eased considerably. However, the feeling that social science should still remain at a respectable distance from policy has had a residual impact. The emergence of a détente between the United States and the Soviet Union and the reestablishment of diplomatic relationships between the United States and China, coupled internally with a growing conservatism with respect to the rights of the poor and to the need for further welfare measures, has led to a situation in which social scientists have become increasingly aware of the commodity value of their researches and the mandarin effects of their findings. Thus, while the amount of social science activity has increased almost as a constant between 1941 and 1974, the character of the association between the social scientists and the political establishment has been tremendously altered over time. The likelihood is that this pattern will continue into the foreseeable future. The very emergence of the game theory as a concept replacing organicism subjects the social sciences themselves to the very analysis under which they have placed the political actors. As a result, the line between social science and political action may have blurred, while at the same time the worth of each to the other has never been more intensely felt.

On the other side of the river among the policy making and evaluating sectors, the demand for social science research findings among government agencies continues unabated, despite reticence on the part of some sectors of the social science community to supply such information and, beyond that, the relatively desultory results thus far obtained in the areas of applied social research. In a recent report before the American Association for Public Opinion Research, Nathan Caplan (1974:172-73) noted the following:

1. There is a need felt among most federal officials for finding better ways to plug research into the decision-making process.
2. Top officials get most of their social science news from newspapers.
3. Policy makers see the need for more large-scale, community-based social experiments, such as the NIT study, along with a widening interest in developing noneconomic measures of social well-being.

One might say of social science what Walter Lippmann long ago said of democracy: it is not a very good instrument for the making of public policy, but it is about the best one available. This does seem to be the case with the social sciences, although on a less philosophical, more pragmatic basis than Lippmann initially had in mind. In the absence of a mass outpouring of democratic persuasion and in the presence of political corruption in high office and political apathy among the ordinary citizens, the social sciences essentially perform the role of cementing U.S. goals and presenting them in such a manner that, at the very least, if it does not provide a rational solution to social problems, prevents the adoption of an irrational solution to those problems. This may not be saying much for the social sciences, but it holds out considerably more promise than any other method of political participation by the social science community under present conditions in American life.

REFERENCES

Caplan, Nathan
    1974   Research cited in *Behavior Today* 5, No. 24 (June 17, 1974):172-73.
de Sola Pool, Ithiel
    1967   The necessity for social scientists doing research for governments. In I. L. Horowitz (ed.), *The Rise and Fall of Project Camelot: Studies in the Relationship between Social Science and Practical Politics*. Cambridge, Massachusetts: M.I.T. Press, (1967). pp. 267-80.
Lasswell, Harold D.
    1951   "The policy orientation." In H. D. Lasswell & D. Lerner (eds.), *The Policy Sciences*. Stanford, California: Stanford University Press, (1951). pp. 3-15.
Price, Don K.
    1965   *The Scientific Estate*. Cambridge: Harvard University Press.
Salomon, Jean-Jacques
    1973   *Science and Politics*. Cambridge: The M.I.T. Press.
Truman, David B.
    1968   "The social sciences and public policy." *Science*, (May 3, 1968), 160 (3827), 508-12.

CHAPTER

9

PROPOSALS ON
THE CONDUCT OF
SOCIAL SCIENTISTS
AND POLICY MAKERS

Recommendations are simple to make but difficult to execute. However, in a work on policy making it would be a dereliction of duty not to attempt some policy recommendations. For the most part, these recommendations flow from the description and empirical contents of what preceded this final set of remarks. But again, as is the case for most forms of policy recommendation, one cannot be entirely sure that speculations are simply being smuggled into a conclusion without sufficient warranty. Be that as it may, we believe that the following set of guidelines may assist those in the European community who are charged with considering the conditions for social science participation in the policy making process and who already have passed the first hurdle and decided that such participation and interaction is a good and useful phenomenon.

The European "welfare" tradition in policy affairs stands in sharp contrast to the U.S. "free enterprise" tradition, which in plain truth, has led to a bureaucratic style in funding that has swelled the ranks of the social sciences but has done precious little to enrich the quality of its policy recommendations. As a result, we would have to recommend a more imaginative sort of funding program: one that would seek greater direct contact between donor and recipient of funds, with a concomitant reduction in the number of administrative middlemen. Such funding should also have a series of built-in follow-up measures to assure a continuing sort of interest in the results and consequences of policy measurement and implementation. The sharp distinction maintained between social scientists who recommend and policy makers who implement is dangerous to both sides, since it creates a network of irresponsibility and ministerpretations that can have disastrous consequences in the real world. The wider the sources of funding for policy, the greater the chances of imaginative and innovative social science. A plurality of funding sources, coupled with a plurality of support for different types of researchers doing the same kind of research, will serve a dual purpose: it will prevent an overconservatized image of the world and avoid the inevitable idiosyncratic consequences of having only one sort of response or report on a major area of policy concern. Finally, we would hope for fewer social scientists working full time directly for federal, state, and city agencies and for more part-time researchers who also have commitments and resources outside the bureaucratic structure—i.e., university affiliations. The multiplicity of linkages enables the social sciences to retain their autonomy and provide honest reporting. It also permits the maximum efficiency on the part of administrative systems at the lowest possible fiscal costs. Social scientists have enough differences from the ordinary sorts of administrative personnel to warrant a careful consideration of the types of employment and deployment of their talents. The results obtained in the United States would indicate that those social scientists who maintain several professional roles serve the needs of the policy sector best and at the same time run the least risk in subverting the canons of science and scholarship that characterize "pure" research situations best located in the university and nonprofit sectors.

The best argument for the widest possible implementation of social scientists in legislative, executive, and judicial branches of government at national and subnational levels is the brake they provide on idiosyncratic decision making that often results from too narrow a consideration of evidence and contexts. The worst reason for more widely using social science talent is to avoid or bypass the democratic processes—a situation in which the role of expertise comes to displace the will of the people on major issues. Between these two poles the tightrope must be walked. Again, there are no magic formulas: populism can degenerate into jingoism, just as assuredly as social science can issue into elitism. But given a context in which decision making becomes increasingly sensitive and complex (and the technological demands are for immediacy of decisions no less than for accuracy of forecasting), there can be no question that the tilt is with the wide deployment of social science. For at this time there is a widespread use of economists as the one group that is held to be reliable and worthwhile in a policy context. And yet, more and more, the problems are at the qualitative rather than the quantitative levels—problems of *how good*, no less than *how much*. Under such circumstances, definitions of what constitutes the good, of how the aims of the society can be meshed and blended to the constraints of the economy, indicate the need for much wider use of psychologists, sociologists, anthropolotists, and political scientists. Indeed, the very proliferation of the social sciences at policy levels will itself provide a democratizing effect on those governments and agencies that at present confine themselves to economists and engineers.

The use of economists and the so-called hard social sciences stands in contrast to the employment of the findings of the so-called soft social sciences. In part, this is an inevitable consequence of the drive of policy makers for quantitative information that can easily be justified, correlated, and tabulated, but it is clearly the case that a great many of the problems that individuals, communities, and nations alike have are precisely in the area of "quality of life" in the more ubiquitous framework of social values and social norms. For that reason, one would hope that the inauguration and implementation of social science research is not limited to simple management techniques or engineering problems but rather takes cognizance of those murky, gray areas of psychology and politics that are perhaps less subject to quantification but at least as useful in their findings for the framing of individual needs and national goals. For that reason, we would urge the use either of a single body of social scientists involving the entire spectrum of disciplines or, failing that, of at least two social science bodies, one reporting on the quantity of goods and services available and the other on the character and quality of those goods and services. The best arrangement will have to be decided by each individual country, since the history of the participation of the social sciences in policy making in each country is obviously unique.

There is such a heavy emphasis on the training of policy-oriented social scientists on behalf of local communities or national agencies that we sometimes forget the essential role of criticism performed by the social sciences. In this context, what we would urge is the widest possible training of social scientists for policy-making roles in counterestablishment institutions no less than in established institutions. The role of social science in setting policy may more readily take place in connection with the advice and support of industrial unions, ethnic minorities, and special-interest groups (such as women, the aged, or youth), and social science may even be used to formulate political platforms of parties that are out of power and out of favor. In short, in considering the role of social science as a policy-making device, we have always to emphasize not simply the subnational levels at which such relationships between science and policy can be maintained but also the ideological content of such social science services. The failure to admit this possibility in the past has led to an undue and unfair assumption that social science was intrinsically a conservative agency working on behalf of the established system. In point of fact, only the widest possible use of social science in counterestablishment institutions can break down those powerfully rooted prejudices that are equally dangerous for both the social scientists and the policy sector, the latter of which, after all, needs the best available information, not the loudest or noisiest forms of patriotism.

One exceedingly important consequence of the high participation of social science in public policy is that the performance of social science itself becomes directly pegged to public-policy definitions of needs and goals. That is, if the problems of ecology and the environment, say, become central, then the fundings open up in that area. This "mandarin effect" signifies several dangerous possibilities: first, that there will be no research outside of policy-stated needs, since no funding will be in the offing; second, that the social science research will be of a crude empiricist variety, veering sharply away from any sort of speculation that might tend to dampen enthusiasm for project sponsorship for future research; third, that social science will set its priorities in strictly fiscal terms and hence fail to challenge prevailing orthodoxies. In some measure, the very tension that must exist between social science and public-policy needs is a safeguard against such a premature atrophy. However, for this "creative tension" to remain intact, sources of funding independent of projects themselves are required. And it is precisely the unwillingness of donors and sponsors to provide for "free floating" funds that jeopardizes social science autonomy.

Social science operates best on public policy when there is a preexisting, broad-based consensus; it operates worst under conditions of public dissensus. Hence, the areas of greatest success are in those areas of denied equity: equal rights for black enlisted men, equal educational opportunities for children of minority background, and equal rights for women. Within this national arena in which a perceived sense of injustice exists, the impact of social science is quite large. When a dissensus exists, such as in the U.S. overseas involvement in Southeast Asia, the efforts of the social sciences are subject to extreme criticism from without and to serious shortcomings at the analytical level—i.e., misevaluations of Vietcong capacities, mistakes over Cuban support for Castro, and so on—from within. When social science services the powerful groups, it is perceived as a reactionary instrument and a fallacious one; when social science services the poor and the oppressed, it is viewed as a legitimizer and an explanatory device. There seems to be an inverse relationship in the perception of social science: as a good thing when operating on shared national aspirations and issues and as a bad thing when operating on a divided set of international aspirations.

All research, like all thinking, is done by real persons, individuals. However "collective" the nature of an enterprise, individual talent and even genius cannot be slighted or ignored. Whether the genius of a Machiavelli, a Hobbes, or a Marx can ever be replaced by a team research effort is a moot point. Suffice it to say that the work of individuals like Morgenthau or Arendt still represents a profound input into the policy process. Sometimes this input is affirmative, as in the work of the "war gamers" of the 1960s, such as Herman Kahn; sometimes it is of a critical, cautionary spirit, illustrating what cannot be done, as in the work of David Reisman. The purpose of mentioning these names is selective, and they are not intended as an exhaustive list of the most important contributors to the social sciences. Support for such individuals or failing that, respect for them, allowing them to survive intact and be taken seriously, is an essential element in any sound federal approach to the relationship between social science and public policy. It is easy to develop the sort of conceit and arrogance that stems from money, influence, and power in high places. The best corrective and antiseptic for such sins of the powerful is the research of the lonely individual, the critical voice raising doubts and even obstacles to what may appear to be self-evident propositions. The European tradition, with its built-in respect for the intellectual tradition over and against the scientific tradition, is perhaps better able to withstand the arrogance of social science power than the American tradition, with its pragmatic predilections, has been. Be that as it may, it is as appropriate to end on a cautionary note as it was to begin this study with an optimistic flavor.

The needs of policy are best met in a context of the free and critical exchange of ideas, and the best place for this in the United States remains the university system. Agencies that become too removed, too distant from the norms of social science scholarship are less likely to affirm and reaffirm an independent stance. The impulse behind private research agencies such as Abt, RAND, Systems Analysis, and so on, was not simply innovation, nor were they simply thought of as a way to avoid university fiscal overhead; rather, they were formed to establish a direct tie-in between donor and researchers that would make applied research less rich in theoretical potential, precisely because generalizability was not a basic value for fiscal donors to research. The danger of such private counseling services are many, but all are wrapped up with a lack of accountability to any larger body of knowers. That is a university's purpose: to establish ground rules for research and hence a system of theoretical accoutability quite beyond the time checks and bookkeeping schedules already kept by such private agencies.

If the university, by its conservatism, greediness in extracting superoverhead profitability, and just plain indifference to applied research, laid the ground for the present entrepreneurial spirit in American social research, it nonetheless affords the best available mechanism for the scientific adjudication of the research process. If research arms should be vigorous and independent in the pursuit of research, even dangerous research, they nonetheless, should not become isolated from the taproots of knowledge itself—and the university is the cultural home for such taproots. The problems of fusing university and policy life are many, but the problem resulting a bifurcation of such a relationship are insoluble; drawing apart leads to arrogance, presumptuousness and hardheadedness, and ultimately to a negation of science as an instrument of criticism as well as construction.

The growth of social science for policy purposes will require a large-scale shift in the understanding of what science in general is all about. Models of science that frankly take into account the role of advocacy procedures, the place of social forecasting, and the need for large- as well as small-scale planning mechanisms must begin to augment the traditional empirical and historical forms of description. The present division between "pure" and "applied" science only serves to permeate and prolong the myth of dualism, the belief that "facts" and "values" or "professionalism" and "occupationalism" are in different realms. The need for cross-fertilization has never been greater, and the rise of policy-making roles for the sciences only points out further this need to maintain a balance between scientific theory and scientifically-based actions. The content of "radicalism" for science is simply the potential of the truth about the world to be implemented over and against the claims of blood ties, impulse, collective will, national rights, and so on. Thus, it is the rational core of science that gives it its special qualities and uses for policy agencies.

APPENDIXES

FEDERAL OBLIGATIONS FOR RESEARCH, BY DETAILED FIELD OF SCIENCE, FISCAL YEARS 1970, 1971, AND 1972 (thousands of dollars)

Field of Science	Actual, 1970	Estimates 1971	Estimates 1972
Total, all fields	**5,601,906**	**5,995,123**	**6,643,584**
Life sciences, total	**1,533,432**	**1,735,136**	**1,945,097**
Biological	684,782	735,295	850,875
Clinical medical	685,633	804,177	874,284
Other medical sciences	144,900	168,361	193,169
Life sciences, NEC	18,117	27,303	26,769
Psychology, total	**113,328**	**125,166**	**140,413**
Biological aspects	45,141	47,379	58,390
Social aspects	64,175	74,569	79,054
Psychological sciences, NEC	4,012	3,218	2,969
Physical sciences, total	**1,010,450**	**1,025,477**	**1,086,483**
Astronomy	210,950	222,196	198,772
Chemistry	243,894	246,627	304,348
Physics	538,333	536,306	568,421
Physical sciences, NEC	17,273	20,348	14,942
Environmental sciences, total	**586,631**	**632,124**	**701,988**
Atmospheric sciences	287,737	311,193	340,301
Geological sciences	188,897	193,223	216,329
Oceanography (excluding biological)	91,222	97,290	112,148
Environmental science, NEC	18,775	30,418	33,210
Mathematics	**102,138**	**103,963**	**111,770**
Engineering, total	**1,967,739**	**2,013,906**	**2,197,655**
Aeronautical	466,464	473,635	474,598
Astronautical	289,525	287,850	328,946
Chemical	117,224	113,299	122,850
Civil	60,771	80,425	106,178
Electrical	354,351	356,340	393,633
Mechanical	140,011	145,327	143,849
Metallurgy and materials	151,549	154,734	159,750
Engineering, NEC	367,844	402,296	467,851
Social sciences, total	**215,852**	**272,994**	**311,018**
Anthropology	8,763	10,412	15,128
Economics	84,332	89,344	98,706
History	4,542	5,006	5,181
Linguistics	1,989	2,012	2,636
Political science	7,417	6,070	7,327
Sociology	38,487	50,009	71,840
Social sciences, NEC	70,322	110,141	110,200
Other sciences, NEC	**72,336**	**86,357**	**149,160**

Source: National Science Foundation, Washington, D.C.: 1973. Federal Funds for Research, Development, and other Scientific Activities.

FEDERAL OBLIGATIONS FOR RESEARCH IN SOCIAL SCIENCES, BY AGENCY AND DETAILED FIELD OF SCIENCE, FISCAL YEAR 1972 (ESTIMATED)
(thousands of dollars)

Agency and Subdivision	Total	Anthropology
Total, all agencies	**311,018**	**15,128**
Department of Agriculture, total	**37,273**	—
Agricultural Research Service	1,146	—
Cooperative State Research Service	16,363	—
Economic Research Service	15,428	—
Farmer Cooperative Service	943	—
Forest Service	3,120	—
Statistical Reporting Service	273	—
Department of Commerce, total	**9,465**	—
Bureau of the Census	944	—
Economic Development Administration	1,591	—
Maritime Administration	550	—
National Oceanic and Atmospheric Administration	1,872	—
Office of Business Economics	4,508	—
Department of Defense, total	**8,110**	**25**
Department of the Army	6,230	25
Department of the Air Force	303	—
Defense Agencies	1,110	—
Departmentwide Funds	467	—
Department of Health, Education and Welfare, total	**116,866**	**2,819**
Health Services and Mental Health Administration	33,517	2,655
National Institutes of Health	1,478	164
Office of Child Development	2,000	—
Office of Education	53,375	—
Social and Rehabilitation Service	12,210	—
Social Security Administration	14,286	—
Department of the Interior, total	**1,810**	—
Bureau of Land Management	58	—
Bureau of Outdoor Recreation	76	—
Bureau of Reclamation	80	—
Office of Water Resources Research	1,596	—

Economics	History	Linguistics	Political Science	Sociology	Social Sciences, NEC	Psychology
98,706	**5,181**	**2,636**	**7,327**	**71,840**	**110,200**	**140,413**
35,274	**155**	—	**45**	**1,543**	**256**	**31**
1,041	—	—	—	48	57	31
15,497	—	—	—	866	—	—
14,696	155	—	45	333	199	—
943	—	—	—	—	—	—
2,824	—	—	—	296	—	—
273	—	—	—	—	—	—
9,016	—	—	—	**449**	—	**1,466**
495	—	—	—	449	—	613
1,591	—	—	—	—	—	—
550	—	—	—	—	—	—
1,872	—	—	—	—	—	853
4,508	—	—	—	—	—	—
868	—	**420**	**1,600**	**4,544**	**653**	**35,705**
725	—	100	1,150	4,230	—	10,142
—	—	—	—	—	303	7,160
—	—	320	440	—	350	13,348
143	—	—	10	314	—	474,489
8,000	—	**716**	**738**	**24,339**	**80,254**	**74,336**
7,360	—	—	738	21,312	1,452	38,678
140	—	451	—	692	31	22,900
500	—	—	—	500	1,000	500
—	—	265	—	—	53,110	9,838
—	—	—	—	1,835	10,375	2,420
—	—	—	—	—	14,286	—
1,093	**23**	—	**260**	**265**	**169**	**68**
58	—	—	—	—	—	—
45	3	—	5	20	3	—
80	—	—	—	—	—	—
910	20	—	255	245	166	68

(continued)

173

Agency and Subdivision	Total	Anthropology
Department of Justice, total	**5,146**	—
Bureau of Narcotics and Dangerous Drugs	471	—
Law Enforcement Assistance Administration	4,675	—
Department of Labor, total	**12,642**	—
Bureau of Labor Statistics	2,617	—
Labor-Management Services Administration	812	—
Manpower Administration	6,680	—
Workplace Standards Administration	2,533	—
Department of State, total	**7,080**	—
Department funds	650	—
Agency for International Development	6,430	—
Department of Transportation, total	**17,455**	—
Federal Highway Administration	1,700	—
Federal Railroad Administration	3,985	—
Office of the Secretary	9,575	—
Urban Mass Transportation Administration	2,195	—
Other agencies		
Advisory Commission on Intergovernmental Relations	487	—
Civil Aeronautics Board	331	—
Environmental Protection Agency	808	—
Federal Home Loan Bank Board	497	—
Federal Trade Commission	460	—
National Science Foundation	41,399	8,222
Office of Economic Opportunity	41,700	—
Office of Science and Technology	20	3
Small Business Administration	205	—
Smithsonian Institution	8,059	4,059
Tennesee Valley Authority	386	—
U.S. Arms Control and Disarmament Agency	634	—
Veterans Administration	185	—

Economics	History	Linguistics	Political Science	Sociology	Social Sciences, NEC	Psychology
—	—	—	**240**	**2,206**	**2,700**	**2,115**
—	—	—	—	471	—	—
—	—	—	240	1,735	2,700	2,115
12,642	—	—	—	—	—	—
2,617	—	—	—	—	—	—
812	—	—	—	—	—	—
6,680	—	—	—	—	—	—
2,533	—	—	—	—	—	—
2,789	—	—	**250**	**1,886**	**2,155**	—
—	—	—	—	—	650	—
2,789	—	—	250	1,886	1,505	—
12,347	—	—	**400**	**1,220**	**3,488**	—
680	—	—	—	1,020	—	—
3,685	—	—	200	100	—	—
7,250	—	—	—	—	2,325	—
732	—	—	200	100	1,163	—
243	—	—	244	—	—	—
331	—	—	—	—	—	—
611	—	—	—	51	146	—
497	—	—	—	—	—	—
460	—	—	—	—	—	—
7,000	1,000	1,500	3,450	2,850	17,377	—
6,400	—	—	—	32,300	3,000	—
3	3	—	7	2	2	—
205	—	—	—	—	—	—
—	4,000	—	—	—	—	—
386	—	—	—	—	—	—
541	—	—	93	—	—	—
—	—	—	—	185	—	—

Source: National Science Foundation, Washington, D.C.: 1973. Federal Funds for Research, Development, and other Scientific Activities.

SOCIAL SCIENCE RESEARCH
WITH FEDERAL AGENCY SPONSORSHIP
(millions of dollars)

Rank	Federal Funds, 1969	Institute	Type*	State	Main Agency Sponsor
1	162,659	Lawrence Radiation Laboratory	a	Calif.	AEC
2	156,295	Jet Propulsion Laboratory	a	Calif.	NASA
3	99,302	Los Alamos Scientific Laboratory	a	N.M.	AEC
4	89,401	Argonne National Laboratory	a	Ill.	AEC
5	76,338	Aerospace Corporation	a	Calif.	AF
6	61,379	Lincoln Laboratory	a	Mass.	AF
7	51,218	Applied Physics Laboratory	a	Md.	navy
8	49,613	Pacific National Laboratory	a	Wash.	AEC
9	48,855	Brookhaven National Laboratory	a	N.Y.	AEC
10	32,702	MITRE	a	Mass.	AF
11	31,030	Stanford Research Institute	b	Calif.	DOD
12	23,552	Stanford Linear Accelerator Center	a	Calif.	AEC
13	20,438	RAND	a	Calif.	AF
14	18,093	Cornell Aeronautical Laboratory	b	N.Y.	DOD
15	16,015	Battelle Memorial Institute	b	Ohio	DOD
16	15,423	System Development Corporation	c	Calif.	DOD
17	13,616	National Center for Atmospheric Research	a	Colo.	NSF
18	12,388	Institute for Defense Analyses	a	Va.	DOD
19	9,961	IIT Research Institute	b	Ill.	DOD
20	9,915	Research Analysis Corporation	a	Va.	army
21	9,218	Center for Naval Analyses	a	Va.	navy
22	8,577	Ordnance Research Laboratory	a	Pa.	navy
23	7,652	Ames Laboratory	a	Iowa	AEC
24	7,404	Plasma Physics Laboratory	a	N.J.	AEC
25	7,231	National Radio Astronomy Observatory	a	W.Va.	NSF
26	5,840	Southwest Research Institute	b	Tex.	DOD
27	5,564	Kitt Peak National Observatory	a	Ariz.	NSF
28	5,241	Riverside Research Institute	c	N.Y.	DOD
29	4,970	Princeton-Pennsylvania Accelerator	a	N.J.	AEC
30	4,900	Sloan-Kettering Institute	c	N.Y.	HEW
31	4,642	Electromagnetic Compatibility Analysis Center	a	Md.	AF
32	4,321	Mayo Foundation	c	Minn.	HEW
33	4,175	Syracuse University Research Corporation	b	N.Y.	DOD
34	3,788	Atomic Bomb Casualty Commission	a	D.C.	AEC
35	3,555	Cambridge Electron Accelerator	a	Mass.	AEC
36	3,527	Southern Research Institute	b	Ala.	HEW
37	3,483	Research Triangle Institute	b	N.C.	DOD
38	3,459	National Accelerator Laboratory	a	Ill.	AEC
39	3,445	Human Resources Research Office	a	D.C.	army
40	3,400	Urban Institute	c	D.C.	HUD
41	3,205	Applied Physics Laboratory	a	Wash.	navy
42	3,089	Midwest Research Institute	b	Mo.	DOD
43	3,080	Hudson Laboratory	a	N.Y.	navy
44	2,770	Institute for Cancer Research	c	Pa.	HEW
45	2,700	Research for Better Schools	a	Pa.	OE
46	2,667	Southwest Center for Advanced Studies	c	Tex.	NASA
47	2,646	Center for Urban Education	a	N.Y.	OE
48	2,487	Southwest Regional Educational Laboratory	a	Calif.	OE

Rank	Federal Funds, 1969	Institute	Type*	State	Main Agency Sponsor
49	2,485	Medical Research Foundation of Oregon	c	Ore.	HEW
50	2,484	Lovelace Foundation for Medical Education	c	N.M.	AEC
51	2,457	Franklin Institute	b	Pa.	DOD
52	2,307	Children's Cancer Research Foundation	c	Mass.	HEW
53	2,067	Oak Ridge Associated Universities	a	Tenn.	AEC
54	2,039	Worcester Foundation for Experimental Biology	c	Mass.	HEW
55	1,978	Jackson Laboratory	c	Me.	HEW
56	1,861	Center for Research in Social Systems	a	D.C.	army
57	1,860	Oklahoma Medical Research Foundation	c	Okla.	HEW
58	1,763	Northwest Regional Educational Laboratory	a	Ore.	OE
59	1,746	Central Midwestern Regional Educational Laboratory	a	Mo.	OE
60	1,710	Southwest Education Development Laboratory	a	Tex.	OE
61	1,707	Coordination Center in Early Childhood Education	a	Ill.	OE
62	1,685	Far West Laboratory for Educational R&D	a	Calif.	OE
63	1,680	American Institutes for Research	c	Pa.	DOD
64	1,613	Institute of Medical Sciences	c	Calif.	HEW
65	1,454	Learning R&D Center	a	Pa.	OE
66	1,404	Retina Foundation	c	Mass.	HEW
67	1,390	Educational Development Center	a	Mass.	OE
68	1,359	Southwest Foundation for Research and Education	c	Tex.	HEW
69	1,350	Mathematics Research Center	a	Wisc.	army
70	1,207	Public Health Research Institute of New York	c	N.Y.	HEW
71	1,200	Center for R&D Learning and Re-Education	a	Wisc.	OE
72	1,180	Analytical Services	a	Va.	AF
73	1,179	Cerro-Toledo Inter-American Observatory	a	Chile	NSF
74	1,169	Salk Institute	c	Calif.	HEW
75	1,131	Wistar Institute	c	Pa.	HEW
76	1,074	Hudson Institute	c	N.Y.	DOD
77	1,041	Space Radiation Effects Laboratory	a	Va.	NASA
78	999	Eastern Regional Institute for Education	a	N.Y.	OE
79	995	Stanford Center for R&D in Teaching	a	Calif.	OE
80	938	Center for R&D in Higher Education	a	Calif.	OE
81	938	Mid-Continent Regional Educational Laboratory	a	Mo.	OE
82	896	Appalachia Educational Laboratory	a	W.Va.	OE
83	862	Southwestern Cooperative Educational Laboratory	a	N.M.	OE
84	820	Regional Educational Laboratory for the Carolinas and Virginia	a	N.C.	OE
85	820	R&D Center in Teacher Education	a	Tex.	OE
86	815	Atomic Power Development Associates	c	Mich.	AEC
87	809	Center for Study of Evaluation of Instructional Programs	a	Calif.	OE
88	800	Upper Midwest Regional Educational Laboratory	a	Minn.	OE
89	790	R&D Center of Educational Stimulation	a	Ga.	OE
90	699	Fels Research Institute	c	Ohio	HEW

(continued)

Rank	Federal Funds, 1969	Institute	Type*	State	Main Agency Sponsor
91	670	Southeastern Educational Laboratory	a	Ga.	OE
92	614	Center for Study of Social Organization of Schools and Learning Process	a	Md.	OE
93	610	Michigan Cancer Foundation	c	Mich.	HEW
94	608	Palo Alto Medical Research Foundation	c	Calif.	HEW
95	587	Policy Research Center	a	N.Y.	OE
96	564	Blood Research Institute	c	Mass.	HEW
97	537	Lowell Observatory	c	Ariz.	NASA
98	519	Center for Advanced Study of Educational Administration	a	Ore.	OE
99	511	Boyce Thompson Institute for Plant Research	c	N.Y.	HEW
100	500	Center for Educational Policy Research	a	Calif.	OE
101	488	Arctic Institute of North America	c	D.C.	DOD
102	457	North Star R&D Institute	b	Minn.	Interior
103	456	Haskins Laboratory	c	N.Y.	HEW
104	449	Gorgas Memorial Institute	c	D.C.	HEW
105	436	Marine Biological Laboratory	c	Mass.	NSF
106	390	Central Atlantic Regional Educational Laboratory	a	D.C.	OE
107	385	Michigan-Ohio Regional Educational Laboratory	a	Mich.	OE
108	379	Research Foundation of Children's Hospital	c	D.C.	HEW
109	346	Rocky Mountain Regional Educational Laboratory	a	Colo.	OE
110	320	South Central Regional Educational Laboratory	a	Ark.	OE
111	320	Pacific Northwest Research Foundation	c	Wash.	HEW
112	280	Institute for Medical Research and Studies	c	N.Y.	HEW
113	241	Cooperative Educational Research Laboratory	a	Ill.	OE
114	205	Hanford Occupational Health Foundation	c	Va.	AEC
115	204	Scripps Clinic and Research Foundation	c	Calif.	AEC
116	169	Bureau of Social Science Research	c	D.C.	HEW
117	166	Carnegie Institution of Washington	c	D.C.	NASA
118	161	National Opinion Research Center	c	Ill.	HEW
119	160	National Planning Association	c	D.C.	HEW
120	41	Institute of Gas Technology	c	Ill.	DOD
121	30	Institute of Public Administration	c	N.Y.	DOD
122	29	The Brookings Institution	c	D.C.	NSF
123	28	Western Behavioral Sciences Institute	c	Calif.	DOD
124	24	Friends of Psychiatric Research	c	Md.	HEW
125	12	New Jersey Mental Health R&D Fund	c	N.J.	DOD

*a: R&D center; b: applied research institute; c: other nonprofit institute.

Source: National Science Foundation, Intergovernmental Science Program Awards, Washington, D.C., Office of Intergovernmental Science and Research Utilization.

FEDERAL EXPENDITURES FOR SOCIAL RESEARCH
AS A PROPORTION OF OTHER EXPENDITURES,
BY AGENCY, FY 1969

Department or Agency[a]	Expenditures for Social Research[b] (thousands)	Column (1) as Percent of Expenditures for All		
		Research	Research & Development	Agency Activities
	(1)	(2)	(3)	(4)
Health, Education, and Welfare	$115,981	9.6	8.7	.2
Agriculture	31,139	12.6	11.9	.4
Office of Economic Opportunity	24,033	100.0	51.6	1.3
Department of Defense	23,358	1.4	.3	*
National Science Foundation	19,695	8.0	7.4	4.0
Transportation	12,901	15.8	4.4	.2
Commerce	10,810	17.2	12.0	1.3
Labor	8,851	97.9	74.4	.3
Interior	4,343	2.7	2.1	.5
State[c]	2,797	18.8	16.1	.1
Housing & Urban Development	2,470	43.3	14.0	.2
Arms Control and Disarmament Agency	1,622	39.2	27.0	16.9
National Aeronautics and Space Administration	1,340	.1	*	*
Justice	1,111	52.5	25.3	.2
All other	8,444	—	—	—
Total	$268,895	4.9	1.7	.1

Sources: Research and development expenditures, *Federal Funds for Research, Development, and Other Scientific Activities, Fiscal Years 1968, 1969, and 1970,* Vol. XVIII, (National Science Foundation, 1969); all agency enpenditures, *The Budget of the United States Government Fiscal Year 1971.* Cited in Harold Orlans, *Criteria of Choice in Social Science Research.* Washington, D.C.: Brookings Institution, 1973: 578.

*Less than 0.1 (0.05) percent.

[a] Reporting expenditures of $1 million or more.

[b] Expenditures for social psychology, psychology not elsewhere classified (but excluding biological psychology), and social sciences.

[c] Including Agency for International Development.

RECENT TECHNOLOGY ASSESSMENTS
INVOLVING SOCIAL RESEARCH,
SELECTED EXAMPLES

Title	Sponsoring Agency	Amount ($ thousands)
1. Report of the Northeast Corridor Transporation Project	Department of Transportation (1970)	12,000
2. Impact of Television on Social Behavior	Health, Education and Welfare (1972)	1,501
3. Jamaica Bay and Kennedy Airport: A Multidisciplinary Study	National Academy of Science / Engineering (1971)	350
4. Social Impacts of Civil Aviation, 1985-1995	Department of Transportation (1972)	236
5. Political and Scientific Effectiveness in Nuclear Materials Control	National Science Foundation (1972)	254
6. Assessment of Biomedical Technology	National Science Foundation (1973)	68
7. Studies of the Social Consequences of Technology	National Science Foundation (1973)	1,500
8. An Investigation of the Interaction between Technology and Our Legal Political System	National Science Foundation (1973)	107.1
9. An Analysis of Voluntary Citizen Group Uses of Scientific and Technological Information	National Science Foundation (1972)	98.5
10. Study Group on the Societal Consequences of Weather Modification	National Science Foundation (1974)	60.5
11. A Study of Certain Ecological, Public Health and Economic Consequences of the Use of Inorganic Nitrogen Fertilizer	National Science Foundation (1972)	282.4
12. The Impact of a Large Recreational Development upon a Semi-Primitive Environment: A Case Study	National Science Foundation (1972)	250

Source: Smithsonian Institute Data Bank, Washington, D.C.: 1973.

FORMER MEMBERS AND PRESENT MEMBERS
OF THE NATIONAL SCIENCE BOARD

Name and Title	Field	Term
Dr. Sophie D. Aberle Special Research Director The University of New Mexico	Medicine, behavioral sciences	1950-58
Dr. Rufus E. Clement President Atlanta University	Education, history	1960-67
The Very Reverend Theodore M. Hesburgh, C.S.C. President University of Notre Dame	Education, religion	1965-66
Dr. Katherine E. McBride President Bryn Mawr College	Education, psychology	1962-68
Dr. Frederick A. Middlebush President University of Missouri	Education, history, political science	1950-62
Dr. Ralph W. Tyler Director Center for Advanced Study in the Behavioral Sciences	Education, behavioral sciences	1962-68
Dr. Malcolm M. Willey Vice-President for Academic Administration University of Minnesota	Sociology	1960-64
Dr. W. Glenn Campbell Director Hoover Institution of War, Revolution, and Peace Stanford University	Economics	1972-
Dr. Roger W. Heyns President American Council on Education Washington, D.C.	Psychology, education	1967-
Dr. James G. March David Jacks Professor of Higher Education, Political Science, and Sociology School of Education Stanford University	Behavioral sciences	1968-
Mr. William H. Heckling Dean The Graduate School of Management The University of Rochester	Economics	1972-
Dr. F. P. Thieme President University of Colorado	Anthropology	1964-

Source: U.S. Senate Committee on Appropriations, Washington, D.C.: 1972.

NAME INDEX

IRVING LOUIS HOROWITZ is Professor of Sociology and Political Science at Rutgers University, and Director of Studies in Comparative International Development. He is also editor-in-chief of *Trans*action/*Society,* the leading multidisciplinary periodical in American social science. Before coming to Rutgers in 1969, Professor Horowitz was Professor of Sociology at Washington University. He has held visiting professorships at the Universities of Stanford, Wisconsin, and California; and overseas at the London School of Economics, the University of Buenos Aires, the National University of Mexico, Queen's University in Canada, and Hebrew University in Jerusalem. *Social Science and Public Policy in the United States* completes a trilogy of volumes on this same theme begun with *The Rise and Fall of Project Camelot: Studies in the Relationship between Social Science and Practical Politics* (1967; rev. ed. 1974); and *The Use and Abuse of Social Science: Behavioral Science and National Policy Making* (1971; rev. ed. 1975).

JAMES EVERETT KATZ is coordinator of the Adult Education Research Project in the Graduate School of Education at Rutgers University. Before coming to Rutgers, he served as Assistant Professor of Sociology at William Paterson College of New Jersey. He is currently researching the broad area of social science policy-making and educational institutions in the United States. His dissertation, written under the direction of Professor Horowitz, was on the subject of *Presidential Politics and Politics for Science and Technology, 1953-1973.* His previous academic training was at Northern Illinois University.

THE DESIGN OF A HEALTH MAINTENANCE
ORGANIZATION
Allan Easton

ENVIRONMENTAL POLITICS
edited by Stuart S. Nagel

ENVIRONMENTAL POLICY: Concepts and
International Implications
edited by Albert E. Utton and
Daniel H. Henning

THE FUTURE OF THE U.S. SPACE PROGRAM
Arthur L. Levine

OCEAN SPACE RIGHTS: Developing U.S. Policy
Lawrence Juda
foreword by Oliver J. Lissitzyn

POVERTY, POLITICS, AND HEALTH CARE: An
Appalachian Experience
Richard A. Couto

SCIENCE POLICIES OF INDUSTRIAL NATIONS
edited by T. Dixon Long and
Christopher Wright